COMMON-LAW WIVES
AND CONCUBINES

By the same author:
The Christian Philosophy of Education Explained, 1992
Christianity and Law, 1993
The Nature, Government and Function of the Church, 1997
A Defence of the Christian State, 1998
The Political Economy of a Christian Society, 2001

COMMON-LAW WIVES
AND CONCUBINES

*Essays on Covenantal Christianity
and Contemporary Western Culture*

by

STEPHEN C. PERKS

KUYPER FOUNDATION

TAUNTON, ENGLAND

2003

Published in Great Britain by
THE KUYPER FOUNDATION
P. O. Box 2, Taunton, Somerset,
TA1 4ZD, England

British Library Cataloguing-in-Publication Data
A catalogue record for this book is available from
the British Library

Printed and bound in Great Britain by
Cromwell Press, Trowbridge, Wiltshire

TABLE OF CONTENTS

PREFACE

WHAT is the nature of Christianity? Is it a religion or a cult, i.e. a personal worship hobby? This question goes to the heart of the modern Church's failure to exercise a world-transforming faith. The Church's abandonment of Christianity as a religion, i.e. as a world-view that structures every sphere of human life and society, has exposed the Western world to the religious influences of secular humanism, New Age-ism (neo-paganism), the Green and ecology movements etc., which are all really modern variations of pagan religion, and which have now begun to transform Western society in a direction diametrically opposed to the principles and practice of Christianity. The result has been that while Christians have maintained their faith as a cult, a system of belief that is little more than a personal worship hobby, when it comes to the question of how Christians should affect the world in which they live they have largely fallen back on trying to clean up secular humanism. In this process the Church has become increasingly irrelevant and powerless as society has been first secularised and then repaganised.

The antidote to this failure on the part of the Church to affect the world, which is her mission field, and the present condition of Western society to which this failure has led, is the rediscovery of Christianity as the true religion, i.e. as an overarching structure to human life that anchors both the individual and the society of which he is a part in God's will for man in Christ. This religious structure the Bible calls the covenant, and it embraces the whole of human life, including politics, education, science, art, welfare, healthcare, marriage, family life, Church, business, economy. Until the Church rediscovers this religious structure for life the Christian faith will continue to decline amidst the rise of other faiths that do provide the individual and society with a religious struc-

ture for life. This is so because man is a religious creature by nature and must express his religious attitudes in all that he thinks,
says and does, both individually and societally. This is just to say
that mankind will either serve the God of the Christian Scriptures
or else some idol of his own making. But the religious nature of
human life is inescapable. Until the Church rediscovers Christianity as the true religion Christians will continue to have saved souls
but live their daily lives as secular humanists without answers for
the desperate problems that face the modern world.

These are some of the main issues addressed in this collection
of assays, most of which were originally published in *Christianity
& Society*, the quarterly journal of the Kuyper Foundation. Their
republication here is the result of requests from readers of *Christianity & Society* for a collection of my essays and articles together in
one volume. All the essays reprinted here have been re-edited for
this volume; the changes made, however, for the most part amount
to no more than minor alterations and typographical corrections.

STEPHEN C. PERKS
SEPTEMBER 2003

CHRISTIANITY AS A CULT

"CHRISTIANITY is not a religion; it is a personal relationship with Jesus Christ." How many times have you heard this statement? Throughout my Christian life I have heard Christians repeat this dictum. It is one of those evangelical shibboleths whose pseudo-wisdom seems incontestable to those who repeat it. Yet it is precisely wrong, not because Christianity is not a personal relationship with Jesus Christ—reconciliation with God in Christ is the heart of the Christian faith. But this is just the point: the relationship with God to which the believer is restored in Christ is inevitably a *religious* relationship. Christianity is a religion, and if our faith fails to have a religious effect upon us as individuals and upon the society to which we belong it fails to accord God the worship he demands of us. What, in fact, the "Christianity is not a religion" theory really means is that Christianity is a *cult*.

We are used today to thinking of a cult as some form of weird belief that takes over a person's life. Examples of such cults are the Moonies, the Mormons, the JWs etc. But this is really an incorrect use of the word "cult." These are religions, not cults, at least if they do indeed take over the lives of their adherents. What then is a cult?

A cult is "a system of religious worship especially as expressed in ritual" or "devotion or homage to a person or thing" (*The Concise Oxford Dictionary*, Eighth Edition, 1990). The term is derived from the Latin word *cultus*, which is the form used most commonly by Christians when they wish to refer to the Church's system of ritual worship (doubtless to distance the Christian Church from the associations that the word "cult" conjures up for most people today). The history of the cult is very interesting. In ancient Rome one could join and practise the rituals of just about any cult one wished to adopt. There were many different cults, and they were very popular. But they were essentially personal devotion hobbies, not religions. The *religion* of Rome was Rome itself as the supreme political power. As long as Roman citizens acknowledged the religion of Rome they were free to practise whatever cult they wished, the cult of Jesus Christ included. It was the early Church's refusal to limit the Christian faith to the status of a cult that brought Christians into conflict with Rome. The practice of Christianity as a *religion* rather than as a cult brought the Church into direct conflict with the *religion* of Rome. This was a clash of religions, not of cults.

What then is a religion? The word *religion* comes from the Latin word *religio*, which means *obligation, bond, reverence for the gods*, from the verb *religare, to bind*. Inevitably, religion brings obligation, *duty*, i.e. life in accordance with an obligation that binds man. The root of *religio* is *lig, to bind*, and is cognate with the word *lex*, meaning *law*.[1] Religion, therefore, structures life; it structures the life of the individual and of society. This is precisely what a cult does not do. A cult is a personal worship hobby. It does not structure man's life nor does it structure society. The Eastern cults that were popular in ancient Rome, such as the cults of Mithras and Isis, did not structure the lives of their adherents—at least not if they were good Roman citizens. What structured the lives of the Romans was the religion of Rome, which was a political religion. What is not often appreciated by Christians today is that it was precisely at this level of politics that the early Church challenged Rome. Refusal to practise emperor worship was considered high treason by Rome.[2] "The officials of the Roman Empire in time of persecution sought to force the Christians to sacrifice, not to any of the

---

[1] "Modern etymologists mostly agree with this latter view [i.e. which links *religio* with *religare*—SCP], assuming as root lig, to bind, whence also lic-tor, lex and ligare; hence religio sometimes means the same as obligatio" (Lewis and Short, *A Latin Dictionary* [Oxford: The Clarendon Press, 1879], p. 1556*af*., cf. p. 1055*b*).

[2] Ethelbert Stauffer, *Christ and the Caesars* (London: SCM Press Ltd, 1955), p. 164.

heathen gods, but to the Genius of the Emperor and the Fortune of the City of Rome; and at all times the Christians' refusal was looked upon not as a religious but as a *political* offence."[3] When the early Christians said "Jesus is Lord" they were not making a cultic statement primarily. Worshipping Jesus as part of a cult of Jesus was not in itself forbidden. The Emperor Tiberius had even proposed to the Senate at one point that Jesus be consecrated as a god.[4] "All religions and all gods could have their place in Rome, as long as the Roman state and its emperor were recognized as the link between the human and the divine orders, the link by whom all others held their continuity and linkage. The issue was this: should the emperor's law, state law, govern both the state and the church, or were both state and church, emperor and bishop alike, under God's law, and under the kingship of Jesus Christ."[5]

Politics is always and inevitably a *religious* matter.[6] All States are religious States. If Christianity were not a religion it could not have challenged the religion of Rome. The cults were permitted precisely because as personal worship hobbies they did not and could not challenge the religion of Rome. They could be absorbed with no detriment to the existing religious order of the Roman Empire. This was not the case with Christianity. Christianity offered the *only* open resistance to emperor worship in the whole of the Roman Empire.[7] "This resistance movement became more and more dangerous through its alliance in the capital itself with the senators of the old school, and through its penetration of the ruling classes, of the court itself, and even the imperial family."[8] One could practise the cult of Mithras or Isis and sacrifice to the Genius of the Emperor without compromising either. One could not

---

[3] Francis Legge, *Forerunners and Rivals of Christianity, From 330 B.C. to 330 A.D.* (New Hyde Park, New York: University Books, 1964), Vol. I, p. xxiv, cited in R. J. Rushdoony, *Politics of Guilt and Pity* (Fairfax, Virginia: Thoburn Press, 1978), p. 304, my emphasis.

[4] Tertullian, *The Apology*, chapt. 5, in *The Anti-Nicene Fathers* (Edinburgh: T. and T. Clark), Vol. III, p. 21*b*f.   [5] R. J. Rushdoony, *op. cit.*, p. 305.

[6] For a more detailed exposition of this point see Stephen C. Perks, *A Defence of the Christian State: The Case Against Principled Pluralism and the Christian Alternative* (Taunton: The Kuyper Foundation, 1998).   [7] Stauffer, *op. cit.*, p. 163.

[8] *Ibid.*, p. 164, cf. Phil. 4:22, where Paul refers to those of Caesar's household.

practise the Christian religion and sacrifice to the Genius of the Emperor without compromising both. Christianity was a direct challenge to the authority of the emperor and of Rome, since it proclaimed a different King to whom all men, including Caesar, owe an absolute obedience and whose law supersedes all other laws, including Roman law—i.e. it proclaims a divine King whose authority and jurisdiction are total.

The early Church, unlike the modern Western Church, refused to reduce Christianity to the status of a mere cult. Christianity for the early Church was not merely a personal system of ritual worship; it was a religion. It structured the whole life of the believer by bringing him under an obligation, a duty, to obey God first in all things. Here was the problem: Christianity teaches that man's first allegiance is to God, in *all* things, not merely in the practice of the Christian religious cultus. The political religion of Rome claimed this primary allegiance for the emperor and for Rome. Man must first of all give political allegiance to Caesar and to Rome. The statement "Jesus is Lord" was primarily, in the context of ancient Rome, therefore, a *political* statement, a direct challenge to the political order of Rome. It was a confession of allegiance to a different political order. Even the New Testament word for church (ἐκκλησία) was not a cultic term but a *political* term, the term used in Greek for an assembly of the people as an organised political body.[9] Rome permitted its citizens to worship whatever god or gods they pleased as members of the various cults. The worship of any god was acceptable to Rome as long as such worship remained essentially a private cult that did not challenge its adherents' primary allegiance to the political religion of Rome. The cults did not, therefore, structure the life of the Roman citizen or of Roman society—Rome claimed that for itself. The early Christians refused to be restricted in this way. They proclaimed Christianity as a religion, as that which structures the whole life of man and society. Jesus is not merely the object of private devotion or the central figure in a popular cult; he is the Lord of glory, the

---

[9] For more on this point see Stephen C. Perks, *The Nature, Government and Function of the Church: A Reassessment* (Taunton: The Kuyper Foundation, 1997), p. 9ff.

one by whom all things were created, before whom all men must, and one day will, bow the knee, Caesar included.

Today in the West the situation is reversed. The Church no longer proclaims Christianity as a religion. By and large, and this is particularly true of evangelicals, Christians insist that Christianity is a mere cult—though of course the word "cult" is not used. The Christian faith is restricted to the status of a personal worship hobby. The idea of Christianity as a system of belief and practice that structures the whole of life and society—Church, family, State and individual life—is, on the whole, anathema to evangelicalism and most other versions of the faith today. The sacred and the secular are different orders. Hence the acceptance of religions such as socialism and evolution by Christians. Christianity does not structure the thinking and the lives of most Christians. It provides them with a cult, a personal worship hobby. What structures the lives of most Christians is secular humanism in one or more of its various forms. The shibboleth with which I began this essay is at least correct in one sense: Christianity is not a religion for most Christians today. But those who proclaim this dubious truth fail to realise that man is by nature a religious being. He will, therefore, inevitably structure his life religiously. If he does not structure his life around the true religion he will structure it around a false religion. Unfortunately, for many Christians, it is the religion of secular humanism, not Christianity, that structures their lives. Christianity is practised merely as a cult, not as a religion.

It is not surprising, therefore, that when non-believers convert to the Christian faith today there is often no practical difference between their former lives as non-believers and their Christian lives following conversion to the faith. Unless someone is involved in something like drug abuse, drunkenness or pornography his conversion to the Christian faith is not likely to change his life very much. The Church is not likely to point out the contrast that conversion to the faith will demand. Neither is the Church likely to teach the principles on which the new life of faith should be based and the practical obligations and responsibilities that go along with faith in Christ. The message is essentially not about life anyway, but about heaven and the afterlife. Jesus is the ticket to the afterlife. This is the message of the Church today. But this is a cult of escapism, not a religion to live by. The only difference that conversion to the Christian faith is likely to make to the *lives* of most people today, therefore, is that they will worship at the local church in the cult of Jesus on Sundays rather than in the cult of DIY at B&Q. In other words, the cult of Jesus is added to the daily life of the convert but does not effect any significant change in his *way* of life. His children will most likely still go to secular humanist schools to be indoctrinated with the religion of secular humanism; he will most likely continue believing the religion of evolution, although God will be given a nominal role in the new syncretistic religion of "theistic evolution"; he will most likely still support the same political party, though now he will have "spiritual" reasons as well as personal reasons to offer as to why society should be structured around his own political ideals; and the Church will seldom, if ever, challenge him to restructure his life and society around Jesus Christ and his revelation, the Bible. Christianity today is not practised as a religion. It has become a mere cult.

But by reducing Christianity to the status of a cult in this way we have defaced it and emptied it of the power to transform our lives in any meaningful way. This is not Christianity. The early Church would not recognise the modern situation in which the Church finds herself as anything other than the equivalent of compromise with emperor worship. The Church has reduced Christianity to a mere cult and has accepted secular humanism as the dominant and controlling religious force in the life of the believer and society at large. Christians worship Jesus as the deity of their personal worship hobby, but secular humanism is the religion that rules their lives. This is a defaced and powerless version of the Christian faith. What the failure to practise Christianity as a religion means is that the believer's relationship with Christ is superficial and ineffectual; it does not transform his life. The notion that "Christianity is not a religion; it is a personal relationship with Jesus Christ" is a perversion of the Christian faith because man's relationship with God is always religious in nature. To deny that fact is to limit God's jurisdiction over man's life. It is to claim, in effect, that Jesus is *not* Lord, that our relationship with him does not bind us to obedience to his law in all things. Christianity involves obligation; it binds us to a new way of thinking and living that is circumscribed by God's word. This obligation is a necessary feature of the believer's relationship with Christ. If it is missing the believer's relationship with Christ will be hindered by his conformity to (i.e. his sanctification in terms of) some other life-structuring law. The Bible calls this *idolatry*. To be reconciled with God in Christ means that one's life must be structured by one's relationship with Christ—i.e. that one's life must be sanctified or set apart to Jesus Christ, to use more "religious" terminology. This brings us to the heart of what religion is.

What those who espouse the notion that "Christianity is not a religion; it is a personal relationship with Jesus Christ" fail to realise is that any relationship between God and man is inevitably a *religious* relationship. In denying that Christianity is a religion this shibboleth denies the biblical concept of sanctification, i.e. dedication of one's *life* to Christ. It asserts personal salvation, i.e. reconciliation with God in Christ, but in denying that the believer's life must be structured religiously by his faith it denies sanctification of the believer's life to God. Unfortunately, the modern Church, including most kinds of evangelicalism, has largely failed to recognise the definitive structure of the Christian religion. Instead, the Church has fallen back on the practice of Christianity as a mere cult. Sometimes this has become a sacramental cult, as with the Church of England for example, and sometimes what has been stressed is the cult of personal piety, as with most Protestant evangelical Free Churches. In each case the faith is redefined in an unbiblical way and the biblical concept of sanctification is allowed to be replaced, often unwittingly, by sanctification in terms of some other religious principle, usually the secular humanistic ideals and principles that Christians subliminally imbibe from the culture that surrounds them. If the Church is to begin practising the Christian faith effectively once more, she must rediscover the identity of

Christianity as the true religion. What is that identity? What is the definitive structure of the believer's relationship with Christ?

All relationships have a structure, and all relationships are structured religiously, i.e. they are structured by law. Without a lawful structure to man's contact with others there is no relationship. The answer to the question "What kind of relationship is this?" will reveal something of the structure of a relationship, e.g. father/son, husband/wife, brother/sister, employer/employee. What kind of relationship, then, does God have with mankind? The answer that the Bible gives to this question consistently is that God relates to mankind by mean of a *covenant*. The Christian's relationship with Christ is a covenantal relationship. Likewise the non-believer stands in a covenantal relationship with God. All men stand in a covenantal relationship to God. As a non-believer man is under the covenant relationship established with Adam. This relationship, through sin, is one of alienation from God. The believer is redeemed from this relationship and stands under a covenant of grace in which he is reconciled to God by Christ. In Adam man stands condemned for his sin. In Christ he is redeemed and reconciled with God. Both are covenant relationships. God always relates to man by means of a covenant.

Christianity, therefore, is a covenant religion. It teaches that God deals with mankind in terms of two main representatives: Adam and Christ. Our personal relationship to Adam and Christ determines our standing with God. In Adam we stand under condemnation for sin. In Christ, i.e. through our relationship to Christ, we are delivered from this condemnation and have peace with God. This new relationship with God, which the believer has through faith in Christ alone, is a personal relationship, but it is not a private relationship. Christ is a public person, as the Puritans used to say. Christ is our covenant head. God deals with us *in Christ*. Our salvation is dependent upon a personal relationship with Jesus Christ, since it is our relationship to Christ that determines our standing with God. But Christ is our covenant head, the representative of a people whom God redeems *in Christ*. God deals with mankind covenantally in terms of these two representatives: Adam and Christ. Our relationship to God is structured, therefore, by the covenant under which we stand. The Christian's relationship to God in Christ is not sacramental nor does it revolve around personal piety: it is *covenantal* in nature. This covenant relationship with Christ should structure (i.e. sanctify) the whole of the believer's life. One aspect of this covenant structure is the Christian public religious cultus—i.e. church worship. But this is not the whole of the covenant by any means. When God delivered the people of Israel from Egypt he gave them his law. The preface to the Decalogue states: "I am the Lord thy God which have brought thee out of the land of Egypt, out of the house of bondage" (Ex. 20:1). In others words, God is the Saviour. *Therefore*, their lives were to be structured by the covenant and they were to obey the covenant law. Obedience to the Commandments did not deliver Israel from Egypt. But having been delivered by God, their Saviour, the children of Israel were now commanded to obey his law and live as a covenant community. One aspect of this covenant, and a very important aspect, was the Temple cultus, since it pointed to Christ. But the covenant was not exclusively cultic. It governed not only the Temple cultus but the life of the family, the life of the nation socially and politically (the State), and the life of the individual; i.e. society as a whole.

In just the same way, Christians are not saved by obeying God's commandments. But this does not mean they do not have to obey his commandments. We are reconciled to God through Christ alone, by faith alone. Therefore, since this is the case, since we are now reconciled to God in Christ, we must obey his commandments. This is what Jesus said: "If ye love me, keep my commandments" (Jn 14:15). The word of God should structure the life of the believer—in other words, the life of the believer should be set apart, sanctified, by conformity to God's word (Jn 17:17). And since we are commanded, as a community of God's people, to go into the world and make disciples of all *nations*, this means also that God's word should structure the life of the nation as well. This new structure to man's life in Christ does not apply only to the Christian cultus, what happens in church; it applies to the whole of man's life. And it applies not merely individualistically; it applies to the new covenant *community* as a whole, which is commanded to bring all nations under the discipline of Christ (Mt. 28:18–20). Obedience to God's law does not, and never did, save anyone from their sin. God's law is not, and never was meant to be, a means of redemption. Rather, its purpose is to structure the life of man and society. God's law is the law of the *covenant* under which man is redeemed from his sin and therefore it is meant to structure the covenant life of the individual and the community of which he is a part. God's law structures the covenant and therefore the believer's relationship with God in Christ. It also structures man's relationship with all other men and things: "Love worketh no ill to his neighbour: therefore love is the fulfilling [i.e. the keeping] of the law" (Rom. 13:10). In the new covenant relationship to which man is restored in Christ, therefore, God's law is written on the believer's heart (Jer. 30:31–34).[10] Consequently, as Thomas Schirrmacher has pointed out, Christianity was often called in the Middle Ages the *Lex Christiana*, the Christian Law, in contrast to the *Lex Muhametana*, i.e. Muslim Law or *lex Antichristi*, i.e. pagan religion.[11]

---

[10]   The law also structures the covenant with Adam, the covenant of works. All those who do not put their trust in Christ stand under this covenant and are therefore condemned as covenant breakers. The same law structures both covenants. God's law addresses all men, therefore, whether they are in Adam or in Christ, and demands their complete obedience—in other words God demands that all men structure their relationship with God, their fellow men and the world in which they live in accordance with his law. Those who refuse to do this come under the condemnation of the law. Thus, the magistrate (i.e. the State), who is a minister of public justice and a servant of God (Rom. 13:1–6), must administer justice in accordance with the principles of equity set down in God's law, which makes the same demands on the believer and the non-believer alike. For those who are in Christ, however, the curse of the law is borne by Christ on the cross (Gal. 3:13). Nevertheless, the law continues to structure the covenant relationship to which the believer is restored in Christ and should therefore regulate both his relationship with God and the world around him. The difference for the believer is that the law is written on his heart by the Holy Spirit (Jer. 31:33) so that he delights in the law of God (Ps. 119:16, 35, 47; Rom. 7:22) rather than seeing it as a yoke from which he desires to escape.

[11] Thomas Schirrmacher, "'Lex' (Law) as Another Word for Religion: A Lesson from the Middle Ages" in *Calvinism Today*, Vol. II, No. 2 (April 1992), p. 5.

The Christian faith is a religion, a religion defined by the covenant relationship that binds the believer to God. This covenant is structured by God's law. It is not a cult; it is a way of life. It affects how we live, at home, at work, in family life, at leisure and in all other human activities. It affects not only the believer's personal devotional attitude in each of these areas; it structures these areas of life totally. This means that the way in which we educate our children must be governed by the covenant; that our family lives must be governed by the covenant; that the way we think and act politically must be governed by the covenant; and how we pursue our vocations must be governed by the covenant. All our relationships, not only our relationship with God in Christ but our relationship with the world in which we live and the society of which we are a part, must be structured by this covenant.

If the way we live, as individuals, families, as a Church *and* as a nation, is not so structured by the covenant we offer God less than he demands of us, and we reduce the faith to a cult. The early Christians refused to do this and this is what brought them into conflict with Rome. Sadly, this is the condition in which much of the Church finds herself today. The modern Church has settled for what the early Christians refuse to accept. Christianity has become a mere cult for many believers today. Their *religion* is secular humanism, because it is secular humanism, not Christianity, that structures their lives. Christianity, however, is a religion *because* it is the reconciliation of man to God, a new covenant relationship with the Lord of Creation. This relationship should affect the whole of man's being and life. The Church, therefore, must cast out her idols and begin once more to structure her life around God's covenant word: the Bible. This means that she must seek to understand how that word applies to the whole of life, and *live* accordingly.

CLEANING UP
SECULAR HUMANISM

MOST Christians in Britain realise that things are desperately wrong in our culture. But there is not the same unanimity about what should be done about this, or indeed if anything should be done at all. (I used to know someone who refused to pray for peace in the world because his eschatology informed him that this is not to be expected in the end times, which he believed we were then in,—although this was about 25 years ago—and he believed that to pray for peace in the world would be, therefore, to pray against God's will, despite the fact that Christ said "Blessed are the peace-makers," Mt. 5:9.) Where Christians are convinced something should be done the usual response is to support Christian lobbying groups. The aim of these groups is to change the law or stop new laws being passed in the hope of preserving what Christians consider to be the Christian character of our society, or some element of it. Thousands of pounds are spent each year trying to stop Christian laws being abolished or non-Christian laws passed. Yet the success of these activities is limited. Even when there is success it is often short lived and a few years down the road the whole battle has to be fought again, and eventually the cause is lost. This is because the underlying culture will not support what Christians want. The wind is blowing in the wrong direction. The fact is, the wind needs to change before such lobbying groups can have any lasting success.

But there is an underlying problem with such activism that is seldom recognised, and it is this, that Christians are often really very much in sympathy with the prevailing direction of the wind in any case; it is just the odd bits of damage that the wind does, the nasty little squalls, that they do not like. The result is that Christian activism in Britain often amounts to no more than cleaning up secular humanism. The reason for this is that despite the desire to do something about the moral deterioration of society, which in itself is of course laudable, Christians often do not have a thought-out biblical world-view to guide their activism. And when confronted by such a world-view, the response of Christians is often one of horror. A Christian agenda for activism, based on a Christian world-view, often fares no better among Christians than it does among non-believers. The Christian activist agenda in Britain is, on the whole, quite humanistic in its perspective.

This is demonstrated by the fact that projects aimed at changing the culture, at doing something with long-term results, are usually met with opposition among Christians. Doubtless this can be explained by the fact that such projects require work and commitment from Christians in their lives, whereas supporting lobbying groups amounts to no more than a financial sacrifice, sending money to help someone else coerce politicians into fulfilling our responsibilities for us by passing and enforcing laws. This is not only a bad strategy for Christians to pursue; it is also an evasion of responsibility, of the Christian's calling to work out his faith.

For example, Christian home schooling is on the whole abominated in Britain by most clergymen and Christians, if it is thought about at all (though in recent years the number of home schooling families has begun to grow). Changing the world-view that underpins our culture (secular humanism) is not on the Christian agenda. (Saved souls are on the agenda, in the sense of brands snatched from the fire.) If the money that has been spent uselessly on trying to reform secular humanist State education in the UK or on trying to get laws passed that will halt the decline in the State education system had been spent on Christian schools and promoting Christian home schooling it would, I believe, have had a significantly more positive and long-term effect in the lives of people that would issue in world-view changes in the next generation, and it is such changes of world-view that are required and produce lasting cultural transformation, not stopping bad laws from being enacted or saving a good law from being abolished. But this requires promoting an unpopular message, namely, that Christians should face up to their responsibilities as parents rather than abdicate everything to the State, and that message is taboo. Trying to get Christians to see this, to understand the pivotal role played by one's world-view, and the fact that if we do not have a Christian world-view we will have a non-Christian world-view, is very difficult in itself. This is because developing a Christian world-view requires thinking, and many Christians do not like thinking about their faith; it is deemed a fleshly or worldly activity. Instead they "feel" things. And too much thinking seems to get in the way of their spiritual "feelings." Trying to get Christians to realise that the education of their children must take place in terms of such a consistently thought-out Christian world-view is even more difficult The result is not simply that Christians unwittingly imbibe a non-Christian world-view, i.e. a non-Christian perspective in terms of which to assess all issues regarded as secular in nature; this unwitting compromise with secular humanism is passed on to the next generation. The problem becomes compounded. When faced with the deterioration of society, instead of seeking to reverse the effects of this compromise, Christians respond by spending a great deal of time and money trying to clean up secular humanism.

The problem is really that Christians on the whole have bought into secular humanism, though they may not realise this. They think they have a Christian perspective if they want to stop pornography and gay rights, but seldom realise that protesting about these sorts of issues on its own will achieve very little unless our whole agenda is anchored in a Christian world-view, and that without such a world-view affecting the whole of our lives, campaigning on these issues will simply amount to cleaning up secular humanism. They will continue to send their children to State schools to be educated in terms of a secular humanist world-view that propagates the very cultural ideals they think they are against but in fact unwittingly support. It is a gargantuan task to re-educate Christians about this. They are simply not interested in thinking about it (not interested in thinking much at all), and yet unless our minds are changed (which is what repentance means) our lives will remain the same. Difficult? Well, yes, but we have to try nonetheless.

And so it is that the work of many Christian lobbying groups, even though their aims are usually laudable aims, amounts so often to no more than an attempt to clean up secular humanism. But this, in the event, is counterproductive, because cleaning up secular humanism simply makes it more attractive to society, both to non-Christians and Christians alike, with the result that real cultural change in terms of the demands of the Christian faith is hindered at best or even abandoned in favour of a respectable secular humanism. But secular humanism, even in respectable dress, cannot save our nation from the moral, cultural and political deterioration that we are now experiencing. Only Christianity can do that. Cleaning up secular humanism will not change our culture; it will certainly not Christianise it, any more than dressing up a pig in a three piece suite will enable it to behave with exquisite manners at the vicar's tea party. We need to replace the secular humanist culture that dominates our society with a Christian culture, not dress secular humanism up as Christianity. I would rather secular humanism wore its dirty ideals on its sleeves than have naive Christians dress it up to look like something it is not. The result of such dressing up is more damaging to our society than leaving it alone so that people can see it for what it really is. Why? Because after the beast has been scrubbed and cleaned and dressed up in fancy clothes, it remains a beast and will continue behaving like a beast, even though it may look more presentable; in other words it will continue to affect our culture according to its real nature. But, and here is the crucial point, it will be able to do its work *subliminally* for most people, who will be unaware of the consequences of its effects on society because of its superficial appearance of respectability. This seems to be particularly true for many Christians, who often fail to recognise the significance of the deeper issues.

For example, Christian lobbying organisations will work for Christian religious education in schools, or for religious education to be mainly Christian, and for controls on sex education etc. These goals are laudable in themselves. But the question of whether State education is a valid Christian ideal is not explored. The issue here is too difficult. Those who front lobbying groups do not wish to be perceived as extremists. They wish to appear reasonable in terms of secular humanistic criteria. They only want things from the government that any "reasonable" person would want.[1] They agree that the State should continue to tax people in order to provide State-funded and State-controlled education. They want only that RE lessons should be mainly Christian and that sex education should reflect our religious heritage etc.

But what about the English lesson, the maths lesson, the science lesson, the geography lesson, the history lesson, the assembly? (And Christians should not think that because the law requires a Christian assembly, their children will get a Christian assembly, or that because a teacher claims the assembly is Christian, therefore the assembly will be Christian.) The influence of the secular humanist world-view in these areas of study is far greater than its influence in the RE lesson, precisely because it is less obvious and in fact more authoritative for most people, including most Christians. Suppose we get schools with Christian RE lessons and no sex education? What then? Do we have a Christian school? Of course not. What if we have a school with Christian RE lessons,

[1] The whole notion of what is reasonable is, of course, also a religious question, since what is considered reasonable rests ultimately on one's understanding of the meaning and purpose of life, which is always and in every respect a religious conviction. Christians, though they believe in Christ as saviour—i.e. have a distinctively Christian soteriology—often fail to understand the implications of such faith for those areas of life that are not strictly within the compass of theology and ecclesiology, and perhaps certain areas relating to sexual and medical ethics. As a result their reasoning about issues considered as "secular" is often governed by the religion of secular humanism, not Christianity. Their world-view is thus syncretistic. But we should remember that what is reasonable for a consistently applied secular humanistic perspective is not reasonable from a Christian perspective. Reason is *God's* gift to man, a consequence of his creation in the image of God. Non-believers are only reasonable creatures to the extent that they reflect their Creator's image in their thinking. Where this is not the case, i.e. where sin determines the way that they think, they are not to be thought of as reasoning at all but as rebelling.

no sex education and all Christian teachers? Do we then have a Christian school? Not necessarily. It depends not only on what teachers are teaching but *how* they are teaching it. If the government, which claims to be religiously neutral, is in control, the ability of teachers to provide a Christian education is severely limited, even if they understand the issues and wish to provide such an education (and not all do). But the government is not religiously neutral, even though it claims to be and even though most people think it is. It is humanistic. Secular humanism is a religion. The modern State is a secular humanist institution, and therefore a religious institution. Likewise for schools. Schools are never religiously neutral institutions because facts never speak for themselves, they are always spoken about by human beings with a theory or several theories. These theories will either acknowledge God's creative will as that which gives meaning to the facts, or they will deny God and his creative will as having any relevance to the meaning of the facts. There is no neutral alternative, no third way to approach the facts. Facts are always interpreted facts. One's interpretation of the facts either acknowledges God as Lord or it does not. We are either for Christ or against him. Either we think (i.e. interpret the facts) obediently, or we think disobediently.

In teaching anything, therefore, a way of understanding is also inevitably conveyed to the pupil, even where this is not understood or recognised, either by pupil or teacher. Teaching anything always involves the imparting of a particular theory of knowledge, which will be either obedient to Christ or disobedient to Christ. Knowledge is not a neutral issue. It is not merely about facts. It is about how we understand and interpret facts. And this is always a religious question because we understand the facts either obediently or disobediently; that is, we think either obediently, by recognising and acknowledging God as Creator and therefore as the one whose interpretation of the facts (his revealed word) is authoritative for the whole of life, or disobediently, i.e. by assuming that the world exists and can be understood independently of the one who created it, continually sustains it, and whose creative purpose defines the meaning of all things. In teaching all subjects the teacher teaches his pupil to think in one of these ways, i.e. he either teaches his pupil to assume the God-created and God-interpreted nature of reality, or he teaches him to assume the autonomous rationality of the human mind, though of course in both cases this may not be done self-consciously. Indeed these presuppositions usually operate quite subliminally in the teacher's world-view and thus also in his teaching of any particular subject, including religious knowledge. Consequently, even Christian teachers who have not understood the epistemological issues may well teach their subjects, unwittingly, from a secular humanist perspective.

In fact this is often the case. And the constant obsession of Christian organisation and lobbying groups with the mere externals of the situation only exacerbates this problem. If only we had more Christians teachers, more Christian RE lesson, less sex education, better discipline, everything would be all right. But it would not. These things on their own will not get at the heart of the matter; they will not on their own automatically produce a Christian world-view. In fact this is quite obvious from our current situation. There is perhaps no other profession where the presence of Christians is greater than that of the teaching profession. State education in Britain is positively awash with teachers who are Christians. Has this produced any real change of basic perspective in the education system? No. It may upset many to hear this, but if the answer were yes would there be the frantic panic exhibited by Christian lobbying groups, who constantly send out mailings encouraging Christians to write to their MP or various Lords about Clause 28 and a host of other measures that overturn Christian virtues in the education system? Of course not. This does not mean that Christian teachers support the overthrow of Christian virtues in education. Of course not (though sometimes this does happen). The deterioration continues relentlessly *despite* the fact that so many Christian teachers are against these deleterious measures. The mere presence of Christian teachers does not, has not, and will not, in itself change the policy. As already mentioned the "victories" of lobbying groups are short lived in this environment (Clause 28 is a good example, since the government remains opposed to it and the issue will come up again,[2] but there are others), and even where there are legal victories, this does not mean that the practical teaching that goes on in schools will become Christian. Passing a law that states RE lessons should be mainly Christian will not produce Christian schools. For that we should need Christian RE lessons to be taught from a *Christian* perspective, not a secular humanistic perspective, and we should also need *all* lessons, including not only RE but maths, English, history, science etc. to be taught from a Christian perspective as well. And not only this. The whole ethos of the school would have to be Christian. Will passing laws achieve this? No. The Christian community's ability to affect areas such as education by lobbying activity is very limited and, in a culture that is as humanistic as ours now is, simply ineffective. But lobbying continues relentlessly, and it costs huge sums of money. For what? Another legal defeat? Perhaps a victory at the first and second reading of some new bill. But eventually the third reading will put paid to all the efforts, which will have then been a waste of money. And if there is a victory at the third reading, the whole venture will more than likely be repeated in a few years, if that, ending in another crushing defeat.

Why? Because the cultural wind, so to speak, is so much against the success of such political fixes. Such measures on their own cannot change our culture. At best they are measures aimed a cleaning up secular humanism. But it does not work. And the money that is spent on this could be spent more tactically and with a greater measure of success, i.e. in a way that would produce long-term cultural reorientation in terms of the Christian faith. But the projects that would do this would require much more than money. They would require hard work and commitment from Christians themselves, rather than the effortless writing of a cheque to fund a lobbying group that tries to make the government pass a

[2] For those readers who are not familiar with the British education system, Clause 28 is a regulation forbidding the promotion of homosexuality in schools. The current Labour government wishes to abolish this prohibition. (Yes, you *did* read that correctly!)

law requiring others to do for Christians what they should be doing for themselves. This is not to criticise the lobbying of government regarding legislation where it is valid, but this on its own
cannot achieve the transformation of society from a non-Christian to a Christian culture. Such transformation requires Christians to put their own hands to the plough. The vast sums that
have been spent by Christian organisations on lobbying government over education law could have been spent with far more
lasting effect on the creation of Christian schools and the facilita-
tion of Christian home schooling through resources and curriculum development, support groups to help and encourage the practice of Christian education by parents and the like. But for this to
happen there would have to be commitment to this by Christians,
by the Churches, and particularly by Church leaders, who are after all responsible for leading their congregations in the faith. What
could have been achieved by this kind of thing by now could have
had significant effects not only in the education of the next generation of Christians but in terms of the Church's witness to the
world.

Instead, Christians seem on the whole so utterly committed to
making sure their children get a good secular humanist education.
Some even deny themselves sacrificially so that they can send their
children to the very best of secular humanist schools, private ones,
and no doubt feel very self-righteous about it. Would that they
were prepared to make the same sacrifice to provide their children
with a Christian education!

What is happening here? This is a strategy guaranteed to produce defeat for the Church. Is there any wonder the Church is so
powerless, has so little influence, is no longer listened to, is so irrelevant to the majority of people in our culture today? Indeed the
Church is little more than an object of ridicule in our society. And
while this continues she deserves no better. To proclaim Christ as
Lord and then send one's children to be educated as secular humanists *is* ridiculous. Is there any wonder that so many of the
children of Christian parents eventually decide that Christianity
is not for them and abandon the faith when they grow up? Of

course, this does not happen in every case. But that does not justify giving our children a secular humanist education. And it happens often enough to cause us to rethink this whole issue.

The only way for Christians to change our culture successfully is for them to get involved in cultural activity. That means that we must engage the culture in which we live in terms of the cultural issues that determine the way we live, but in a way that brings the gospel to bear on those issues. If Christians want Christian education for their children they must provide it, not expect the government to pass a law requiring someone else to provide it for them. What is Christian in the least about that? If Christians want society to behave in a Christian manner they must get involved with creating the cultural conditions and means for that to happen; e.g. they must establish Christian schools that will provide Christian education for non-believers also, many of whom would be willing to send their children to Christian schools for the sake of their education (this is not hypothetical; such schools do exist, though there are far too few of them).

Likewise, if Christians wish to see the homeless problem and unemployment dealt with they must get involved with providing Christian services for those in need based on Christian work ethics, rather than leaving it all to the State—such an abdication of our responsibility to help the destitute does not fulfil the divine command of Scripture (James 2:14–16). If Christians wish to see the arts and media transformed by the gospel—and this is a vital area since these spheres are so formative for the life of our whole culture—they must get involved with the arts and the media. If Christian wish to see the political life of the nation Christianised and raised to a better level they must get involved with the political process, *not* in order that Christians might be relieved of their Christian responsibilities by the State however, but that they might be enabled to shoulder their responsibilities. For example, taking the issue of education again, a Christian political perspective would not be geared to relieving parents of their God-given duties in the education of their children, e.g. provision of State-funded and State-controlled schools (not even State-funded *Christian* schools), but rather tax reform that would empower parents financially to provide for their children's education themselves.

These are just a few of the areas that face us as Christians and demand that we engage with them as ambassadors of the gospel of God. Our remit in bringing the gospel to bear on life is as wide as life itself. No area of our life, individually or jointly as a society, is excused from this calling to bring all things into subjection to Jesus Christ.

This will require the development of a Christian world-view. Without this our ability to think and act consistently as Christians in the cultural melting pot will be severely inhibited.[3] God will still save individuals. God will always save his elect. But we are commanded not merely to snatch brands from the fire; we are commanded to disciple the *nation* to Christ, the whole nation (Mt. 28:19). This cannot be achieved by means of lobbying activities. This is not meant to deny that such activities have a legitimate role; but such a role exists in a limited sphere, quite simply because politics is only one part of life, and we are never to look to it as an idol, i.e. as that which provides meaning and guidance for the whole of life. Only Christ provides such meaning in our world. Lobbying groups cannot take the place of Christian activism. And by activism I do not mean political *protest*, which is what it has often now come to mean for many. Rather, I mean hands on cultural engagement with the world that Christ came to redeem. This is our calling both as human beings created in the image of God (Gen. 1:28), and as redeemed sinners who serve Christ in the power of his Spirit (Mt. 28:18–20).

Christians must decide whether they want a Christian culture or whether they merely wish to clean up secular humanism. The way we answer this question, consciously or unconsciously, will produce very different results, because it will determine *how* we seek to affect our culture, how we seek to be active in society as Christians, and therefore it will determine the consequences of

---

[3] For a good introduction to the need for developing a Christian world-view see John Peck and Charles Strohmer, *Uncommon Wisdom: God's Wisdom for our Complex and Changing World* (London: SPCK, 2001).

those actions. Our calling is to disciple the nation to Christ, to create a Christian culture, a Christian society and nation, not to clean up secular humanism. Our strategy must be geared to this. Therefore we must start *thinking*, and thinking not as a ghetto waiting for the end, but as an army poised to transform our culture for Christ. "For as [a man] thinketh in his heart, so is he" (Pr. 23:7).

3

COVENANT SIGNS AND SACRAMENTS

COMMUNION, like baptism, is a sign of the covenant. It is not a sacrament. There are no sacraments in the Bible. Sacrament is a concept foreign to biblical thinking. It is interesting to observe that where sacramental thinking is strong, covenantal thinking is usually very weak, often non-existent. The whole context of Scripture is covenantal, and the so-called "sacraments" are not sacraments at all, but covenant signs and seals.

The term "sacrament" is derived from the Latin word *sacramentum*, which was the sum of money deposited with the magistrates by Roman citizens who went to court; it was also used to denote the military oath of allegiance. From this military use it came to mean more generally an *oath* or *solemn engagement*. In later times and in ecclesiastical usage it acquired the meaning of *something to be kept secret*, a *mystery*, and *the office of the ministry*.[1] According to Augustine, "Signs, when they relate to divine things, are called sacraments,"[2] and "A sacrifice, therefore, is the visible sacrament or sacred sign of an invisible sacrifice."[3] The word was also used by Jerome in his Vulgate version of the Bible in Eph. 5:32 where Paul speaks of marriage as a mystery signifying the relationship between Christ and his Church: "Sacramentum hoc magnum est . . ." ("This is a great mystery . . ."). Oddly, therefore, we can perhaps say that marriage is a sacrament, but then that would not

---

[1] C. T. Lewis and C. S. Short, *A Latin Dictionary* (The Clarendon Press, 1879).

[2] "Signa, cum ad res divinas pertinent, sacramenta appelantur" (*Epistulae*, 138, cited in Lewis and Short, *op. cit.*, p. 1612).

[3] *The City of God*, (Edinburgh: T. and T. Clark, 1872, translated by Marcus Dods), X.6 (Vol. I, p. 388).

be the biblical concept of a covenant sign or seal. The word acquired the meaning of the mysteries of the Christian faith, the
gospel revelation, but of course there is nothing mysterious about
baptism and the Lord's Supper in this sense, since they are not
hidden things, but revealed truth, signs and seals of the covenant.

Unfortunately, the biblical signs of the covenant denoted by
this Latin term (and certain other rites not to be found in the Bible
as covenant signs) eventually came to be understood in a way quite
contrary to the biblical meaning attached to covenant signs and
acquired the status of magical rituals that confer spiritual blessings regardless of the participant's attitude of heart and requiring
no practical response from him. They are believed to work *ex opere
operato*, by the mere performance of the rite. Their efficacy is perceived to be in the sign itself and in the act of partaking of this
sign, much as the efficacy of preaching is seen by romantic Protestants to be in the act or "event" of preaching itself, and in the
experience of listening to a great preacher, not in the results this
event produces in the lives of those who listen to him by their
equipment for the work of service in the Kingdom.[4] With regard
to the Lord's Supper (though not baptism) this is so for many
evangelicals and Reformed people no less than Roman Catholics,
though the rationale may be different. It is true that Protestants
require faith in the recipient if the rite is to be effective, and they
do not believe in transubstantiation. But the belief in a rite that is
efficacious in itself, conferring on the communicant a spiritual blessing that is unrelated to the wider context of his life and requiring
no practical response that would constitute a real antithesis between the Christian way of life and that of the non-believer is
practically, if not theoretically, on a par with the Roman Catholic
belief. The fact is, most evangelical and Reformed people show
great zeal when it comes to protecting their communion tables

---

[4] On the biblical concept of preaching and the office of teacher in the New
Testament see Chapter Thirteen, "The Implications of the Information Revolution for the Christian Church"; see also, Stephen C. Perks *The Nature, Government and Function of the Church: A Reassessment* (Taunton: Kuyper Foundation, 1997),
Appendix B, pp. 92-99.

and Reformed Churches show equal zeal in protecting their pulpits (since preaching is a third, and perhaps the primary, sacrament in modern Reformed Churches[5]), but blithely send their children to be educated in spiritual brothels (secular schools) without batting an eyelid, a scandal that must surely be greater than what is often perceived as the heinous spiritual crime of permitting one's children to take the Lord's Supper, and just as surely must be the very denial of the meaning attached to, and the responsibilities entailed in, the baptism of a child. This is as good a case of straining at a gnat and swallowing a camel as ever there was.

The history of the doctrine of the Eucharist has been a process of theological algebra in which theologians have attempted to find the value of x, the real presence. This process was not helped by the fact that in part mediaeval theology amounted to what could perhaps be described as a game of Chinese whispers. Theologians relied on compilations of the sayings of the Fathers as their authority. Over time, however, these quotations of the Fathers were increasingly subject to embellishment, reinterpretation, and outright distortion, and before the printing press there were no definitive editions to which appeal could be made for the correct reading. Despite the claim that what the Church taught was an uninterrupted tradition going back to the Church Fathers and ultimately to the apostles and Christ himself, mediaeval theology had travelled a long way from its biblical origins. And the Bible itself, at least in the West, was not immune from this process of distortion, since the Latin Vulgate translation of the Bible, which was held up as inspired, was subject to the same proliferation of different readings through the many hand-written copies that were made of it that any other document was subject to, a fact that surely invalidated the Papacy's claim that the Reformers' reliance on the Greek text of Scripture rather than the Latin Vulgate was vitiated by the vast number of variant readings in the different

[5] On preaching as a sacrament see Colin Wright, "Restoring the Idea of the Throne to Christian Preaching," *Christianity & Society*, Vol. v, No. 2 (April, 1995), p. 18ff.

Greek manuscripts; Roman Catholics had precisely the same problem with their own Latin Vulgate version.

The Renaissance, which placed an emphasis on the newly discovered original Greek texts of classical authors, brought a much needed reform to mediaeval scholarship. The emphasis on getting as near to the original source material as possible had significant repercussions for the Church. It gave the Western Church the text of the Bible in the original languages. The Reformers, many of whom received a humanist education, brought this emphasis to the study of theology, with startling results. But Rome was not built in a day. And neither could it be demolished in a day. The Reformers were still mediaeval thinkers in many ways. It was as difficult for them to break away completely from the modes of thought that characterised their time as it is for the modern scholar to break away from post-Enlightenment modes of thought. And so it was with their doctrine of the Eucharist. This is quite understandable. The pioneering work of the Reformers led the Church into a new and more biblical emphasis and this in turn eventually led to a reconstruction of the social landscape of Northern Europe. But their work was not a complete break with the mediaeval attitudes of the past, nor could it have been. What Abraham Kuyper said of Calvinism is true of the Reformation as a whole, namely that "the underlying characteristic of Calvinism must be sought, not in what it has adopted from the past, but in what it has newly created."[6] The Magisterial Reformers did retain much from the past in their understanding. With the exception of Zwingli and those who followed him in this matter, this was also true of the Reformers' understanding of the Eucharist.

Of course the Reformers abandoned transubstantiation, though not all to the same degree; and they rejected the notion of a repeated sacrifice in the Eucharist. But despite their rejection of a *local* or *corporeal* presence in the Eucharist, they were unable or unwilling to abandon altogether, or at least were ambivalent about, the notion of a *real presence* in the Eucharist, however mystically or spiritually they variously interpreted it. Calvin, for example, says,

[6] Abraham Kuyper, *Lectures on Calvinism* (Eerdmans, [1931] 1976), p. 102.

"we must not dream of such a presence of Christ in the Sacrament as the craftsmen of the Roman court have fashioned—as if the body of Christ, by a local presence, were put there to be touched by the hands, to be chewed by the teeth, and to be swallowed by the mouth."[7] But he also states that the flesh of Christ is given in the Lord's Supper: "That we really feed in the Holy Supper on the flesh of Christ, no otherwise than as bread and wine are aliments of our bodies, I freely confess"[8] and "I confess that our souls are truly fed by the substance of Christ's flesh."[9] The Magisterial Reformers, however, also held to orthodox Christology as this was expounded at the Council of Chalcedon in A.D. 451, which maintained that the two natures of Christ are inseparably united but not confused.[10] The human nature did not become divine, nor the divine human. Nevertheless, neither could the two natures be separated, since they are united in one person. According to Calvin, therefore, "The Sacraments direct our faith to the whole, not to a part of Christ,"[11] and "When, therefore, we speak of the communion which believers have with Christ, we mean that they communicate with His flesh and blood not less than with His Spirit, so as to possess thus the whole Christ."[12]

But there is a problem with this. Calvin also understood that Christ's human nature is limited by the same constraints that limit any human being: "For as we do not doubt that Christ's body is limited by the general characteristics common to all human bod-

---

[7] *Institutes of the Christian Religion* (Philadelphia: Westminster Press, 1960, translated by Ford Lewis Battles), IV.xvii.12 (p. 1372).

[8] Corpus Reformatorum, 20:73, cited in R. S. Wallace, *Calvin's Doctrine of the Word and Sacrament* (Edinburgh and London: Oliver and Boyd, 1953), p. 199.

[9] C.R. 9:70, cited in Wallace, *op. cit.*, p. 199.

[10] There was, however, a significant difference between the Lutherans and the Reformed on this point. The Lutherans sat much more loosely to the orthodoxy of Chalcedon, maintaining a *genus maiestaticum* (majestic genus) in which there is a real rather than a mere nominal communication of attributes, i.e. the human nature partakes of the divine attributes. Hence the Lutheran insistence on the ubiquity of Christ's body, which was essential to the Lutheran concept of consubstantiation.

[11] *Institutes*, III.xxi.9, as cited in Wallace, *op. cit.*, p. 200.

[12] *Opera Selecta*, ed. P. Barth and W. Niesel (Münich, 1926-36), 1:435, cited in Wallace, *op. cit.*, p. 199.

ies, and is contained in heaven (where it was once for all received) until Christ returns in judgement, so we deem it utterly unlawful to draw it back under these corruptible elements or to imagine it to be present everywhere."[13] The ubiquity of Christ's body is denied. How, then, can the believer communicate with the whole Christ, flesh and blood as well as Spirit, not just a truncated half-Christ, if Christ's body is not ubiquitous and remains in heaven? Calvin's answer to this problem was to argue that the believer, when participating in the Lord's Supper, is raised up to heaven by the Holy Spirit and there communes with Christ's body: "Christ, then, is absent from us in respect of His body, but dwelling in us by His Spirit, He raises us to heaven to Himself, transfusing into us the vivifying vigour of His flesh . . ."[14] Thus, "No extent of space interferes with the boundless energy of the Spirit, which transfers life into us from the flesh of Christ."[15] The difference between Calvin and the Magisterial Reformers on the one hand, and the Roman Catholics on the other, was not in *what* is received in the Eucharist, but rather in the manner of its reception.[16] Thus Calvin writes:

But greatly mistaken are those who conceive no presence of flesh in the Supper unless it lies in the bread. For thus they leave nothing to the secret working of the Spirit, which unites Christ himself to us. To them Christ does not seem present unless he comes down to us. As though, if he should lift us to himself, we should not just as much enjoy his presence! The question is therefore only of the manner, for they place Christ in the bread, while we do not think it lawful for us to drag him from heaven. Let our readers decide which is more correct. Only away with that calumny that Christ is removed from his Supper unless he lies hidden under the covering of bread! For since this mystery is heavenly, there is no need to draw Christ to earth that he may be joined to us.[17]

Calvin rightly believed the Roman doctrine of transubstantiation to be an unacceptable fable. But he seems not to have realised that the notion of the faithful being transported mystically into heaven,

<hr>

[13] *Institutes*, IV.xvii.12 (p. 1373).   [14] C.R. 9:33, cited in Wallace, *op. cit.*, p. 206.
[15] C.R. 27:48, cited in Wallace, *op. cit.*, p. 206.   [16] Wallace, *op. cit.*, p. 199.
[17] *Institutes*, IV.xvii.31 (p. 1403).

there to partake spiritually of Christ's flesh, could be perceived as equally absurd. This shows how, despite their break with Rome in so many ways, the Reformers were still to some extent constrained in their understanding by the attitudes and cultural milieu of their age—as indeed all men are, the modern scientist no less than the ancient Greek.

But this is certainly not to deny that the Reformers also broke new ground and provided a new direction and new material with which later generations could build—and this is no less true in the matter of their understanding of the Lord's Supper. The process of doctrinal development from one generation to the next is part of the Church's task. And almost always, it should be remembered, this process of development has taken place in the context of the Church's defence of the faith against heresy. Heresy has always been the catalyst for the further development of Christian orthodoxy, a truth to which the apostle Paul seems to have pointed (1 Cor. 11:19). This is why a refusal to engage in debate with heresy is fatal for the Church's intellectual development, fatal to sound doctrine. Where the faith is not vigorously defended, where the *reasons* for belief are not articulated and taught against the prevailing heresy, atheism and paganism of the day, the Church finds herself in decline, and compromised with that very heresy, atheism and paganism against which she should stand fast and bear testimony.

This was, of course, the history of the Church in twentieth-century Britain. And the problem remains still. The faith is no longer defended by the Church. Modern scholarship has in the main merely cast aside much of the good building material that the men of faith of former centuries fashioned out of the new opportunities of their day and placed at our disposal. This is understandable in the light of the modern liberal/Arminian ethos in the Church. What is not so understandable is the stagnation that seems to exist among Reformed and conservative evangelical Christians in the matter of the theology of the Eucharist. There has been little real doctrinal development here since the Reformation, though re-inventing the wheel has become popular in some circles. The only real difference between the Romanists and the Protestants on the matter of the Eucharist often boils down to the fact that Protestants have not yet found the value of x. So the game of theological algebra goes on undiminished in Protestant Churches. But whereas the Romanist thinks he has found in transubstantiation the value of x, i.e. the real presence, the Protestant knows that this is the wrong answer but cannot find an adequate replacement. Looking at this rite from a mere covenantal point of view rather than a sacramental (i.e. magical) point of view seems so much less satisfactory to many and requires a response few are inclined to make willingly. Hence the game of theological algebra, with x, the real presence, never being defined nearly enough for us to know what it really is. Of course, all good Protestants know that a sacrament is "an outward and visible sign of an inward and spiritual grace," the definition given in the Catechism of the Book of Common Prayer.[18] But this has become a mere jingle for many; the real meaning of the Christian "sacraments" still eludes them. These Protestant sacramentalists know some things for certain though, or so they claim, namely, that x does not

---

[18] The Prayer Book definition continues with the words "given unto us, ordained by Christ himself, as a means whereby we receive the same [i.e. an inward and spiritual grace—SCP], and a pledge to assure us thereof." The inward and spiritual graces signified by these visible signs, the Prayer Book tells us, are "death unto sin, and a new birth unto righteousness." This is largely the same definition as that given by the Council of Trent: "A Sacrament is a visible sign of an invisible grace, instituted for our justification" (*Catech. Trident.* II.i.4, cited in John H. Blunt, ed., *Dictionary of Doctrinal and Historical Theology* [London, Oxford and Cambridge: Rivingtons, 1871], p. 669*a*). These definitions are derived from that given by Peter Lombard in the twelfth century: "A sacrament is the visible form of an invisible grace, bearing the likeness and existing for the sake of that same grace" ("Sacramentum est invisibilis gratiae visibilis forma, ejusdem gratiae imaginem gerens, et causa existens"—*Sentences*, lib. iv. dist. i, cited in J. H. Blunt, *op. cit.*, p. 669*a*). This definition was, in turn, derived from Augustine: "On the subject of the sacrament, indeed, which he receives, it is first to be well impressed upon his notice that the signs of divine things are, it is true, visible, but that the invisible things themselves are also honored in them, and that the species, which is then sanctified by the blessing, is therefore not to be regarded merely in the way in which it is regarded in any common use" (*On the Catechising of the Unin-structed*, Chap. 26:50: *Nicene and Post-Nicene Fathers* [Edinburgh: T. and T. Clark], First Series, Vol. III, p. 312*a*]; see also the quotation at note 3 above).

mean transubstantiation, nor does it mean covenant sign, since the former would involve them in Popery and the latter would require them to shoulder their covenant responsibilities, i.e. practise the faith rather than just praying about it, a fate worse than being a half-baked Papist no doubt.

Standing at a greater distance from the Reformation than the Reformers themselves stood, and with the benefit of the developments in covenant or federal theology that took shape in the century and a half following the Reformation, we are in a better position; we are able to build on their work and go beyond it. Looked at from a consistently covenantal perspective the theological gymnastics of the Roman, Lutheran and Reformed doctrines of the Eucharist seem unnecessary and unrealistic, even bizarre. The Eucharist can be conceived more consistently and biblically in terms of a covenantal perspective and context, as a rite signifying covenantal unity in and with Christ. And when the Lord's Supper is so conceived covenantally, rather than sacramentally, the issue of whether covenant children should participate comes much more sharply into focus. The participation of covenant children becomes not only valid, but essential, just as it is essential to the covenantal view of baptism. In many ways it seems something of a mystery as to why the Reformed Churches developed a consistently covenantal doctrine of baptism, over against the Roman doctrine of baptismal regeneration, but continued to adhere to a sacramental view of the Eucharist.

Since communion, like baptism, is a covenant sign, it is reasonable to expect it to be administered on a covenantal basis, not a rationalistic basis, much less a superstitious basis (the "sacramental" viewpoint). It is not drinking wine and eating bread that brings blessing to those who are faithful, nor judgement on those who fail to discern the body, but covenant faithfulness or breaking the covenant, abusing it, as did the Corinthians in their agape feasts, treating each other despicably. They failed to discern the body of Christ—i.e. they ill-treated it, namely, each other, the Church. The damage done to the body of Christ was not through the physical eating and drinking, but through the abuse of each other, members of Christ's body, the unity of which is symbolised in communion for sure. In this sense, therefore, to refuse to give communion to those who are members of the Church, children included, is to fail to discern the body. Ironically, therefore, refusing to give communion to baptised Christian children is the very abuse that anti-paedocommunionists think they are avoiding by not giving it. Children are excommunicated for a man-made offence—i.e. not being intellectually advanced enough to satisfy man-made theological criteria, a demand that is nowhere to be found in the Bible as a qualification for participation in the covenant signs, though of course profession of faith is required of adults. Nevertheless, saving faith is naive; there is an important sense in which we are saved by *who* we know, not *what* we know. In the Passover the whole family was involved, including the children (Ex. 12:24–27); and communion is the Christian Passover. But this is a covenantal argument not a sacramental argument, and sacramentalists do not think in these terms (i.e. biblical terms). Teaching on the covenant is virtually absent from evangelicalism of all brands today—at least in Britain.

Ironically, in many Protestant Churches the criteria for permitting a child to take communion, namely passing an intellectual test, exists side by side with an extreme form of anti-intellectualism when it comes to the issue of how much adults are expected to understand of the faith. This is odd. Children must pass an intellectual test to get communion, but adults are not required to pursue a vigorous understanding of the faith at all, despite the fact that Christ commanded us to love the Lord our God with all our heart, soul, strength and *mind* (Mt. 22:37; Mk. 12:30; Lk. 10:27). In fact, it is often the case that adults know very little about what the Lord's Supper means, but they are given it regardless of their grasp of its meaning. There are children with a far better grasp of what communion is about than many adults, but they are still not permitted to participate, because, it is said, they do not understand. Even though they can explain the meaning of the Lord's Supper they are deemed not to have a proper understanding, whereas adults who cannot articulate two sentences on the meaning of the

Lord's Supper are deemed to understand despite their inability to express their understanding. Strange indeed it is, that Churches that are so anti-intellectual and anti-theology should apply such strict intellectual and theological standards for children, while waiving them for adults, who, if they are thought to have a "simple" faith are on that account deemed more spiritual. This is especially odd in the light of the fact that Christ gave us as an example of such simple faith, not the adult ignoramus, but the unaffected trust that characterises the faith of children (Mt. 18:3–6), who, in fact, are often far more zealous to know more about the faith (and most other things) than many adults, since the simplicity of their faith, which is what Christ holds up as an example, is not the product of intellectual laziness, as so often it is with adults, but of their naive trust. Adults are encouraged to have faith in Christ in the same way. This trust does not require a developed intellectual understanding. Neither does it exclude it. If many adult Christians were as eager to know more about the faith as children are to know more about anything, the faith included if they are brought up as Christians, the Church would be in a far better condition today.

Of course, transubstantiation dealt paedocommunion a hard blow. Paedocommunion was practised in the early Church and in the Western Church for the first 1200 years of the Church's history. It is still practised by the Eastern Churches today.[19] According to Christian L. Keidel: "References to infant and child participation in the Lord's Supper continue in the west throughout the period of Charlemagne and following. But with the emergence of the doctrine of transubstantiation and the doctrine of concomitance (i.e., that Christ is present entirely under either kind), this ancient practice was soon discontinued. The fear that infants and children might spill the wine and thereby profane the actual body and blood of the Lord appears to have been the primary reason for this discontinuance. This gradual abrogation of communion under two kinds led Pope Paschalis the Second, in the 12th century, to emphasize in a letter to Pontius, abbot of Cluny: 'As Christ

---

[19] Christian L. Keidel, "Is the Lord's Supper for Children?" in *The Westminster Theological Journal*, Vol. XXXVII, No. 3 (Spring 1975), pp. 301-341.

communicated bread and wine, each by itself, and it ever had been so observed in the church, it ever should be so done in the future, save in the case of infants and of the sick, who as a general thing, could not eat bread.' This letter shows that infants were accustomed at that time, in the western church at least, to partake only of wine in the Lord's Supper, since it was harder for them to eat the bread. Thus when the cup was withdrawn from infants, it *ipso facto* meant the cessation of any involvement in the Lord's Supper as well. Additional justification given for this discontinuance was that infants received all that was necessary for salvation in baptism, and that little children, therefore, were not in danger of losing their salvation if they waited until the age of discretion before partaking of the eucharist, at which time they would eat with more respect and understanding."[20] But of course, if children receive all that is necessary for salvation in baptism, or more correctly, if baptism signifies all that is necessary for salvation, on what grounds can they be denied the rite that signifies continuation in that salvation?

At the very least, Christ said "Suffer the little children, and forbid them not, to come unto me" (Mt. 19:14) and warned us that it would be better for us to have a nasty accident in some water than hinder the children from coming to him (Mt. 18:6). If it is said that he was referring to harming them, then I can only say that refusing them covenant membership in Christ's body is the greatest harm that can be done to anyone. And if they are members of the Church, which is after all what is signified by baptism, at least looked at covenantally (rather than sacramentally), what right has anyone to excommunicate them. It seems to me that refusing to give baptised Christian children communion is precisely a case of hindering them from coming to Christ.

It is not surprising, therefore, that when children are forbidden to take part in the life of the Church until they reach a certain age they are then not interested and leave the fold. This is judgement indeed. People keep their children at arms length from the faith until they are old enough to "make a decision for themselves"

[20] *Ibid.*, p. 302f.

and when they decide they've had enough of this man-made Sunday religion (I am not referring to the Church's rituals but to lives that deny the meaning of those rituals) their parents are surprised and sad that they have left the faith. The trouble is that often it is the parents who first abandon the faith practically by not bringing their children up in the nurture and admonition of the Lord (i.e. they abandon their covenant responsibilities), preferring mere rituals to God's ordinances, i.e. denying the practical meaning and reality signified by those rituals, which the children were never allowed to take part in anyway (and children see through shallow superficial rituals, they see when these things are done but do not really mean anything in practical terms to those who do them— again I am not referring to the rituals *per se*, since ritual is a part of human life, but to the denial of the reality that the ritual is meant to signify).

But this is now a much broader subject, though indeed by no means unrelated to communion. Covenant signs are meaningless in the context of a life that is devoid of covenantal content, i.e. covenant faithfulness (Rom. 2:25–27). But by the same token, they are highly meaningful in the context of a life of covenant faithfulness, and to deny them to those who are seeking to live the Christian life faithfully, but who still fail, as we all do, and who recognise their need to repent and renew their faith in Christ, which is also what communion is about, is to hinder them from coming to Christ. This is as true for children as it is for adults. Children need to know they are sinners and that they need to repent and be forgiven also. Why bring them up as Christians if they are then denied participation in the covenant rituals that signify the very heart of the Christian message and way of life? This is standing the gospel on its head! And if they are being brought up as Christians, believing the truth, they need to come to communion just as much as any adult sinner. It seems totally wrong to me that they should be brought up to live as Christians but denied participation in one of the central covenant rituals. They need to remember that Christ died for their sins, they need to proclaim his death, and they need to renew their faith in Christ; and they need to do all these things at the Lord's Supper just as adult believers do. If they are not being brought up to understand these things in what sense are they being brought up as Christians? And if they are being brought up to believe and live the faith, who can rightfully deny them the Lord's Supper?

Communion is about the constant need for sinners to come back to Christ, to repent of their sins and seek his grace continually, to be continually renewed in the faith. This does not exhaust the meaning of communion, but it is at the heart of it. But children are told throughout their youth that they cannot have this, and what's more, that they do not *need* it. That is the message they get, notwithstanding that is not what is intended. They are denied the rituals that signify the very thing Christian parents want them to believe, that signify the heart of the Christian gospel. This is undoing with one hand what both Church and Christian parents try to do with the other. No wonder when they reach early adulthood they leave the faith. They have been taught to understand it is not for them, that they do not need it, by their being denied participation in one of the central rituals of the faith. This is refusing to let them come to Christ. We cannot even say that they get a different message from the sermons in most church services because they do not listen to them. They are sent out to Sunday school. And even when they do stay in church, at "family" services, they are fed nothing but mindless pap under the pretence that they cannot understand anything else—though the difference between this and what adults get each week is usually one of degree only. They are treated like people who cannot understand, and in the end they behave like people who cannot understand. This is the message that is drummed into them by their exclusion and in the end they agree, they do not understand, and they leave.

Of course, to change this requires much more than merely permitting baptised children to receive communion. It requires a teaching programme, a constant drip, drip, teaching programme that will orient the Church towards understanding the faith and covenant faithfulness, i.e. practice of the faith. And if people do not understand the faith, what it means, how it should change their lives, they cannot practise it. But perhaps permitting baptised children to receive communion accompanied by a teaching programme aimed at explaining both the ritual and the reality it signifies is a good starting point (and baptism *should* always precede communion, since baptism is the rite of *initiation* and communion the rite of *continuation*, i.e. covenant renewal). Perhaps the two could be linked together initially. In other words, perhaps baptised children of Christians could be given communion where parents are prepared to attend explanatory teaching sessions and thereby show themselves willing to understand and shoulder the responsibilities this entails for the parents of covenant children. Such would help to stem the flow of the youth from the Church far better than youth clubs and Sunday school, things that, no matter how well-intentioned, still do not have the virtue of being rites, covenant signs of our participation in Christ, instituted by the word of God, such as are baptism and the Lord's Supper.

4

SOCIALISM AS IDOLATRY

IT seems that conformity is increasingly one of the idols of the age in which we live and that the Church has also succumbed to this form of idol worship. This is sad because Britain traditionally was a society tolerant of differences, a society that even celebrated its differences. Yet at the same time as individualism has been abominated (sometimes legitimately, but often not so) and community stressed, what we have achieved is not community at all, but mere conformity. It seems to me that community cannot exclude individuality and that to try to achieve community by vilifying individuality only produces a conformist society devoid of true community. Of course, we need both community and individuality. The one does not take precedence over the other. But there are sorts of good individualism and bad individualism and not all kinds of community are good.

My assessment of this is based on my experience, i.e. British society. Britain is a socialist State. I have many American friends who will respond to this by saying something such as "It's getting that way in the USA too." But I'm not convinced it is. The US government can be very totalitarian at times. But, and this is the important point, the people don't like it on the whole (at least not the people I have met as opposed to the people who represent the USA in the media and politics) and they resist it. Here, most people *want* to be ruled by a nanny State. They lap it up! The British government often seems less totalitarian than the US government (a fact explained, according to some Americans, by the underestimated Teutonic influence on American society and culture), but this masks a sad fact: namely, that this can seem so only because there is so little resistance to governmental tyranny in the UK.

Most people want a totalitarian government in Britain today. Britain used to prize its freedom. The British have happily given it away now and become slaves of the nanny State in return for government run "social security" programmes, i.e. the Welfare State. Of course, British totalitarianism is not of the Russian and Nazi kind. "Soft totalitarianism" I've heard it called. But the effect is the same.

But it seems to me that the creation of the ideal socialist society is actually achieved by the destruction of real community, because the State becomes a surrogate for everything. Family, welfare, jobs, everything becomes subordinated to the State, which becomes the replacement for the community that used to exist. This was community more of the Christian kind. The growth of socialism has gone hand in hand with the destruction of Christian society in our nation. But I do not believe that the new society that socialism is trying to create works; it is a pseudo-community. It vilifies the individualism of capitalism, but fails to recognise that capitalism was not the whole of society. It does not recognise the true community that was part of Christian society prior to the triumph of socialism. Socialism sees things only in terms of economics and politics. But capitalism was part of a social order that did not view everything in terms of economics and politics. Because socialism does see everything in terms of economics and politics (i.e. because it idolises these things and reduces everything to them rather than having them in their proper place) it misses what really made the Christian community a true community, what made it work. Christianity is to be dumped now (though doubtless it can still be exploited for voting purposes every now and then—usually when a political party has lost a general election and is reduced to scratching around for support in every nook and cranny of the franchised but otherwise to be ignored population). Yet our sense and practice of community prior to the creation of the brave new socialist world came from our shared religious world-view. When Christianity was dominant even non-believers thought and acted like believers. Now, under the new world order of socialism, Christians think and act like non-Christians.

But along with the rise of this new State-run society individualism has not ceased, it has just been stripped of all the virtues and qualities that Christianity imparts to life. We now live in a godless State. Our community is godless, and our individualism is godless. But because man can only find his true meaning in God this means that community and individuality as they should exist are corrupted. We have conformity now much more than we used to have, but community is breaking down everywhere. Yet, although individualism is today vilified as capitalistic and selfish and socialism trumpeted as more caring and community oriented, we are more individuals than ever—witness the rise of a culture in which what counts more than anything is the individual and his self-fulfilment. Hence the breakdown of marriages and the breaking up of families. The "me first" culture is much more common now. People are much more motivated now by pure self-interest regardless of the consequences for others than they used to be when Christianity dominated our culture as the prevailing world-view.

The problem of course is not individualism, it is sin. But the Church has seriously failed to preach the gospel in its fullness here. As a result things do not seem to be much better in the Churches on the whole. Most Churches are characterised by a strong sense of conformity and at the same time a rather weak sense of real community. If one does not conform to the prevailing ethos of the Church one is not permitted to make a significant contribution to the life of the Church since it is perceived that such would inevitably "rock the boat." This ethos, however, is usually a kind of mindless respectability devoid of any rational foundation underpinning it as an attempt to work out a biblically informed culture. Even in the area of concern about "social issues" that Christians still consider relevant to the faith, there is little in the way of an attempt to develop a specifically Christian world-view as a foundation for human social action. Instead, the Church follows the world by sanctifying its deeds with pious platitudes. Being "concerned" about social issues for many Christians means being a middle class socialist, or is considered equivalent to being a Social Democrat in one's politics (why are so many Christians in the UK mesmerised by the claim that "third way" politics is Christian?). The Church seems to follow, quite mindlessly, the world, repeating its political and social shibboleths. And in the Church, as in society at large, the socialist world-view has crowded out true community with mere social conformity.

In falling prey to this kind of idolatry the Church has abandoned her true mission. She has ceased to be the salt and light of society and is consequently in no small way responsible for the destruction of our society. She follows the world instead of leading it to the truth. The truth has become an embarrassment for the Church. But judgement begins at the house of God: "For the time is come that judgement must begin at the house of God: and if it first begin at us, what shall the end be of them that obey not the gospel of God?" (1 Pet. 4:17). God has judged the Church and the judgement is now moving into society at large. All that we need for evil to triumph is for good men to do nothing. And that is what has happened. The Church has done nothing; she has fiddled while Rome burned.

The State has replaced God in our society and therefore it has become the institution that ultimately provides meaning for the nation. Because men inevitably look to their gods for meaning, modern society looks to the State to create community, to structure society and to provide meaning. But in doing this the State has replaced true community with itself, and the culture of self has triumphed in a society where true community is in decline.

In contrast, in a Christian society community should flow from the meeting of people in common life, which requires a common faith, or at least the prevalence of this and its acceptance in society, even if not everyone accepts its religious basis. In other words, society requires a shared world-view, a shared set of presuppositions about the nature and meaning of life. Where this is absent there can be conformity but not real community. In the context of a shared world-view, however, individuality is not lost but given meaning. It does not exist on its own but in a context; it therefore partakes of the characteristics of the world-view that dominates a society generally. In a Christian society this means that individuality finds meaning in terms of the truth, not in terms of some false idol, as it does today, be that idol money, fame, political power or whatever. Likewise, community finds its meaning in terms of the truth, not some idol, e.g. the State. Where the State replaces God as the source of the meaning of life and orders the life of the nation according to the ideology of socialism, or where anything else in the created order replaces God as the focus of life, whether communally or individually (i.e. where men engage in idolatry rather than worshipping the God of Scripture), man loses the true life he was meant to have, communally and individually, since his true life is found in God.

5

COMMOM-LAW WIVES
AND CONCUBINES

WE live in an age when Christian institutions are the target of
social reformers who are intent on nothing less than the total liberation of the individual and society from the oppressive practices
of the Church and the unreasonable requirements of the Christian faith. Doubtless this is the prelude to a new golden age in the
eyes of these social saviours and their cohorts. Perhaps it will even
come up to the standards of the golden age of Greek civilisation,
tempered by a lavish dose of feminism of course. Though one
wonders if it has ever occurred to these latter-day visionaries that
hardly any of the golden ages of past, or even present, civilisations outside the influence of the Christian faith would have toler-
ated anything like feminism. Such a liberal notion would never
have been allowed to find expression. That it has been allowed to
find expression in Western society is due in great measure to the
kind of civilisation that Christianity has created in the West. It is
well-known, at least well-known to Church historians—obviously
less well-known to modern feminist ideologues—that the Christian faith has always been favourable to the plight and rights of
women. Greek women of the first century A.D. found in Christianity a consideration as equals and co-workers with men (though
not an equality of vocation) that they could not have dreamed of
as part and parcel of their former pagan way of life. This was a
practical liberation of women from the tyranny of ancient non-
Christian civilisation that we can hardly comprehend today, so
thoroughly conditioned are we by the blessings and privileges that
living in even a post-Christian society has conferred upon us.

Unfortunately, such blessings are taken for granted today, and it is common for social evils, and sometimes things that are indeed not social evils, even social blessings, but which are reputed social evils by modern thinkers, to be blamed on the Church or the Christian faith and the limitation of men's and women's potential that Christianity has, supposedly, perpetrated through social pressure and stigmatisation. Thus, for example, modern man's discontent with the lifestyle that unemployment or disability creates is not infrequently blamed on the Protestant work ethic. Of course ancient Greece knew no such social problems of unemployment or disability as we have today—slaves seldom have the privilege of being unemployed, and a disabled child would probably not have lived to an age at which he could have contemplated his plight. Nor is such a child likely to fare any better in the new golden age of secular humanism that looms before us. Exposure at birth was the simple method of dealing with this problem in the golden age of Greek culture; amniocentesis has relieved the modern, post-Christian world of even this unpleasantness and the problem of disability can now be dealt with quickly and clinically, obviating the necessity of even giving birth.

§1

The Assault on Christian Marriage

Marriage too, of course, has had to bear its share of the blame for the modern condition, whatever it happens to be. The Christian institution of marriage and family life has had to bear the full weight of secular humanism's frontal attack on the Christian religion. Marriage is now thought to be outdated, an oppressive relationship unsuited to nurturing the brave new world that the progressive thinkers of our day are intent on creating. Though, rather inconsistently, white weddings and all the trappings that go with them are as popular as ever. No expense is spared on the lavish arrangements that are thought essential to a proper church wedding. It is just that for many people in modern Western society the ceremony means virtually nothing, and divorce is now almost as popular as marriage. This is a strange phenomenon. The cost of a wedding today seems to be inversely proportionate to the value that is attached to the institution of marriage—though the cost of children's birthday parties is hot on the heels of the kind of expense lavished on a wedding in some cultures. But of course the meaning is irrelevant; it's the style that matters. This is just one more element in our increasingly superficial culture, which stresses the outward appearance, the image and mere style as the all-important component of modern life, and rejects the content and meaning, the real purpose of human relationships and indeed of human existence. It is not surprising, therefore, that we now hear of pressure groups and think tanks that are working for the complete abolition of marriage as it has hitherto been conceived—i.e. *Christian* marriage—and its replacement with ten-year, renewable or cancelable "marriage" contracts and the like.

For some, though, even this kind of commitment is too much. Living together without any kind of marriage contract is now the preferred option of many couples. It is not uncommon, however, for this state to be referred to as "common-law marriage," and the woman deemed to be the man's "common-law wife." Furthermore, in the eyes of some it is thought that a man can have a legal wife *and* a "common-law" wife at the same time, and it is not entirely unknown in this country, though it is certainly uncommon, for a man to maintain a relationship with two such women at the same time, the one his legally married wife, the other his reputed "common-law wife." The notion, however, is completely false. Not only is the relationship with the woman who has not gone through any marriage ceremony adulterous and sinful; if it were indeed a common-law marriage it would be bigamous, since English law does not recognise marriage to more than one spouse at the same time as legitimate, whether that marriage is considered a common-law marriage or a civil or ecclesiastical marriage. It is impossible in the eyes of the law to have two wives; one marriage must be illegal and adulterous. The only question that the law addresses is, *which one is the legal, i.e. the valid, marriage?*

Of course, in cases where the term "common-law wife" or

"common-law marriage" is used today there has been no ceremony of marriage of any kind at all. As already stated, for a married man or woman to go through a marriage ceremony of any kind with a third party would be bigamous in the eyes of the law, and this has always been the case under English common law. But mere cohabitation, no matter for how long, does not constitute common-law marriage, even when the two cohabiting parties are not married to anyone else, and, moreover, it *never* did. This estate of mere cohabitation is one of concubinage not marriage, and English law does not, and never did, recognise it as anything more than concubinage. But concubinage is not a pleasant term, and it conveys a nuance of disapprobation—at least in a Christian or post-Christian culture. The term "common-law wife" sounds much more acceptable, and brings with it the supposed advantages of being dissolvable at will by either party. This whole notion is, however, completely false. A man who lives with a woman in a relationship of physical union without marrying her has a concubine, and neither common law nor canon law recognise, or ever have recognised in the past, anything in such a relationship but the fact of mere concubinage.

§2
A Brief History of Marriage in England

The English law of marriage has a long and complicated history. As early as the time of Glanvill (mid-twelfth century) it was recognised that matters of matrimony were exclusively within the jurisdiction of the ecclesiastical courts.[1] The English law of marriage was thus the canon law of the Church as practised in England.[2]

---

[1] For a brief history of the development of English law at this time, including the separation of the secular and ecclesiastical courts, see Stephen C. Perks, *Christianity and Law: An Enquiry into the Influence of Christianity on the Development of English Common Law* (Whitby: Avant Books, 1993).

[2] Frederick Pollock and Frederic W. Maitland, *The History of English Law Before the Time of Edward I* (Cambridge University Press, Second Edition, 1911), Vol. II, p. 367f.

When a question pertaining to the validity of a marriage came before a common-law court it was referred to a bishop to be settled by canon law. Common-law marriage, therefore,—i.e. marriage recognised as such by the common law—was marriage that was recognised by the ecclesiastical courts. In short, common-law marriage was by definition a *Christian* marriage, a Christian institution. The mediaeval ecclesiastical courts punished concubinage as fornication and gave those involved the option of marrying or separating.[3]

It was the view of the early canonists, including Gratian (1090–1150), that where there was no physical union the marriage was not valid.[4] But this opinion did not prevail. According to Pollock and Maitland its demise was due to the influence of Peter Lombard and the fact that if there were no indissoluble bond created by the ceremony itself—i.e. if physical union was essential to marriage—Joseph and Mary could not have been married at the time of Christ's birth.[5] The canon law of marriage thus stated that *consensus non concubitus facit matrimonium*—"agreement not copulation makes marriage."[6]

Before the Reformation in Europe, and before Lord Hardwicke's Act in England (1753), marriage was either informal or formal—the latter being conducted at the door of the church (*in facie ecclesiae*—literally "in the face of the church"). Marriage was entered into by the consent of the parties to the marriage. In an informal or non-ecclesial marriage all that was required was a simple agreement of the parties in words of the present tense (*sponsalia per verba de praesenti*), e.g. "I receive you as my wife/husband . . . etc." or a promise to marry in words of the future tense (*sponsalia per verba de futuro*), which created a contract that was considered consummated either by words in the present tense or by the act of physical union. Before consummation, however, this amounted to an engagement and the relationship could be dissolved by mutual consent.[7] Where there was no physical union,

---

[3] J. H. Baker, *An Introduction to English Legal History* (London: Butterworths, Third Edition, 1990), p. 547.   [4] Pollock and Maitland, *op. cit.*, p. 369.   [5] *Ibid.*
[6] Baker, *op. cit.* (First Edition), p. 255.   [7] *Ibid.* (Third Edition), p. 546.

therefore, the validity of the marriage depended on the form of words used in the ceremony. If the words were said in the present tense the marriage was made; if in the future tense the marriage was not complete and could be dissolved.[8] Such informal marriages were irregular, and the Church disapproved of them,[9] but the words created an indissoluble bond of marriage.[10] Any subsequent marriage by one of the spouses to a third party, even if celebrated formally at the door of the church, was made null and void by the previous marriage, "constituted by a mere exchange of consenting words."[11] Either party, however, could compel the other to solemnise their marriage *in facie ecclesiae*,[12] and the Church could compel them by means of spiritual censures to do the same.[13]

Formal marriages were essentially the same as informal marriages, except that they were celebrated at the door of the church (*in facie ecclesiae*), received the priest's blessing and were followed by a nuptial mass inside the church.[14] Although this gave a degree of certainty to the marriage, in that it was a formal ceremony blessed by the Church and witnessed by the community, the Church did not marry the couple, but merely solemnised the marriage. As with informal marriages, "The parties were *not* married by the priest's blessing or the other ceremonies; *they married each other*."[15]

The problem with marriages not conducted *in facie ecclesiae*, formally at the door of the church, was that they might be difficult to prove. It was possible to marry in complete secrecy, without witnesses, by the simple exchange of words in the present tense. Such marriages were valid marriages that created an indissoluble bond, but nevertheless unprovable. Canon law required at least two witnesses for proof of any matter—and in this the Church followed the general biblical requirement: "at the mouth of two witnesses, or at the mouth of three witnesses, shall the matter be established" (Dt. 19:15 cf. Mt. 18:15–16; Jn 8:17; 2 Cor. 13:1). Thus,

---

[8] *Ibid.*   [9] Pollock and Maitland, *op. cit.*, p. 372.   [10] Baker, *op. cit.* (Third Edition), p. 546.   [11] Pollock and Maitland, *op. cit.*, p. 367.
[12] L. I. Stranger-Jones, *Eversley's Law of Domestic Relations* (London: Sweet and Maxwell, 1951), p. 14.   [13] Pollock and Maitland, *op. cit.*, p. 372f.
[14] Baker, *op. cit.* (Third Edition), p. 548.   [15] *Ibid.* My italics.

as Pollock and Maitland point out: "If A and B contracted an absolutely secret marriage—and this they could do by the exchange of a few words—that marriage was for practical purposes dissoluble at will. If, while B was living, A went through the form of contracting a public marriage with C, this second marriage was treated as valid, and neither A, nor B, nor both together could prove the validity of their clandestine union."[16]

An unfortunate result of this was that the ecclesiastical court would have to admonish A and C to live together in a state of continuous adultery.[17] Since this was immoral however,—the first marriage, between A and B, being valid but not provable—theologians were forced to concede that A and B should for conscience' sake live together as man and wife, thereby disobeying the Church and suffering excommunication as a result, secure in the knowledge that they would be absolved on the Day of Judgement.[18]

For obvious reasons, therefore, both the secular and ecclesial authorities were keen to put an end to these informal, unsolemnised marriages. In 1200, in a council at Lambeth, Archbishop Hubert Walter promulgated a constitution requiring all marriages to be celebrated *in facie ecclesiae*, in the presence of a priest, and only after the publication of the banns of marriage on three successive occasions prior to the ceremony.[19] Those not married in the regular way after publication of banns were not to be admitted into a church without a licence from a bishop.[20] In 1215 at the Lateran Council, Pope Innocent III made this rule effective over the whole of Christendom.[21] Regular marriages, i.e. marriages celebrated at

---

[16] Pollock and Maitland, *op. cit.*, p. 385.   [17] *Ibid.*   [18] Baker, *op. cit.* (Third Edition), p. 548.   [19] Pollock and Maitland, *op. cit.*, p. 370.   [20] *Ibid.*

[21] *Ibid.* This was not a new ecclesial doctrine however. Lanfranc (1005-1085) had issued a constitution stating: "No one may give his daughter or kinswoman to anyone without the blessing of a priest; if he does otherwise, it will not be judged a lawful marriage but a fornicatory marriage" (ut nullus filiam suam vel cognatam det alicui absque benedictione sacerdotali; si aliter fecerit, non ut legitimum coniugium sed ut fornicatorium iudicabitur—cited in *ibid.*). One may well wonder how a valid marriage can be considered a fornicatory marriage; but the canon still sees the condition entered into by the informal ceremony as one of matrimony, if irregularly celebrated. It is not concubinage. See Pollock and Maitland's comments in *ibid.*

church according to this constitution, had, from then on, certain legal advantages over informal, unsolemnised marriages. For example, only when a marriage was celebrated at the door of the church could the bride be endowed.[22] But the wife's personal property became vested in the husband and her real property was vested in her husband during coverture,[23]—i.e. while she was married to her husband and thus under his protection. Nevertheless, informal, unsolemnised marriages did not cease. The mere decree of the Church did not bring the custom to an end, and rather than declare such irregular marriages null and void the Church continued to accept them. Such marriages were deemed sinful in the eyes of the Church, but they were still accepted as marriages and invalidated any subsequent marriage *in facie ecclesiae* by one of the spouses to a third party. As Pollock and Maitland put it: "On the one hand stands the bare consent *per verba de praesenti*, unhallowed and unconsummated, on the other a solemn and a consummated union. The formless interchange of words prevails over the combined force of ecclesiastical ceremony and sexual intercourse."[24]

This situation continued in England until Lord Hardwicke's Act of 1753. Registration of marriages began in the sixteenth century, but the registers were not universal and they were not always well preserved. The Council of Trent outlawed informal marriages and required the presence of a priest for the celebration of a marriage to be recognised as valid.[25] But England, a Protestant nation, was unaffected by this. Informal, or clandestine marriages, as they were called, continued to be made. In 1598 even Chief Justice Coke, who was the attorney-general at the time, married his second wife in a private ceremony, for which he was censured by the Archbishop.[26] In 1694 marrying without banns or a licence was made a criminal offence, but such marriages were still considered valid. Clandestine marriages, again, did not cease; indeed from the mid-seventeenth century onwards they had become more popular.[27] The main reason for the 1694 legislation, in any case,

---

[22] *Ibid.*, p. 375.   [23] Baker, *op. cit.* (Third Edition), p. 552.   [24] Pollock and Maitland, *op. cit.*, p. 372.   [25] Baker, *op. cit.* (Third Edition), p. 548.   [26] *Ibid.*
[27] *Ibid.*, p. 548f.

was not to end clandestine marriages so much as to facilitate the taxation of matrimony.[28] Other attempts were made to end informal clandestine marriages during this period. But it was not until Lord Hardwicke CJ introduced a bill to end the practice in 1753 that the situation changed.[29] This Act abolished clandestine marriages altogether.[30] Henceforth, a valid marriage in the eyes of the law required either the publishing of banns or the purchase of a licence, for which parental consent was required in the case of those under 21 years of age, the presence of two witnesses and the recording of the marriage in a public register, falsification of which became a capital offence.[31] Jews and Quakers were exempted from getting married in church but not Nonconformists and Roman Catholics. The royal family was also exempt from the provisions of the Act as were marriages celebrated with the special licence of the Archbishop of Canterbury.[32] The Act covered only England and Wales. Regarding marriages entered into outside England and Wales English law recognised the law of the place in which the marriage was celebrated.[33] This accounts for the popularity of Gretna Green amongst eloping couples. As the nearest place in which one could get married outside the provisions of the Act for the majority of people resident in England it became the most frequently used venue for eloping couples under 21 years of age. The Marriage Act 1836 introduced a civil ceremony, which could be celebrated in a registry office or a registered building, e.g. a Nonconformist chapel.

---

[28] *Ibid.*, p. 549.   [29] An Act for the better Preventing of Clandestine Marriages, 26 Geo. II, c. 33.

[30] The term "clandestine" did not refer only to marriages that were entirely secret and without witnesses. The term was used to denote what has been called informal marriages above. "There are various degrees of clandestiny which must be distinguished. The marriage may be (1) absolutely secret and unprovable . . . But a marriage may also be called clandestine (2) because, though valid and provable, it has not been solemnized *in facie ecclesiae*, or even (3) because, though thus solemnized, it was not preceded by the publication of banns." Pollock and Maitland, *op. cit.*, p. 385.

[31] Baker, *op. cit.* (Third Edition), p. 549.   [32] *Ibid.*, 550.   [33] *Ibid.*

§3
The Common-Law Doctrine of Marriage

To the extent that the terms "common-law marriage" and "common-law wife" referred to an informal marriage unsolemnised by the Church, the notion these terms represented was abolished completely in 1753 by Lord Hardwicke's Act. In this sense, therefore, there is no such thing as a common-law marriage any more in England and Wales. The term is incorrectly used to denote a relationship based on mere cohabitation and physical union. Such a relationship is concubinage, nothing more, and English law, common or ecclesiastical, never recognised it as anything more than concubinage. In another sense, the only real meaning of the term "common-law marriage" or "common-law wife" is a marriage or wife that is recognised as such in common law. To the extent that the term has any validity today, therefore, it refers to all valid marriages whether ecclesiastical (Church of England marriages) or civil marriages (e.g. marriages in a registry office or in a Nonconformist chapel), and in England and Wales it refers *only* to such marriages, since the term can only mean a valid marriage in English common law.

As we have already seen, common law prior to the 1836 Marriage Act recognised marriage as the domain of the ecclesiastical courts and accepted as a valid marriage what the ecclesiastical courts accepted as a valid marriage. The English law of marriage was the canon law of marriage. The common law did not have a doctrine of marriage peculiarly its own; it certainly did not have a doctrine of marriage different from that of canon law.[34] It merely deferred questions relating to the validity of marriage to the ecclesiastical jurisdiction. Common-law marriage, therefore, however it might be conceived, was always a *Christian* institution, an estate judged to be valid in the eyes of the Church and therefore accepted as such in common law. To the extent that the term represents the informal marriages of the mediaeval period it was still

[34] Pollock and Maitland, *op. cit.*, p. 374.

a Christian institution, i.e. an institution validated by the Christian Church, though canon law did not require the presence of a priest or solemnisation by the Church for a marriage to be valid, despite its continual efforts to secure these as the regular form of marriage and the extirpation of clandestine marriage.[35]

In short, the common-law doctrine of marriage was the Church's doctrine of marriage. Whatever else common-law marriage was, therefore, it was not merely an agreement to cohabit, a state that in no way affected a union of any kind in the eyes of the law. There had to be words of marriage in the present tense or in the future tense that had been consummated by words in the present tense or by physical union. Without these essential words of marriage, i.e. without the couple marrying each other, there was no marriage and the common law did not accept their cohabitation as marriage in any sense.

Of course, modern concubines, of which there are very many in our society, do not like the term that most accurately defines their relationship to the man they live with. The word comes from the Latin, *concubinatus*, meaning *"Union of a man with an unmarried woman*, usu[ally] of a lower social grade than himself."[36] The truth is unpleasant to modern liberated women so the term "partner" or some such circumlocution is used to describe the sexual relationship they have entered into. In the light of all the talk that we get from feminists about the liberation of women from the oppression of Christian marriage, it seems odd that they should be so content with having reached that most exalted of all female conditions: concubinage.

§4
Consequences of the Abandonment of Christian Marriage

The increase in concubinage and divorce and the demise of marriage as a life-long institution has had serious consequences for

---

[35] *Ibid.*, p. 372f.   [36] Charlton T. Lewis and Charles Short, *A Latin Dictionary* (Oxford: The Clarendon Press, 1879), p. 404*b*.

modern Western society. These deleterious social trends, combined with the heavy taxation policies of modern governments and, not insignificantly, the loss of faith and belief in the Christian world-view, which for a millennium provided the religious foundations of Western culture, have proved fatal to the health of the Christian institution of marriage and family life, and indeed fatal to the health of our society generally. The result has been the creation of a dysfunctional generation that has hardly any concept of the Christian social order upon which the nation drew for its strength and vitality in the past. The decline of the family as one of the pillars of society has also contributed to the growing homelessness among the young—and State handouts and welfare are not the answer to this problem; the State is no substitute for the family. Without a strong Christian family ethic society lacks a stable and secure environment in which to nurture the next generation, and thereby an essential means of preserving social order.

Since individual freedom has largely been suspended by the envious State and the Church has already been dismantled from within as a pillar of society, only the State remains as a major prop of the social order in modern Western nations. Virtually all other institutions have now been subordinated to the State. The result has been tyranny. Without a strong Church, a strong family and individual liberty there is no means of checking the absolutist ambitions of the modern State. Neither Church nor family have any real power or authority in society any longer and the all-powerful, predestinating State now controls and governs the life of the individual and the nation.

§5
The Christian Social Order

The time is surely ripe for reversing this trend. Part of the answer is the restoration of the Church to her rightful position and role in society. Part of the answer also, and a very significant part, is the restoration of the Christian institutions of marriage and the family in the life of the nation. Of course, this can only happen as the Christian faith is embraced and the Christian virtues practised in the lives of the individuals and families that constitute the nation. This is a change that must begin in the heart. But it must not stop there. Pietism cannot solve the problems that afflict our nation. If the change of heart effected by regeneration is not demonstrated in a man's outward life, we must seriously question whether there has been a change of heart in the first place, since Christ taught us that it is by the *fruit* they bear that we shall know who are his, not by a mere confession of faith. Only the Christian faith can save our society from its present plight. But it can only do that as individuals, families, Churches and politicians work out the faith in all the spheres of life and culture proper to each.

A healthy society—i.e. a *Christian* society—requires not only a strong Church, but a strong family ethic, a strong ministry of public justice (the State), and individual liberty. These are the four pillars upon which a Christian social theory and practice rests. All four are essential to a healthy society, and they are equally essential. A Church-centred society is not the Christian ideal; neither is a libertarian society or a patriarchal society, certainly not a totalitarian society. The Christian ideal requires all four principles: a strong Church, a strong family, a strong magistrate,—and by "strong" I mean a *just* magistrate also—and individual liberty, all operating within the parameters and boundaries, and observing the proper limitations of authority, set down for these institutions in God's word. These are the ideals upon which Christian society is founded. The demise of one of these institutions means, ultimately, the end of a Christian social order. All of these vital institutions must be restored in society if we are to save the nation from ruin and judgement. One must not be stressed to the exclusion of the others, and none may take precedence over the others.

6

CENSORSHIP

SOME years ago the retiring chairman of the British Board of Film Censors stated on a Radio Four interview that "There are no subjects which are off limits or taboo. It is only the way in which they are treated which may result in censorship." This comment was used to justify the granting of a certificate to allow the distribution of a film whose subject matter was necrophilia. What are Christians to make of this statement? Was he right?

My answer to this is that there are no subjects that are off limits to the Christian in his attempts to come to a correct understanding of the world in which he lives; i.e. the Christian has to be able to assess all things from a Christian point of view. This means that he must be able to think about all things from a Christian perspective, a Christian world-view, even those things with which he disagrees and that he believes to be utterly immoral. For example, homosexual practices and paedophilia are immoral and forbidden. But the Christian must come to a proper understanding of these things, and this means that he must think through these issues in order to determine the correct Christian response, especially in an age of moral delinquency such as our own is. And the Christian has to be able to articulate and explain the correct Christian response to non-believers as part of his witness to the faith.

Cinema films and television programmes are forms of art. But art also communicates a message, and these media are very effective means of communication. In an age like the present, when so many people are unwilling to go to church and listen to the preaching of the gospel, the Christian artist and dramatist may be able to communicate the Christian message regarding such things to non-believers much more effectively than the preacher, at least as the first point of contact. But in order to do that he has to deal with the issues. In this sense, therefore, we must agree with what the censor said. But this does not mean that we should necessarily condone what he would condone. The question is, "What is the message being put over by this drama?" This goes not only for the vile things we see on television and on the cinema screens but also for the seemingly harmless things. It is a question that is as pertinent to the *Blue Peter* programme[1] as it is to the sexual immorality and violence portrayed on television.

Christians often get indignant about the graphic portrayal of sex and violence in the media and complain, but fail to see the real problem entirely, namely, the non-Christian world-view that underpins such dramas. They complain about television programmes and movies being shown at the cinema, but send their children to schools that indoctrinate their children into the very same world-view that produces such dramas in the first place: secular humanism. This is the real problem. The most damaging programmes are those that convey the message of secular humanism subliminally, not those that convey it obviously, because people do not really see the programmes that convey the message subliminally for what they are, namely, propaganda for secular humanism. If God is dead and there is no meaning to life except what one makes for oneself, what one imposes on one's own life, then sexual immorality and gratuitous violence will be the inevitable consequences, since men are slaves to sin until they find their true purpose in life in serving God. If I choose my own meaning and purpose for life, if I am at the centre of the world and all things exist for me, if "The world is my idea," to use the words of Schopenhauer, then all that we see in the media today in terms of mindless violence and the selfish abuse and mistreatment of people by each other will inevitably follow. Merely complaining about the depiction of mindless violence and sexual immorality without getting to the real cause of the problem, the kind of world-view that pro-

[1] For those not familiar with British television *Blue Peter* is a children's television programme. It has won many awards and is widely regarded as children's television at its best. The content is mainly topical and informative, not fictional.

duces such entertainment, and, of course, the realities of modern life that such entertainment depicts, is not enough. Not only is such a superficial approach an insufficient answer for the problems facing our culture today; it is part of the problem itself, because it fails to challenge sin in the human heart, and therefore condones, unwittingly, the sinful attitude itself, the idolatry of the human heart, while condemning only certain expressions of such a sinful attitude. Christians condemn the sinful *effects* of human rebellion against God—and rightly so—but often fail to condemn the *attitude*, the disposition of the heart, the world-view or mind-set, that produces these sinful effects. This attitude of the heart is not merely a question of feelings and passions; it is an intellectual attitude and an attitude of will just as much as an attitude that affects the passions and desires. The term *heart* is here used in the biblical sense to indicate the soul or religious centre, the mind, the essential nature of man. The attitude of man's heart affects the whole of his culture, not merely his sexual appetites, lust for vengeance etc. It affects his view of the meaning and purpose of life and therefore informs and controls his whole view of life generally.

Christians must be careful not to get into a mode of thinking in which they merely wish to clean up secular humanism. This is the danger of much Christian thinking on these issues. There is a difference between being a Christian and merely being prudish. Children's television can be as degrading and immoral as adult television—and I'm not thinking here of the obvious candidates, but those programmes that parents often think are good, wholesome programmes. Though the graphic portrayal of violence and sex may not be there, this does not mean that the corrupting message of secular humanism is not there, that children are not being encouraged to see the world and everything in it from a purely self-centred point of view and to see the world as a godless place. It is the philosophy or world-view underpinning the drama that is at question. What is the message? Does the message glorify God or man? A children's television programme can be just as degrading in its own way as one of these nasty and perverted movies about sex and violence, and because the degradation of the chil-

dren's programme is not as easy to see, it is actually more dangerous in the long run.

The same argument applies to the kind of world-view in terms
of which education takes place at school and university. Facts are
never presented or taught on their own; they are taught as part of
an overall world-view, a particular theory of knowledge and understanding of life, its origin, meaning and purpose. Those who
teach may not be conscious of the way in which their religious
attitude of heart affects what they teach. But it will affect their
teaching subliminally nonetheless. If their attitude of heart denies
God and worships the creature instead of the Creator, this will be
reflected in the kind of world-view they embrace, and therefore
this attitude of heart will colour everything they see and everything they teach. It is not only the overtly religious aspects of education that will be coloured by this attitude of idolatry, but the
maths lesson, the history lesson, the biology lesson, the science
lesson. The whole curriculum will be subject to this world-view. It
is not the facts taught that are the problem, but the theory, the
world-view, in terms of which the facts are understood.

For Christians, therefore, the real problem is not X-rated movies. It is rather the fact that they send their children to be educated
by those who believe and teach the God-denying world-view of
secular humanism. How will God see this? Christians may stand
outside the cinema protesting against some X-rated movie or write
to the BBC about the depiction of some sexual activity on the
television, but if they then send their children to be educated in
terms of the very same world-view that produces such movies they
are no better than those they are complaining about, perhaps even
worse. They are hypocrites. Unfortunately, this is precisely what
much "Christian" lobbying is about: cleaning up secular humanism.[2] But when all the graphic sex and violence has gone from the
television screen the perverted and degrading philosophy of secular humanism remains and continues to contaminate the education of the youth because it is this same philosophy that underpins
the world-view that children imbibe in the secular schools. Unless

2 See Chapter Two, "Cleaning up Secular Humanism."

Christians are committed to living differently themselves, which includes providing an education for their children that does not revolve around this secular humanistic world-view, any gains from such protestations outside cinemas, or petitions sent to politicians, will be short lived because the cause has not been dealt with; all that has happened is perhaps that the symptoms have been repressed for a short while. But the cancer remains, and continues to produce its consequences in the next generation. Merely cleaning up secular humanism, whether in the cinema, on the television screen, or in the schools, is not enough. Christians need to have Christian answers, Christian alternatives to secular humanism's culture of death.

The flip side of pietism, ironically, is that much of life is not redeemed but left as it is. Christians run away from the world instead of redeeming it. But where they have not redeemed it they then become thoroughly subject to it. A sort of schizophrenia seems to have got hold of much of the Church. The population must not be permitted to watch the sex and violence that rebellion against God produces, but one may send one's children to be educated into the world-view that brings forth such rebellion. Such is the implicit message of much "Christian" lobbying for censorship.

In fact the Bible gives us some very gruesome, violent and sexually immoral stories, stories about incest, homosexual acts, ritual sacrifice of children etc. One story particularly that I have always found utterly gruesome, utterly nasty, is the story of the Levite who cut up his concubine, who had been raped to death by the men of Gibeah, into twelve pieces and sent a piece to each of the leaders of the tribes of Israel, with the result that all Israel made war on the tribe of Benjamin (Judg. 19 to 20). And many more such horrific stories are related in the Bible. The Bible is not a prudish book and those who are intent on bowdlerising the Bible do themselves and their fellow men a great disservice. If God has revealed himself in a particular way there must be a purpose to it. If we soften that revelation in translation—which often happens because modern translators find the Bible too coarse or graphic or insufficiently poetic—there will be an inevitable knock-

on effect in our understanding of who God is, because in the Bible
God reveals himself to man. Such softening of the biblical message will change our view of God. God's revelation is corrupted
by such prudish translations. This is a form of liberalism because
it panders to man's desires, to what he wants to hear, not what
God says. Pietism has been one of the results of such a softening
of the Bible's message and in turn has become a major cause of
the effeminate type of "Christianity" that is popular today. Pietism
has vitiated the gospel in an age when the truth needs to be heard
clearly. The Bible is very graphic in its depiction of man's sin, and
very hard in the message it conveys to sinners. No subject is taboo
in God's word. It speaks to man's situation. It is realistic in its
portrayal of mankind in the state of slavery to sin.

But the Bible is never gratuitous; there is always a moral purpose to its depiction of man's sin. This is not the case with the
modern depiction of sex, violence or other gruesome things in the
cinema and on television. Violent acts and acts of sexual chaos
are depicted gratuitously, and there is a serious message underpinning the portrayal of such gratuitous violence and sexual chaos.
What such dramas are saying, in effect, is this: "There is no God.
Men can kill, rape and torture with impunity. The only thing one
can do is to murder, rape and torture back. This is a godless world.
There is no meaning except one's own self-fulfilment and happiness." But this is an immoral message whether it is conveyed by
graphic images of violence and sexual perversion, or whether it is
conveyed subliminally by a *Blue Peter* children's television programme on evolution. The Bible, and therefore Christian drama
that is glorifying to God, will deal with the same subjects, but say
instead "There is a God who is just, and he does not wink at sin.
Those who live by the sword will die by the sword. God will rec-
ompense. The only deliverance for man from this state of degradation is faith in Jesus Christ." I am not saying that this message
will be an overt message in the drama, as it would be in a sermon
on the same subject. It may well be very subliminal; and surely
that is what art is about to a great extent. It may very well be far
more effective because it is subliminal. But that is the message.

Therefore, the Christian dramatist, artist, not only may, but surely must, deal with these things.

How such things are depicted is another thing. If the depiction of these things means that those involved in performing the drama have to sin, then obviously this is not acceptable to the Christian dramatist. Some would say this restricts the artist. But surely art is also about craftsmanship, creativity and invention. Art is not merely a message. It is a message that is creatively packaged to heighten its poignancy. If the artist/dramatist cannot put his message over without recourse to sinning then he is only saying he is a poor artist. The Christian message about homosexual practices being immoral can be put across without having to show two men performing a homosexual act. If the dramatist says it is necessary for him to have the actors do this immoral thing, or simulate it, all he is saying is that he lacks the creativity as an artist to convey his message effectively through his art.

Nevertheless, much overt "Christian" art today is rather sickly sweet and unrealistic. Art and drama surely must deal with the reality of life, not run away from it. But it must deal with it from a Christian perspective. If there is nothing to redeem then Christianity has nothing to say. It is irrelevant. But if there is no redemption either, likewise, Christianity becomes irrelevant. This is as true for the Christian artist and the Christian dramatist as it is for the clergyman, the missionary et al. The Christian artist must practise his art redemptively. Indeed, we must all live redemptively. Our calling is to take the things of this world and elevate them to a higher state than they where in when we found them. This is the job of the artist consummately.

It is the *world* that must be redeemed; but it must be *redeemed*. For the Christian artist or dramatist to neglect either side of this equation is to fail in his calling as an artist. The task of living redemptively in this way embraces the whole of man's culture. There are no areas that are off limits to the Christian dramatist, the Christian artist, because there are no areas where sin has not corrupted the life of man. Man is totally depraved until he is touched by the grace God. And there are no areas that are off limits to God's grace. The redemption that Christ has purchased by his blood covers the whole of human life and culture. Man is also saved totally by the God's grace. There are no areas of human life that are off limits to the gospel. Therefore, there are no areas that are off limits to the Christian artist or the Christian dramatist; his subject matter is the whole of human life and culture. But he must, in his own way, bring the redeeming message of the gospel to everything with which he deals, and thereby raise it from its state of degradation through sin to a higher level. The Christian artist, dramatist, must practise his art redemptively.

7

PREACH THE GOSPEL AND
HEAL THE SICK

Jesus came preaching the kingdom of God and healing the sick (Mt. 4:23; Lk. 4:18–19); and he commanded his disciples to preach the Kingdom and heal the sick (Mt. 10:7–8; Lk 9:2; 10:9). This commandment has been understood historically as a command to Christ's Church, not merely to the apostles and the seventy. Doubtless these days, as a result of claims for miraculous healings and the exercise of the charismatic gift of healing in many Churches, the texts supporting this understanding have been applied in a far narrower way by those who affirm the cessation of the charismatic gifts of the Spirit—although one does not hear the argument that preaching the Kingdom was also limited to the apostles and the seventy, which is the logical corollary of such a narrow application of the text. The fact is that wherever Christianity has gone, the healing of the sick has accompanied it. Hospitals were not invented by compassionate secular humanists with an eye on the greatest good for the greatest number in society. They were the consequence of the Church's taking her commission to heal the sick seriously and of the Christianisation of society.

A belief that the healing of the sick must go hand in hand with preaching the gospel does not commit one to a charismatic perspective therefore. All Christians ought to take this command of Christ seriously, and the Church has throughout history. We are commanded not only to preach the gospel of the kingdom of God, but to heal the sick. This command binds the Reformed Churches no less than the charismatic. Nor is it to be understood merely in terms of providing medical care. Of course, the provision of medical care is an important part of it. But to restrict the command to such would be to interpret it in a way that does not find support in Scripture. Christ and his apostles were not physicians and did not provide this healing by means of contemporary medical practice. Nevertheless, they healed the sick, miraculously. Even Reformed and non-charismatic Churches and believers pray for divine (i.e. miraculous) healing—or at least should do so, since it is commanded in Scripture (James 5:13–15). Such prayer does not commit one to a charismatic perspective.

Let me make it clear, therefore, that I am not going to argue for a charismatic understanding of this command. I am not going to argue the case for the contemporary commitment to the charismatic gift of healing. Neither am I going to argue against it, at least not here. My point is simply that this command has been understood historically (leaving aside the contemporary debate about the charismatic gifts) as having a present application. This command binds us as Christians, whatever our perspective on the charismatic gifts, to the healing of the sick in Christ's name as an inevitable accompaniment of the preaching of the kingdom of God, and not only by the use of medical science, which for sure is not excluded,—indeed it is a necessary aspect of it (cf. James 1:27; 2:15–16)—but also by means of prayer for miraculous healing. As already indicated, to understand the command as *not* involving such divine intervention would be to interpret it in a way that is not consistent with the record of the Church's practice in the Scriptures themselves. In other words, the command does not apply exclusively to miraculous healing, but this is at least an important part of it, because there are situations in which modern medicine does not have the answers. Such an understanding of this command does not, in itself, argue the case for the continuation of the charismatic gift of healing. Quite the contrary, we are given instructions as to what we are to do when sickness strikes: the elders are to pray over the sick person and anoint him with oil, praying that any sins that have been committed be forgiven (James 5:13–15). This all Christians should accept as the ongoing practice of the Church without denying that God can work outside this context as well. This is healing by God directly in response to prayer without the intervention of medicine. Nevertheless, even when medical science is the direct means of healing we must trust ourselves primarily to God as the healer, and medical science as one means that he uses in his mercy. We must not be like Asa, king of Judah, who trusted himself to the physicians instead of to God (2 Chron. 16:12).

But we find ourselves in a difficult situation today. The healing of the sick is at best a hit and miss thing in the practice of modern Christianity. However much we might like to dress it up otherwise and pretend that the Church exercises a healing ministry, the Church does not heal the sick in any convincing way today, not in any way that is convincing to non-believers, and not even in a way that is convincing to many believers. And this is true on both fronts of the Church's healing activities, i.e. the practice of medical science and prayer for miraculous healing.

Let us look at the medical side first. The Church's commission to heal the sick has been taken over by the State on the medical front. This is not meant to be a criticism of the many Christians who work in the medical profession. But the fact is that people do not see the Church as an institution that provides healing in any sense today on the whole. They see the *State* as the institution that provides healing. Is there a problem in the Health Service? Most Christians in Britain would probably see the answer as somehow involving State funding of the NHS more adequately (i.e. via taxation or borrowing). But the Bible does not even recognise the State as legitimately acting in this sphere at all. Christian answers to the problems that face our society cannot be found down a route that is in principle not in accord with biblical ideals of social order. If even Christians trust the State rather than God to provide healing, is there any wonder non-believers do not recognise the Church's mission in this area. Whereas the Church in times past was recognised as providing for society significantly in this area, especially for those who were not able to provide for themselves—the poor—the Church has virtually abandoned all claim to this role today. The State has taken over completely. This is just another aspect of the State's usurpation of roles that belong to other organisations, but essentially with healing the result has been to create a trust in the State; i.e. people see the State as the author of salvation in this area.

Now of course, I use the NHS. I am not suggesting that Christians stop going to see their NHS doctor or stop using NHS hospitals. Why? Because we are now, as a Christian nation, effectively in a state of occupation by the enemy: secular humanism. We cannot realistically do otherwise—at least for the time being. But being in a situation where we have to accept that the NHS is the primary provider of medical health care in society (which we are forced to pay for via taxation anyway) does not mean that we should be ideologically committed to State health provision in principle. Unless we are prepared to think through and develop a distinctively Christian approach to the provision of health care we shall never be able to free ourselves from our enslavement to the State in this sphere. Most people cannot afford private health insurance in a society as socialist as ours is. And in any case, Britain does not really have an optional private health service. The private system in Britain is largely a queue jumping system, since the doctors who service the private system are the same ones who service the State system. Having private health insurance means usually that you see your NHS trained and NHS employed physician at a time when someone else on the NHS is waiting for an appointment. The doctor gets paid for the appointment via the insurance policy (i.e. privately); but he also works in the NHS and the time spent with a private patient means a time delay for the NHS patient next on the list. Or he may get an appointment for you to see a specialist at an NHS hospital a good deal earlier than if you had waited on the NHS list; but even then, the specialist would be taking time out of his NHS list to see his private patients. This is not a private system at all; it is a queue jumping system. This is not meant to be a criticism of those who use this private queue jumping system. My purpose is merely to point out that we do not have a proper alternative private system in Britain. Nor is it meant to be an argument against private medical health care. Quite the contrary; it is an argument *for* a proper private system. (Neither is it to argue that the free market will provide suitable heath care for all. I do not believe it will, though I do believe it will provide a significant part of it). But we need to stop pretending we have a private health system. We do not. We have a private queue jumping system, which those who can afford pay for.

This is a far cry from the Christian ideals upon which Christian health care works. Health provision for society as a whole in our nation was born out of Christian ideals, and the Church still has a responsibility in this area. But the State has taken over because the Church has withdrawn. So now people look to the State where once they looked to the Church; and Christians on the whole in Britain seem to think this is a good thing. But the consequence is that the Church in this area, as in so many others, is now irrelevant; she has no role, and people do not look to the God she proclaims as having any role in their lives when it comes to such things. Why? Well, in part the Church has been telling us that this is the job of the State. The State must fund health care by taxes. Our nation has even been told this is a Christian ideal. And yet in the very practice of it virtually every Christian virtue is under assault in the State-run health service (witness abortion and the attempts to legalise euthanasia), just as Christian principles are under attack in the State education system (witness the stripping of Christian values from education on just about every level). Under the State-run system we now have the absurd situation in which one can get a "sex change" on the NHS but those who suffer from multiple sclerosis cannot get the latest and most effective drugs to alleviate their condition. To argue that this is immoral is seen as religious bigotry by secular humanists. The Christian values underpinning medical health care have gone.[1] Now we have the ethics of State-run health care, which is supposed to be religiously neutral.

[1] Anyone who doubts this need look no further than the incident related in the article "Prison—After Saving Their Boy's Life" by John Smeaton in *Pro-Life Times*, Issue No. 5 (September 2000), reproduced in *Christianity & Society*, Vol. x,

This will not stop or be reversed in the State systems of health care or education despite the considerable money that Christians pour into trying to halt the decline each year under the misguided notion that they can "Christianise" a pagan system. The effect of such actions is at best to clean up secular humanism. But that is simply not good enough. It does not fulfil the Church's commission. For the time being we have to abide in the situation we have. But we can start building for the future if only the Church will awake from her slumber. But this means there must be leadership, and this is where the Church has fallen down. The Church's failure today is a failure of leadership. A Christian health care system would operate on criteria different from the secular humanistic criteria of the State-run system across the board. But one would not know this from the stance taken by the Church, which on the whole supports the idea of a State-owned health service.

What about the other front, i.e. the Church's prayer for the sick (miraculous healing)? Well, it's all a bit hit and miss really. I'm not saying people never get healed. But they do so far less than is claimed and the dubious stories we so often hear and read of today in the name of divine healing hardly inspire trust in God as our healer. The Church's witness to God in terms of healing in this respect is often a bad one. People do not see the Church as a source of compassion and healing for their diseases, but rather as a group of con-men trying to claim miracles as a testimony to a particular sect or charismatic leader. In other words, people do not see this infatuation with miraculous healing as a genuine concern for the sick or the glory of God (though doubtless it is on the part of many Christians).

In this respect the words of John Owen are pertinent: "It is

No. 4 (October, 2001), p. 17. The article relates the story of how members of a family were imprisoned after clashing with medical staff in hospital over whether their disabled nephew should be allowed to live. The family had been told that it was in the boy's best interests to allow him to die but his mother had intervened to stop doctors giving her son a diamorphine drip that would have led to his death. Two aunts and an uncle of the boy were prosecuted for their part in helping the mother save her son's life under a law intended to deter drunken violence in hospitals.

not unlikely but that God might on some occasions, for a longer season, put forth his power in some miraculous operations; and so he yet may do, and perhaps doth sometimes. But the *superstition* and folly of some ensuing ages, inventing and divulging innumerable miracles false and foolish, proved a most disadvantageous prejudice unto the gospel, and a means to open a way unto Satan to impose endless delusions upon Christians; for as true and real miracles, with becoming circumstances, were the great means that won and reconciled a regard and honour unto Christian religion in the world, so the pretence of such as either were absolutely false, or such as whose occasions, ends, matter, or manner, were unbecoming the greatness and holiness of Him who is the true author of all miraculous operations, is the greatest dishonour unto religion that anyone can invent."[2]

The fact is, neither non-believers nor even believers on the whole turn to the Church for healing today, whether of the miraculous kind or as a provider of medical care. And when they do turn to her for miraculous healing in response to prayer they are usually disappointed. Why is this? I should like to suggest a possible answer to this in what follows. It is not meant to be a dogmatic statement, but rather to suggest a reason for the Church's current lack of credibility not only in her mission to heal the sick, but also in her mission to preach the gospel with any significant results for individuals or society (by results here I do not mean merely bums on seats or money in coffers, but rather changed lives and a changed society, something that is seldom observed as a result of modern evangelistic campaigns or in modern conversions even where people have genuinely come to belief in Christ as Saviour of their souls[3]).

I suggest that the reason the sick are not healed by the Church today, or in a rather hit and miss and shoddy fashion, is that the gospel is preached in a rather hit and miss and shoddy fashion. In other words, I suggest there is a direct link between the two parts

---

[2] John Owen, *A Discourse of Spiritual Gifts* in *The Works of John Owen* (Edinburgh: Banner of Truth), Vol. 4, p. 475.

[3] For an explanation of this see Chapter One, "Christianity as a Cult."

of the command, between the preaching of the gospel and the healing of the sick. That is to say, unless we preach the gospel properly, we shall not be able to heal to sick properly, and the proper preaching of the gospel will lead to the proper healing of the sick. If your Church, therefore, has a rather poor record of healing the sick in its services, as most Churches in Britain do, or in providing for the sick in others ways, as most do, the real problem lies not on the "heal the sick" side of the equation but on the "preach the gospel" side, because it is my belief that the gospel is preached very poorly in our land today. I am not referring to preaching by liberals and the like, who often do not even claim to believe in the God of the Bible (I do not think the Church's problem lies with them, but rather with the evangelicals who have handed over custodianship of the faith to them without a fight, and who content themselves with sitting around tut-tutting about all the terrible things that the liberals are doing in the Church but seldom try to do anything about this in real terms). I am referring to the gospel preached by evangelicals, however that term should be defined or understood.

Why should we expect God to heal the sick in answer to our prayers if we refuse to preach the gospel in its fulness? If we preach a cut-down version of the kingdom of God, can we not expect a cut-down version of the healing of the sick? Evangelicals preach a gospel of sorts, but it is generally a truncated version of the one given us in the Bible. It is often little more than "pie in the sky when you die." Consequence: not much healing of the sick. A cut-down preaching of the message of salvation brings with it a cut-down healing of the sick. If we preached the gospel, we should be able to heal the sick. But we do not, we preach convenience religion, catatonic comfy-zone evangelicalism instead of the kingdom of God. Why? Because the Kingdom brings discomfort and challenge, and what Christians seem to want in Britain today is comfy-zone Christianity. We don't want any tribulation. By tribulation here I do not mean being thrown to the lions and the like; I mean the challenge that living life as a Christian brings. Whatever that challenge is, the answer too often of the Church, of individuals and of Church groups, is "We can't do that," which, translated into what people usually think rather than what they say, means "I don't want to do that, it would be inconvenient." Well, being thrown to the lions is a major inconvenience. A lot more inconvenient than providing your children with a Christian education instead of the secular humanist one they get down at the local State school (including State-funded C. of E. schools, which are usually little different from other State schools), or at a prestigious private school, which is much more convenient, and in the case of the former paid for by someone else on the whole. But so often we will not endure even the lesser tribulations that living the Christian life requires, both individually or as Churches. So we tailor the gospel to suit our tastes, to fit in with our comfy-zone. The result: catatonic Christianity. At all costs, the world must not be turned upside down; that would be too inconvenient. Yet we are told that we must enter the kingdom of God through much tribulation (Acts 14:22), and unless the world is turned upside down by what we preach, we are preaching a defective gospel. One consequence of this, but by no means the only one, is that the sick will not be healed, or at least not in any convincing way that demonstrates the Church's passion for God or her compassion for the sick.

Of course, there are many Christians who are desperately committed to the healing of the sick, both in medical terms and as miraculous answer to prayer. But perhaps the problem is sometimes that the cart is put before the horse. In other words, healing ministries come before the preaching of the gospel in its fulness. Jesus did not tell us to set up healing ministries. He certainly did not tell us to set up healing ministries and then heal the sick on a hit and miss basis. He did not promise to heal the sick on a hit and miss basis. But neither did he tell us to preach a gospel of personal salvation at death devoid of any real meaning for our lives in the here and now. He did not tell us to preach "pie in the sky when you die." He told us to preach the kingdom of God and to pray for his will to be done *on earth* as it is in heaven. The gospel we are given in the Bible is a gospel that impacts on our daily lives now, or at least should, to the extent that when people begin living it out it will turn their world upside down (Acts 17:6).

Perhaps in times past when our society was more Christian this characteristic of Christianity was less obvious, though I'm not entirely convinced of such an argument. But today we live in an aggressively anti-Christian society. If our preaching of the gospel does not challenge both ourselves and the world, it is defective preaching. Unless the Church is turning the society of which she is a part upside down something is missing. We are not *being* the Church effectively. We may go to church, sing all the hymns and choruses, say all the right things, but still fail to live effectively as Christians. This is not to deny the salvation of individuals. But one can have a saved soul and wasted life. If all the Church does is to go through rituals, good as those rituals are, we are not *being* the Church effectively. We have to stop thinking about planting and building up churches as the business of Christianity (i.e. building institutions dedicated to the Christian cultus) and start thinking about how we are to *be* the Christian Church, the body of Christ, a Christian community of faith, to the society God has put us in. I suspect this is at the heart of the Church's problem today. The gospel we preach is a cut-down version and the Churches we are part of are cut-down Churches. What people get when they come into contact with Christianity is quite simply the cut-down version. Just as some people buy the cut-down version of computer programmes, which cannot do all the things that the full versions can do, because the full versions are too expensive for them, so also Christians find the full version of the Christian faith too inconvenient, too much hassle in their lives, so they settle for the cut-down version; they are content to be brands snatched from the fire, to have a saved soul and a wasted life.

So what is the nature of this cut-down version of the faith? Primarily it is a gospel that treats salvation as deliverance from hell and an eternal home in heaven at death—hell-fire insurance. It emphasises the eternal only. As one evangelical lady once said to me: "I think death is the most wonderful thing in the world, I'm looking forward to it." But Jesus said that he came that we might have *life* more abundantly (Jn 10:10), not that we might have death more abundantly. Of course, as Christians we believe in the resurrection of the body and the life everlasting. This is a cardinal doctrine of the faith; without it there is no salvation ultimately. But the faith addresses our lives here and now in a decisive way. It changes everything, not merely our eternal destiny. So why do so many Christians have this truncated view of the gospel?

The answer to this question lies in the gospel that is preached. The evangelical gospel of today is not biblical. It is devoid of true religion: i.e. it is devoid of an overarching religious structure that anchors man in God's will for his life. Put in more biblical terms, it is devoid of the covenant. This does not mean that Christians are not regenerate, that they do not exercise saving faith. But it does mean that due to the lack of teaching in the Churches about what the faith is the evangelical practice of the faith is one-sided. Evangelicalism on the whole lacks a biblical paradigm for structuring this present life in such a way that it provides a meaningful context for the expression of the Christian faith. Where is such a paradigm to be found? In the concept of covenant, and, particularly as it refers to this present life, in the Old Testament. Of course, many Reformed Churches preach covenant theology. But even this is usually a cut-down version of the covenant with a narrow focus on soteriology and ecclesiology. The biblical covenant (the covenant of grace) and thus the biblical gospel is much broader that this, and to restrict the covenant to soteriology and ecclesial matters is to misunderstand the nature of the biblical concept of salvation.

Thus, the evangelical gospel of today, including that preached by most Reformed Churches in Britain, is unbiblical precisely because of its neglect of the covenant. As a result, evangelicals often do not have the biblical tools or raw material with which to work in determining the Christian attitude to many issues. While the evangelical Churches concentrate exclusively on New Testament Christianity they will miss the significance of the faith for this life and the salvation of our society and culture as well as our souls. And in doing this they will continue to preach an unbiblical gospel that has no basis in the New Testament either, but only in a truncated view of the New Testament. How is this?

When the New Testament speaks of Scripture it speaks of the Old Testament. When Christ spoke of the "Scriptures" he was referring to the Old Testament (Mt. 21:42). When he rebuked the Pharisees, telling them that they erred because they did not know the "Scriptures," he was referring to the Old Testament (Mt. 22:29). It is these Scriptures, says Jesus, that "testify of me" (Jn 5:39; Lk. 24:27). Likewise, when Paul speaks of the "the holy scriptures, which are able to make thee wise unto salvation through faith which is in Jesus Christ" and says that "All scripture is given by inspiration of God, and is profitable for doctrine, for reproof, for correction, for instruction in righteousness, that the man of God may be perfect, throughly furnished unto all good works" (2 Tim. 3:15–17), he speaks of the Old Testament. The believers of the apostolic era did not have a New Testament, though they did have the teaching of the apostles, which was founded on the doctrines of the Old Testament (cf. Mt. 5:17–19; Eph. 2:20). The Old Testament, which testifies of Christ, is the foundation of the New, and the New cannot be properly interpreted outside of the context of the Old. As Augustine said, "The New Testament is latent in the Old, and the Old is patent in the New."

But today we here of "New Testament" Christians. This mentality is symptomatic of the cut-down version of the faith that prevails among evangelicals, but it is a less powerful gospel, and a distorted gospel. Christ's own teaching of the gospel of the kingdom, of his purpose in coming to die for sinners, strikes at the heart of this reductionist version of the faith. The Old Testament is not an optional extra for the serious minded or the religious enthusiast. It is at the heart of the Christian faith. That is how it is presented in the New Testament and in Christ's own teaching. The Old Testament is fundamental to the gospel itself. Christ says to the Jews: "Had ye believed Moses, ye would have believed me: for he wrote of me. But if ye believe not his writings, how shall ye believe my words?" (Jn. 5:46–47). Unless we understand Moses we shall misunderstand Christ.

Yet a desire to understand Moses is hardly a characteristic of modern evangelicalism. Christianity for most evangelicals is a New Testament affair. The greater part of Scripture is neglected. This neglect then results in a distortion of the faith. For example, in one evangelical church I heard the message that basically God had three plans. The first two, the cultural mandate and the giving of the law through Moses, went wrong, so God sent his son to die for sinners instead (this is not too far removed from the schoolboy's quip about why God gave everyone four cheeks). This is the heart of the evangelical gospel today: the gospel supersedes the cultural mandate and the law of the covenant.

Jesus told us plainly that this is *not* what he came to do. He did not come to negate the law and the prophets but to fulfil them, i.e. to bring them into their full expression (Mt. 5:17–19). Thus, Jesus says that unless we understand Moses we will not understand him. His gospel cannot be separated from his word in the law and the prophets. If we cut ourselves off from the whole message of the Bible, either by using only the New Testament or by spiritualising the Old Testament away, we will end up with a cut-down version of the faith, and inevitably a cut-down experience of the Christian life, including answers to prayer for healing.

If we want to heal the sick we *must* preach the whole gospel. If we preach a cut-down gospel we shall have cut-down healing. What is the gospel? It is the good news about the kingdom of God. It involves the whole word of God for the whole of life. This means that we must cease practising Christianity merely as a personal worship hobby and make it our *religion,* i.e. what structures our whole lives in thought, word and action. We must bring the Word of God incarnate into the whole of our lives by looking to the word of God in Scripture to guide the whole of our lives. It is no good merely asking Jesus into our hearts—that is, to save our souls. We must bring him also into the life of our society at all levels, into our family life, our economic life, our leisure life, our work life, our political life, our medical life, our children's educational life, by listening to his word and seeking to conform ourselves to his word in all areas of life. Unless we subject ourselves to Christ and his word in this way the gospel we preach will be a cut-down version. But where do we go to get teaching, principles for action, understanding, for all this? The New Testament alone does not provide this. The Old Testament is a vital deposit of God's word for these areas of life. The New Testament does not claim to supersede all the teachings of the Old in these areas; it claims rather to be based on the Old Testament and to bring it up to date, so to speak, to show us how to bring the teachings of the Old Testament into fuller expression now that Christ has come and given his Great Commission to his disciples, i.e. the discipling of the nations. How shall we do this if we neglect the very words of Christ in the Old Testament, which comprises the larger part of the Bible? The result will be a distorted and a defective gospel.

The reason, I suggest, that the world is cynical about the Church's claims of miraculous healing is that there is little substance to these claims. This is because there is little substance to the Christian faith itself as practised by the Church in Britain today. The problem is not really that there is little substance to the claims of healing; rather the problem is that there is little substance to the practice of the faith across the whole of life, and this inevitably affects the Church's healing ministry. In short, if we preached and lived the gospel more fully we should find that the sick would be healed more convincingly. And this would have repercussions not only for the healing of the sick but also in other areas, including politics, economics, education, etc. The effect surely would be to turn the world upside-down. If we do not want Christ to rule our political, social, vocational, economic and educational lives, why should we expect him to jump every time we ask him for healing when we are ill?

For many years full-time Christian work has been seen as the work of the clergy and possibly medical missionaries. It is true that in recent years there has been a reaction to this in which whole body ministry has been stressed, but this ministry has still been narrowly conceived as ministry within the walls of the institutional church; in other words, its emphasis has been to share out the minister's job among a greater number of people. I suggest this is a wrong-headed notion to some extent. Not because I think Church leadership should be a one-man band. I do not. But because it focuses too narrowly on what Christian work is. It confines it to the institutional Church instead of seeing it as our cultural mandate in the world. Still the emphasis is only on the narrow soteriological and ecclesial aspects of the faith and also on the medical and the healing of the sick. Perhaps this has been because of a failure to understand the meaning of the command to preach the gospel and heal the sick, as if Church and hospitals are the only areas of life that Christ is concerned about. The rest of life is neutral. There's no such thing as Christian art, Christian music, Christian politics etc., just art, music and politics, which, because of their association with the world must be avoided. In this perspective Christ has not come to redeem the world, only individual souls. On the contrary, the gospel is for the whole of life. God commands us to bring all things into obedience to his Word incarnate by submitting to his word in Scripture as our rule of life.

What does this mean in practical terms? It means a lot of things. But because our nation is now occupied by the enemy our ability to do a great deal on all these levels is limited. That does not mean we should not try, but it does mean we shall progress slowly. But there is an example in which our ability to respond to God's call upon us is not so limited—at least here in Britain. It is an area where the Christian still has a great deal of freedom and where he is able to do something significant and constructive. Let us use it as a test.

The area I speak of is the education of our children. God requires us as Christians to give our children a Christian education. Christians are not expected to hand their children over to secular humanist schools for their education. Of course, there are few Christian schools. But home schooling is also an option, and it is growing in this country. Those who home school their children are no longer isolated individuals. "Oh, that is not for me! I can't do it" you say. Christ does not offer you a choice. He commands you to raise your children in the nurture and admonition of the Lord (Eph. 6:4). That includes, though is by no means limited to, their education.

The Christian Church (i.e. the Christian synagogue) has more in common with a school than it has with a temple, which does not feature in the new covenant as a place of worship. The Church is the community of faith, and in the institutional Church education has a central role to play. At the very least, therefore, supporting Christian education is a vital role of the Church, the community of faith. This is why in centuries past Christians set up schools as well as hospitals. Our schooling system was originally largely the product of a Christian society, as were our hospitals. Both have now been given over to the State, which, as the new god of our secular society, provides health and education for its citizens. One always looks to one's god for these things. Health care and education are intensely religious social functions. In our secular humanist society they are run in terms of the religion of secular humanism, as is our politics, which is also always an intensely religious activity.

Well, what are you going to do? Wait until your child is asked to engage in homosexual family role play activities in school? Don't think this will not come.[4] Clause 28 is as good as gone. Christian lobbying groups may stave off the debacle for a while. But as with all the other victories achieved by trying to play secular humanists at their own game (power politics) they will not last long. But suppose I am wrong and Clause 28 stays (and this is only an example, there are many other problems to consider); if your children are left in a secular humanist school they will continue to be educated in terms of a secular humanist world-view (and secular humanism is a *religion*), regardless of whether they attend the Christian cultus on Sundays and participate in some third rate Sunday school programme for an hour that isn't even aimed at undoing the effects

---

[4] Since this essay was written such role play has actually been advocated in educational material recommended by the Scottish Executive for sex education lessons in Scottish schools (Clause 28 has already been abolished in Scotland). See Stephen C. Perks, "Up Yours! The New Approach to Sex Education in Scotland" in *Christianity & Society*, Vol. XI, No. 3 (July 2001), p. 2f.

of what they are bombarded with in school all year. In other words your children will continue to be educated as secular humanists not as Christians. This is not merely a matter of sex education and discipline. Christ is concerned with more than our sexual behaviour; he is concerned with the whole of life, all the actions that are necessarily the result of our thought life, and it is the whole of this thought life that secular humanist education seeks to affect. State schools are responsible for the academic, physical, moral, psychological and spiritual growth of the child; i.e. the whole person. And raising children in the admonition of the Lord is equally concerned with all these things, with the whole person, not merely RE in the narrow sense. There are no neutral areas.

Of course, there are other issues to consider besides education. But this is a good place to start because it is one of the few areas where Christians are able to do so much. If you are not alone get together with other Christians in your Church and area who want to home school their children. Pull your children out of school and start home schooling them. Ask your pastor to support you and the whole idea of Christian education. If the Church will not support you in seeking to promote Christian education do it alone. Be prepared to be the only one. Make your faith count. This is *not* too difficult for you do (Mt. 11:30).

This will just be the start. There's more to come, but we have to start somewhere and, well, the other things we have to do will probably be much more difficult and contentious. Don't expect success elsewhere if you can't provide leadership here. Leadership training starts in the family not the work place (1 Tim. 2:4, 12). How are we going to set up Christian hospitals, Christian law courts operating at the local level (1 Cor. 6:2), a Christian political party, ministries and services to the homeless based on the Christian work ethic (2 Thess. 3:10), and perhaps most difficult of all Christian *Churches*, if we cannot lead our own families? (1 Tim. 3:4–5) We have more freedom, ability and power to educate our children in the faith than we have to affect just about any other field of human endeavour. If we fail here how can we expect to succeed elsewhere?

We have to create a Christian society, a Christian nation within a nation that will in time supplant the pagan society that now exists. Waiting for the rapture will not achieve this. When we start doing this—discipling the nation, as Christ commanded us to do (Mt 28:18–20)—we can expect to see the sick healed along with a lot more things we presently pray for but do not see. But don't expect much more than phoney claims of healing until we rid ourselves of the phoney gospel that is preached and lived today.

There is no lack of those who want to see the sick healed in the Church today, but there are many who do not want to preach the uncompromising gospel of the kingdom of God, and we all have to fight the sin in our own hearts that militates against the desire to live it out. The catatonic comfy-zone Christianity that presently prevails in Britain is the easy option: pie in the sky when you die. But don't expect the sick to be healed, and don't expect society to turn to Christ. The choice is yours. Don't wait for someone else to do it first. God calls you now to live out the gospel in word and deed. You can start now with what is within your power and ability to do: a Christian education for your children either at home or in a Christian school if there is one in your area. God does not call us to do the impossible, because with God all things are possible (Mt. 19:26). Either we believe it or we don't. If no-one else in your Church or area believes it, at least you do. Make your faith count, and make the words of Joshua your own: "As for me and my house, we will serve the Lord" (Josh. 24:15).

8

WHAT IS SPIRITUALITY?

"Spirituality" and "spiritual" are terms constantly used by Christians, yet seldom defined. No Christian would question the need for spiritual development, but what this means is left to the individual to work out. When spirituality is discussed and taught it is often vaguely defined at best, and the result is that spirituality is equated with a sort of mysticism or spiritual experiences and charismatic gifts. Yet seldom is the subject explored from the biblical perspective. Even among charismatics there is often little exegesis of scriptural texts relating to spirituality (as opposed to texts relating to spiritual gifts); rather, assumptions are made about spirituality, which remains unexplored biblically. To be sure, spirituality is understood as being "in tune with the Lord" or "walking close to the Lord" etc., but again these ideas are often very vague and undefined. And now, not only are Christians and other people who are perceived as "religious" types using the term. Teachers in State schools, for example, are now held responsible for the intellectual, social, physical, moral and *spiritual* development of the child.

But what does this mean? We now have New Age spirituality, which hardly sits well with Christian spirituality; though among evangelicals today all sorts of ideas about spirituality are popular. Celtic spirituality, for example, seems particularly popular at the moment—though I have not as yet found anyone who really seems to know what it is, at least sufficiently to be able to explain it to me. Hence it is just another type of mysticism.

Whatever notion of spirituality is adopted, it seems that being spiritual or spiritually mature is regarded as essential to knowing how to live the Christian life properly, especially when it comes to that old problem of *guidance*. And here it is that the Church so often finds herself adrift on a sea of changing ideas and fashions, tossed to and fro by all manner of strange phenomena claiming to be the latest work of the Spirit of God in our midst. Some get guidance from the Spirit directly, through impressions in the mind, "words from the Lord" and the like, while others evidently do not. Does this make the former more spiritually mature than the latter, who are less "in tune with the Spirit"? Doubtless to some it does, even if it is not overtly stated.

Then there is the common contrast between the spiritual and the intellectual, in which the mind or intellect is set up in some kind of antithesis to the spirit or spiritual understanding. Intellectual knowledge is often perceived as dangerous and detrimental to the development of spiritual understanding and the reception of Spirit-inspired guidance. In this perspective the use of the mind is rejected as a sort of fleshly temptation. In some charismatic Churches and movements the concept of spirituality that prevails could perhaps be described more accurately as a kind of spiritualism, so important are beliefs about genealogies of demons and demon possession of particular human blood lines, problems with being afflicted with curses, deliverance ministry and the like. Even to question this kind of spiritualism is often taken as a sure sign that one is "not sensitive to the Spirit." Such ideas seem more akin to animism than Christianity.

Yet when we look at the effects of such an understanding of spirituality we see not the spirit of a sound mind, the order and discipline that the Bible tells us should characterised the lives of those who are followers of Christ (1 Tim. 2:7), but rather the very opposite, i.e. a tendency to mental instability, disorder and even chaos that affects both congregational meetings and individuals. The "Toronto blessing" is a pertinent example. The nearest biblical incident of a man behaving like a beast I can think of is Nebuchadnezzer, who was driven to live like an animal until he acknowledged that sovereignty belongs to God (Dan. 4:28–37). Yet at Holy Trinity Church, Brompton, London, I saw men acting like animals under the pretense that they were receiving some bless-

ing from the Holy Spirit. One man, who got up to give his testimony, was so constantly racked with a violent jerking of the knees
and head that initially I thought he was severely disabled. As he
gave his testimony, however, it became clear that he had no disability. His behaviour was a blessing from the Holy Spirit! When
the "Toronto blessing" came upon the participating congregation
as a whole at the end of the service I saw people running up and
the down the aisles imitating cockerels, roaring like lions and imitating various other assorted farmyard animals. Along with this
there was the jabber and insanity of various other "manifestations" recorded throughout history in times of "revival": violent
shaking, uncontrollable weeping, crying and laughing, stamping
and paddying. The anarchy and lack of discipline of such meetings is in stark contrast with the obedience to God's law and the
discipline and order that the Bible demands of believers in their
worship. Even in small meetings and Bible studies those who claim
to have the gift of "speaking in tongues" will continually babble
away under their breath (with just enough volume to make sure
everyone knows what they are doing), despite the fact that we are
told clearly in Scripture to pray with the *mind* as well as the spirit (1
Cor. 14:15) and forbidden to speak in tongues without a translation (1 Cor. 14:28).

This contrast between obedience to Scripture and the reputed
manifestations of the gifts of the Spirit, being "in tune with the
Spirit" etc., has not diminished with the decline of the charismatic movement as such, but has in some respects become more
common as the influence of charismatic ideas has become more
widely diffused within evangelicalism, though in a more diluted
form. The result is that evangelical Churches are no nearer being
able to act on biblical principles of guidance than they were before the advent of this era of spiritual gifts. And this reputed great
movement of the Spirit in the charismatic Churches seems to have
had no effect whatsoever on the decline of the Church and of the
faith in Britain.

When it comes to pastoral matters this situation only makes
things worse. People sit around waiting for God to speak rather

than seeking to understand and apply the biblical principles of life that have already been revealed in Scripture. The answer to all sorts of problems in the Christian life is seen as a new revelation from the Spirit rather than the development of a Christian mind through the study and understanding of Scripture.

So what is spirituality? What does it mean to live a spiritual life? How is spirituality to be defined biblically? The answer is given very clearly in Rom. 8:1–16, where walking in or according to the Spirit is contrasted with walking in the flesh. But what does it mean to walk in the Spirit? In itself this gets us no further. We still need an explanation. And which spirit is being referred to? Ours or the Holy Spirit? And Christians who use this term profusely should, at least these days, stop to consider how the term is used more generally, because non-Christians now use the terminology of spirituality a great deal. What is spirituality to a non-Christian? Do we mean the same thing? Hardly. New Agers use the term, and unless we understand the difference and are able to explain it clearly to others who do not share our faith, our use of the term in the present cultural/religious climate will be misleading. Personally I try to avoid the term because of this, though its use by Christians prior to the advent of New Age spiritual ideas was not altogether well defined or helpful. And what of teachers who are to promote the spiritual development of their pupils?

Well, walking in the spirit could mean living according to our own spirit, i.e. getting in touch with our own spirit—the New Age idea of getting in tune with oneself at the deepest level. Or it could mean living in tune with the Holy Spirit. I shall take it as granted that for Christians the latter is the correct meaning. But this still leaves a lack of focus and room for much difference of interpretation and misunderstanding because what Christians believe about the Holy Spirit differs so much.

Fortunately, Paul does not leave us guessing about these questions. He explains what it means to walk in the Spirit very clearly. Interestingly, the criterion clearly set out by Paul as characterising living in the Spirit in contrast to living in the flesh is seldom mentioned in the context of discussion about spirituality, at least not in a positive sense. The criterion Paul gives us is *obedience to God's law* (Rom. 8:7). The one who walks or lives in the flesh is hostile towards God, we are told, because the *mind* does not subject itself to the *law* of God.

Now this is interesting because discussion of spirituality among Christians, at least in my experience, seldom revolves around the criterion Paul uses here. Spirituality is not usually seen in terms of adherence to God's law. More often the law of God is assumed mistakenly to be the "law of sin and death" mentioned in v. 2. Yet Paul shows clearly that the inability to subject ones *mind* to God's *law* characterises those who walk according to the flesh, not those who walk according to the Spirit, because the law, he tells us in v. 14 of chapter 7, is *spiritual*. The one who walks in the Spirit is the one who is prepared to subject his mind and thus his whole life to God's law, according to Paul. He is the spiritual person. Indeed, Paul even goes so far as to say that God sent his Son in the likeness of sinful flesh as an offering for sin in order that the requirements of the *law* might be fulfilled in those who walk in or according to the *Spirit* (8:3–4).

Clearly, therefore, when we come to understanding what spirituality is we must take into account this doctrine. If we fail to understand that salvation is essentially deliverance *from* bondage to sin (i.e. disobedience to God's law) into obedience to God (as he has set down his will for man in his law) we shall fail also to understand the true nature of spirituality. All sorts of ideas foreign to the Bible, or biblical ideas that have been twisted in our understanding, will then come to dominate our ideas of spirituality and guidance. Such foreign and twisted ideas have been common in the Church through the ages and are still common.

We are now in a better position to answer the question "What is spirituality?" from a biblical perspective.

1.   The spiritual man, i.e. the one who "walks in the Spirit," as defined by the Bible, is first one who is a son of God: "For as many as [i.e. all who are] led by the Spirit of God, they are the sons of God" (Rom. 8:14). The spiritual person is one who has received the Spirit of God, who has been delivered from his sin,

i.e. from his bondage to disobedience to God, through faith in
Christ by the working of the Holy Spirit, who has received the
Spirit of adoption, and has God as his Father (Rom. 8:15–16). First
of all, therefore, to be spiritual, or spiritually minded (let us not
forget that the spiritual man is one whose *mind* is subject to God's
law), is to trust God in Christ for salvation. It is to recognise that
one cannot save oneself by one's own works, one's own righteousness, and it is to trust oneself solely to Christ as the one who delivers us from our sins. The Holy Spirit is the Spirit of *faith*, trust in
Jesus Christ (1 Cor. 4:13–14). Therefore those who are Spirit-led
are those who trust Christ for salvation.

We shall go on to consider the necessity of obedience as the
fruit of this faith; but here I want to stress that the beginning of
true spirituality is the abandonment of our own righteousness,
our own works, as a means of reconciliation with God; it is to trust
oneself totally to Christ. Salvation is the gift of God in Christ, not
the reward of self-righteousness. Those who will be saved must
turn to God in Christ and trust in him as the one who delivers
men from sin. Only this work of grace in the human heart by the
Holy Spirit, granting faith to God's elect, makes one a spiritual
person, i.e. one led by, or living according to, the Holy Spirit.

This faith is the gift of God, not the product of the human
will or the reward of our own works: "For ye are saved by grace
through faith; and that not of yourselves: it is the gift of God: Not
by works, lest any man should boast" (Eph. 2:8–9). The spiritual
person is one who has received the gift of faith in Christ by the
working of the Holy Spirit in his heart, and who is therefore a son
of God. The spiritual person is one who has been freed, delivered,
from the power of sin and death by the Spirit of life in Christ, and
who is thus no longer under condemnation for sin (Rom. 8:2).

2.   This deliverance from sin involves a complete change of
mind. The word *repentance* in the New Testament (μετάνοια) means
a change of mind. Repentance is the changing of one's mind about
God and his will for one's life. It should manifest itself therefore in
the whole of a person's outlook.

The Bible has much to say about the mind. Many Christians

today have a wrong understanding of the mind. As we have seen, the mind is often seen in some kind of antithesis with the spirit or spiritual understanding. This perspective is foreign to the Bible. On the contrary, the Bible defines true spirituality as a *mind* set on the law of God (Rom. 8:6–7). You know the old proverb: "A man convinced against his will is of the same opinion still." A man who says he is Christian and believes in Christ, but whose mind has not been changed, is a man who has not repented. Christianity is not a form of fire insurance against being thrown into hell. It is not something we take on just in case something nasty happens, like the Last Judgement. It does not consist in the saying of mere words or creeds. It involves a complete change of *mind*, a turning away from what had been our unbelieving attitudes, views, aspirations etc. to *subjection of the mind to God's law*. Conversion to the Christian faith involves a change of mind.

Now, this emphasis on the mind is a biblical emphasis. Paul describes the unbeliever as one given up to a depraved *mind* (Rom. 1:28). The carnal *mind*, he tells us, is hostile towards God (Rom. 8:7). Non-believers live in the vanity, or futility, of their *minds* (Eph. 4:17). Paul warns the Colossians not to be misled by those who have a "fleshly *mind*" (Col. 2:18); he tells them they were once alienated and hostile in *mind* towards God and therefore involved in evil deeds (Col. 1:21). The unbelieving Israelites were people whose *minds* were hardened (2 Cor. 3:14). Non-believers have their *minds* blinded by the god of this world (2 Cor. 4:4). Paul expresses his concern for the Corinthians lest their *minds* should be led astray (2 Cor. 11:3).

In contrast with this unbelieving mind, Christians are those to whom God has given the Spirit of a sound *mind*[1] (2 Tim. 1:7). The new covenant is one in which God puts his *laws* into our *minds* and hearts (Heb. 8:10). We are commanded to love the Lord our God with all our *mind* (Mt. 22:37). Christians are those who have left aside the old self with its corruptions, lusts and deeds, and are being renewed in the spirit of their *minds* (Eph. 4:22–23). God shall

---

[1] On the meaning of the term translated as *sound mind* by the AV in this text see the discussion at note 8 below.

keep the hearts and *minds* of believers in Christ (Phil. 4:7). Peter tells us to gird up our *minds* for action (1 Pet. 1:13) and writes his epistle in order to stir our *minds* (2 Pet. 3:1).

The Christian is one who has changed his *mind*, whose mind has been renewed. Spirituality is the development of a renewed mind that is subject to God's law. Guidance in the Christian life, therefore, comes from the development of a renewed understanding that is subject to God's word, i.e. governed God's law.

3.   This change of mind resulting from belief in Christ leads to a different kind of lifestyle. What is this lifestyle? As already mentioned, it is a life that is subject to God's law, which is God's revealed standard of justice or holiness. As we have already seen, Paul shows us that the spiritual mind is a mind that is subject to God's *law* (Rom. 8:6–8). But there is more.

(i)   Paul says that the fruit of the Spirit, i.e. the fruit of living in conformity with the Spirit, is *love*, joy, peace, patience, kindness, goodness, faithfulness, gentleness, self-control; against such there is no law (Gal. 5:22–23). (Notice that he does not say that the fruit of the Spirit is pietism.) And he says elsewhere: "And now abideth faith, hope, charity [i.e. love, *agape*], these three; but the greatest of these is charity [*agape*]" (1 Cor. 13:13). Love (*agape*), we are told, of God and of one's neighbour, is the sum of the whole law and of the prophets (Mt. 22:37–40). But what is the love (*agape*) spoken of here? Paul tells us plainly: love (*agape*) is the fulfilling, i.e. the *keeping*, of the *law* (Rom. 13:10). The context makes this even plainer. Paul says "Owe no man any thing, but to love one another: for he that loveth another has fulfilled the law" (Rom. 13:8). But what does this mean? Paul explains immediately: "For this, Thou shalt not commit adultery, Thou shalt not kill, Thou shalt not steal, Thou shalt not bear false witness, Thou shalt not covet; and if there be any other commandment, it is briefly comprehended [i.e. summed up] in this saying, namely, Thou shalt love thy neighbour as thyself." (Rom. 13:9). Why? Because "love worketh no ill to his neighbour: therefore love is the fulfilling [i.e. the *keeping*[2]] of the

[2] Joseph Henry Thayer, *A Greek-English Lexicon of the New Testament* (Edinburgh: T. and T. Clark, 1901), p. 518*b*.

law" (Rom. 13:10). Christ tells us: "If ye love me, keep my commandments" (Jn 14:15); and John tells us that we know we have come to know Christ by keeping his commandments (1 Jn 2:3) and that anyone who claims to be a Christian but who does not keep the commandments is a liar and the truth is not in him (1 Jn 2:4). The one who has the fruit of the Spirit is one who loves both God and his neighbour, and love is the keeping of the law, both with respect to God and one's neighbour. Here again, therefore, spirituality, i.e. living in conformity with the Spirit, is defined as obedience to God's law.

(ii) We get the same result if we look at this from another angle, that of the purpose of the sending of the Holy Spirit. Christ says: "It is expedient for you that I go away; for if I go not away, the Comforter will not come unto you; but if I depart, I will send him unto you. And when he is come, he will reprove [i.e. convict] the world of sin, and of judgement, and of righteousness" (Jn. 16:7–8). The spiritual person is one who lives in conformity with the Spirit, one who is sensitive to the will of the Spirit in his life. But what is it that the Spirit comes to do? To convict the world of sin, judgement and righteousness. Let us look a little more closely now at these three convictions that the Holy Spirt comes to work in the world.

(*a*) The Holy Spirit comes to convict the world of sin. But what is sin? The Bible leaves us in no doubt about what sin is: "Sin is the *transgression* of the *law*" (1 Jn, 3:4). Thus, where there is no law, neither is there transgression (Rom. 4:15). The Spirit comes to convict the world of sin, to reprove man for his disobedience to God's law, which is God's revealed will for man.

(*b*) The Holy Spirit comes to convict the world of judgement. What does this mean? The word used (κρίσις), from which we get the English word *crisis*, means *a separating, selection,* or *a decision, judgement.*[3] The Spirit comes to convict the world of the judgement that must necessarily come to a world of sinners who have disobeyed a righteous God. God is not politically correct. He dis-

---

[3] G. Abbott-Smith, *A Manual Greek Lexicon of the New Testament* (Edinburgh: T. and T. Clark, 1986), p. 258.

criminates. And the basis on which he discriminates, the criterion he uses to discriminate, is his righteous law, which is perfect justice. Those who transgress are judged and condemned. But for those who trust in Christ the judgement fell on Christ at Calvary. This is what it means for Christ to bear our sin.

(c) The Holy Spirit comes to convict the world of righteousness. But what is righteousness? The word used for righteousness in the New Testament (δικαιοσύνη) means "conformity to the Divine will in purpose, thought, and action."[4] But then what is the divine will? Where do we find it? How do we know what God requires of us, how he requires us to purpose, think and act? By looking into the perfect law of God, which is a perfect transcription of God's righteousness. "The law of the Lord is perfect, converting the soul: the testimony of the Lord is sure, making wise the simple" (Ps. 19:7). "The statutes of the Lord are right, rejoicing the heart: the commandment of the Lord is pure, enlightening the eyes" (Ps. 19:8). "For the commandment is a lamp; and the law is a light; and reproofs of instruction are the way of life" (Pr. 6:23). Righteousness is conformity to God's will as revealed in his law, in purpose, thought and action. Thus, righteousness means *justice*, since what is just is defined by God's law. The Spirit, therefore, comes to convict us of righteousness, to show us not only that we are sinners, disobedient to God's holy law, but that we must also conform to the law if we are to be righteous.

Now, someone will say that our righteousness is Christ and that we are justified by his righteousness, not our own. This is true. This is the gospel. But Christ's righteousness is perfect conformity to the divine will in purpose, thought and action. The definition of righteousness is the same. We are saved by his righteousness, by means of his substitutionary life and death on our behalf. But the nature of righteousness remains unchanged. And though we are not delivered from our sins by our own law keeping, i.e. our own righteousness, but by Christ's righteousness, we are delivered from our sin so that the requirements of the law might be fulfilled in us, i.e. so that we might live obediently to God's law (Rom. 8:4). Thus

[4] *Ibid.*, p. 116.

Paul says "How shall we, that are dead to sin, live any longer therein?" (Rom. 6:2). In other words, how can those who have been delivered from sin, from bondage to disobedience to God's law, continue to live disobedient lives. The life of the believer is to be characterised by obedience, not disobedience. Our obedience is the response of faith, not the cause of it. Obedience to God's law does not save us, but it is still required of us, and the Spirit comes to convict us of this, to show us that we must obey and to lead us into the truth (Jn. 16:13) that we might obey God's law. Therefore Paul says that by faith, i.e. through faith, "we establish the law" (Rom. 3:31).

In these three particulars, therefore, we see that the work of the Holy Spirit is a work of enlightenment, but enlightenment of a specific kind, namely a work of *conviction*. The Spirit does not come to enlighten the world with mystical revelations and spurious spiritualistic experiences. He comes to convict us that we have sinned, transgressed against God's righteous law, God's *spiritual* law, that God judges those who transgress against his law, and that his righteousness is the standard of behaviour, the rule of life, that he requires of us. The law shows us what it means to conform to the divine will in purpose, thought and action. Of course we are convicted also that we cannot escape the judgement that awaits those who disobey God's law except by faith in Christ. So Jesus says, "He [the Holy Spirit] shall glorify me: for he shall receive of mine, and shall shew it unto you" (Jn. 16:14). The Holy Spirit convicts us of sin, judgement and righteousness, all concepts that relate to God's righteousness as it is revealed in his law.

So the one who is Spirit-led in the way he lives is one who is convicted, convinced, of the righteousness of God's law, of man's sin in disobeying it, of the inevitability of God's righteous judgment against that disobedience, and of man's need to conform to that law in purpose, thought and action; and he is one who knows, to whom the Holy Spirit has revealed, that only in Christ is there forgiveness and reconciliation with God. This is the truth into which the Holy Spirit leads men.

Being Spirit-filled or Spirit-led by this definition begins now to look much more familiar, more recognisable as the kind of behaviour that the Bible requires of us. Being Spirit-led is not being led astray by all sorts of spurious experiences into some kind of "Christian" spiritualism such as we often see in those Churches that claim to have direct revelations from God—revelations that seem to lead people into ever more bizarre and disturbing behaviour, mental instability, the breakdown of personal and congregational discipline and increasing chaos, so that the Church begins to resemble some kind of mystical sect rather than the congregation of a people who have received the Spirit of discipline (2 Tim. 1:7).

The Bible has no time for the heretical notion that the law of God and the Spirit of God are in opposition to each other. The law is spiritual (Rom. 7:14) and the Spirit comes to convict the world of the need for conformity to God's law, that the requirements of that law might be fulfilled in those who walk in the Spirit, i.e. in those who are spiritual (Rom. 8:3–6).

But what of Paul's statement that in Christ we are set free from the "law of sin and death"? (Rom. 8:2). The law of sin and death spoken of here is *not* the law of God. How could it be? Paul has told us that by faith we *establish* the law of God, that the law is *spiritual*, that the Spirit comes to lead us into conformity with that law. What then is "law of sin and death"? It is simply the *ruling power* of sin and death. Paul does not refer to God's law as being a law of sin and death but rather to the dominating power of sin in producing death. The "law of sin and death" is the ruling power, the dominating influence of sin in its capacity to produce death.

This is not a novel interpretation. For example, C. E. B. Cranfield writes in his commentary on Romans: "It would seem that Paul is here using the word 'law' metaphorically, to denote exercised power, authority, control, and that he means by 'the law of sin,' the power, the authority, the control exercised over us by sin. It is a forceful way of making the point that the power which sin has over us is a terrible travesty, a grotesque parody, of that authority over us which belongs by right to God's holy law. Sin exercising such authority over us is a hideous usurpation of the prerogative of God's law."[5] Likewise John Murray: "'law' in this instance is used in the sense of rule or principle of action. The usual signification of law, however, as that which propounds and demands action need not be suppressed. 'The law of sin' may be conceived of as not only impelling to action that is antithetical to the law of God but also as dictating such action"[6] And Calvin says: "I would not dare, with some interpreters, take *the law of sin and death* to mean the law of God."[7]

There is, therefore, no antithesis between the Spirit and the law of God; rather, the antithesis is between the Spirit of life, who comes to free us from disobedience to God's law (sin) and to enable us to obey God's law, and the law of sin and death (i.e. the ruling power of sin), which leads us to disobey God's law.

4.   The Holy Spirit is the Spirit of a *sound mind*, or a *disciplined mind*. "For God hath not given us the spirit of fear, but of power, and of love, and of a sound mind" (2 Tim. 1:7—note again the reference to love [*agape*], which is defined biblically as obedience to God's commandments [see 3(i) above]). Modern translations usually have ". . . of power, and love, and *discipline*." Ultimately it comes to the same thing since discipline, the ability to correct oneself according to God's word, is essential to wisdom and thus to a sound mind.[8]

What is clear from this is that a mind that is Spirit-filled or

[5] C. E. B. Cranfield, *The Epistle to the Romans* (Edinburgh: T. and T. Clark, 1975), Vol. I, p. 364.

[6] John Murray, *The Epistle to the Romans* (Eerdmans, 1959), Vol. I, p. 264f.

[7] John Calvin, *The Epistles of Paul the Apostle to the Romans and Thessalonians* (Edinburgh: The Saint Andrew Press, 1961), p. 157.

[8] It is worth noting, however, that according to Kittel's *Theological Dictionary of the New Testament* this word (σωφρονισμός) "has a definite act[ive] sence [*sic*] in secular lit[erature]: 'Making to understand,' 'making wise.' Inasmuch as understanding is the basis of virtue and an upright life (Plat. Charm., 164d) it also means 'admonition to do better,' Strabo, 1, 2, 3; Plin. Cato Maior, 5, 1 (I, 338 f.); Jos. Bell., 2, 9; Ant., 17, 210; 18, 128; Philo Leg. All., III, 193. More rarely it can mean 'discretion' in the sense of 'moderation,' 'discipline.' Plut. Quaestionum Convivalium, VII, 8, 3 (II, 712c); Iambl. Vit. Pyth., 30, 174." (Ulrich Luck, "σωφρονισμός" in Gerhard Kittel and Gerhard Friedrich, *Theological Dictionary of the New Testament* [Grand Rapids, Michigan: Eerdmans, 1971, trans. G. W. Bromiley], Vol. VII, p. 1104).

Spirit-led is a disciplined mind. It is not characterised by instability regarding one's understanding and practice of the faith. The Spirit is also a Spirit of order. Congregational meetings that are Spirit-led will be orderly meetings, meetings characterised by discipline (cf. 1 Cor. 14:40). Paul counsels the Corinthians that non-believers who see the Church acting disorderly will think they are mad (1 Cor. 14:23). Therefore they are to make sure everything happens in an orderly fashion. Disorderliness in church meetings is *not* a mark of the Spirit, nor is disorderliness and indiscipline a mark of the Spirit in the individual. The Spirit-led person is one whose life is characterised by discipline in the faith, including stability in understanding and practice of the faith, i.e. wisdom.

This gives us a very clear benchmark against which to assess claims that people or Churches are being led by the Spirit. Is this spirit of discipline what we find among those individuals and Churches that claim to be led by the Spirit, who claim that they have received directions and revelations from the Holy Spirit? If not then the claim to be Spirit-led is vain. Those who engage in disorderly and chaotic meetings, and those with disorderly and chaotic lives have not understood the meaning of spirituality. Indeed, we tend to find quite the reverse, namely, that those who proclaim loudest that their Churches and lives are Spirit-led tend to display greater disorder, an observable lack of discipline, lack of understanding and an inability to act in terms of biblical wisdom—in other words immaturity in the faith. One thinks immediately of the "Toronto blessing" phenomenon, but this is merely the latest fad in a long established tradition of idiocy in the charismatic movement. The experience of many is that those who claim a never-ending stream of revelations and "words" from the Holy Spirit are least concerned of all about knowing, understanding and applying God's law to their lives and Churches in order that they might live in a disciplined way according to biblical wisdom. It would not be going too far to say that on the whole charismatic Churches least of all can be said to be characterised as disciplined Churches, and often an element of mental instability can be observed (and I think this latter observation can be explained to some extent by the fact that the unbiblical ideas of spirituality that tend to prevail in such Churches are inherently destabilising mentally). Least of all could it be said of charismatic Churches that they are characterised by the spirit of a sound mind.

I have been asked to discuss the nature of spirituality and to explain my assertion that to be spiritual is to trust and obey God. This is not meant to be a pogrom against charismatic Churches. I have written on this subject because I have been asked to do so.[9] But if I am to acquit myself properly of this task I must deal with the relevant issues pertaining to it. I must highlight the serious problems relating to the practice of faulty spirituality, not because I wish to lambast particular people or Churches (I do not wish to do so), but because misunderstanding of what constitutes biblical spirituality has issued in a serious failure to practise the Christian faith properly, a failure that is particularly relevant to the charismatic Churches, and a failure that seriously inhibits the Church's mission in the world as this is defined biblically. All of us fall short. But knowing that we do and where we fall short is half the battle in overcoming our lack of true spirituality, and this is impossible if use of the mind in accordance with biblical teaching is automatically viewed with suspicion as unspiritual. Why? Because, as we have seen, it is through the renewing of the *mind* by the Spirit that we grow in our faith and in our understanding of the faith and thus become more spiritual in our thoughts and actions.

So what is a sound mind or a disciplined mind, biblically speaking? What is spiritual discipline?

(i) Spiritual discipline is the ability to use scriptural wisdom as a means of guidance. It is not reliance on every impression that enters one's mind as a means of guidance, nor is it being tossed about with every whim or fashion of "spiritual" experience that blows in one's direction. It is the disciplining of the mind according to God's word.

[9] This essay was originally written in response to a letter in the correspondence column of *Christianity & Society* (Vol. X, No. 3 [July 2000]) asking for clarification on and biblical justification for my assertion that spirituality is simply trusting and obeying God.

The most difficult battle that anyone ever has to face is the conquest of the mind. And it is here that we see the Holy Spirit at work in the sanctifying process, because as a man thinks, so he is (Pr. 23:7). We are what we think, the Bible tells us, not what we eat. The way we think determines the way we speak and act. If we are to conquer our words and our actions we must first conquer our minds. Renewing of the mind by the Holy Spirit is what leads to obedient living, i.e. sanctified living.

This spiritual discipline involves understanding God's word and the ability to apply it. This is not mere theological knowledge, knowledge of or commitment to Reformed creeds and doctrine, as some seem to think. Knowledge of doctrine, valid as it is, even vital as it is, does not on its own constitute true spirituality. True spirituality is more a question of developing a Christian mind, a Christian world-and-life view, and living in terms of this, something that Reformed Churches as much as any brand of Christianity tend to depreciate. This is a matter of developing a biblical wisdom (to use John Peck's definition[10]), i.e. the discerning ability to recognise one's situation and apply biblical principles of life appropriately. This is something that is *learned*. We put on Christ, Paul tells us: "put ye on the Lord Jesus Christ . . ." (Rom. 13:14). Wisdom is acquired through learning and practice in the submission of one's mind to God's word.

Neither is wisdom something that exists in a vacuum, i.e. divorced from an understanding of the world in which we live. It cannot co-exist well with retreat and isolation from the world because as a work of the Holy Spirit in our lives the purpose of the acquisition of biblical wisdom is to enable us to live redemptively *in* the world, i.e. to live in such a way that we bring ourselves and the world in which we are placed and to which we relate continually into subjection to Christ. We are commanded to go out into all the world with the message of Christ (Mk 16:15). Pietism, therefore, is not a manifestation of biblical wisdom. It is rather the opposite of biblical wisdom, namely an attempt to escape in some

---

[10] See John Peck and Charles Strohmer, *Uncommon Sense: God's Wisdom for our Complex and Changing World* (London: SPCK, 2001), *passim.*

way from the world, to abandon the world or at least significant aspects of it. Pietism is the opposite of living redemptively in the whole of life. The purpose of biblical wisdom, or the development of a Christian mind, a Christian world-and-life view, is to enable us to live redemptively in the world and therefore transform it, bringing everything we touch into subjection to the obedience of Christ (2 Cor. 10:3–5).

(ii) A disciplined mind or a spirit of self-discipline leads to *reasonable* service. Paul says, "I beseech you therefore, brethren, by the mercies of God, that ye present your bodies a living sacrifice, holy, acceptable unto God, which is your *reasonable* service" (Rom. 12:1). Some translations have "spiritual worship" instead of "reasonable service." The words used (λογικὴν λατρείαν) mean "reasonable" or "rational service." The AV is the better translation. The word translated as "reasonable" is the word from which we derive the English words *logic* and *logical*. According to John Murray "The service here in view is worshipful service and the apostle characterizes it as 'rational' because it is worship that derives its character as acceptable to God from the fact that it enlists our *mind*, our *reason*, our *intellect*. It is rational in contrast with what is mechanical and automatic. A great many of our bodily functions do not enlist volition on our part. But the worshipful service here enjoined must constrain intelligent volition. The lesson to be derived from the term 'rational' is that we are not 'Spiritual' in the biblical sense except as the use of our bodies is characterized by conscious, *intelligent*, consecrated devotion to the service of God."[11] The word "service" does not refer merely to worship services, either privately or in church, but rather to a whole life of service to God. Paul is not speaking merely about what we do in church or at Bible studies or in family devotions; he is speaking about the character of our whole lives, which are to be lives of reasonable, *rational*, service to God.

This has some significant implications for the way we live our lives and the way we worship together in congregational meetings. According to Paul here there is no room in the Christian life

[11] Murray, *op. cit.*, Vol. II, p. 112; my emphasis.

of service for the mindless emotional binges that have become common in the "worship" services of many evangelical Churches, nor insane antics such as those to be observed at "Toronto blessing" meetings. Our service to God, our life of working for his Kingdom in all its aspects, is to be *rational*. Mysticism and gnosticism are not part of the Christian religion. The Christian faith is a reasonable, a *rational* faith. Therefore we are required to be able to give a reasoned defence of the faith to all who ask (1 Pet. 3:15).

Here again we see that the use of the mind in defending the faith, which the Bible commends, indeed demands of us, is often incorrectly deprecated by Christians who have come to believe that defending the faith with reasoned argument is not a spiritual activity because it involves intellectual effort, and intellectual effort is perceived often as the antithesis of being spiritual. Spirituality in this perspective is divorced from the use of the intellect. The Bible denies this dichotomy. The spiritual person, i.e. the Spirit-led person, is one who is always ready to give a *reason* for the hope that is in him, i.e. a reasoned defence of the faith. God requires the service of our *minds* in the whole of our life of service. To fail to use our minds in the service of God is to offer a worship that is not acceptable. Acceptable worship to God is rational worship, worship that "enlists our *mind*, our *reason*, our *intellect*."

(iii) Spirituality, or the Spirit-led life, is a life of dominion in our callings to bring all nations under the discipline of Christ (the Great Commission, Mt. 28:18–20) and all areas and aspects of life into conformity with his word (the Cultural Mandate, Gen. 1:28).

I said earlier that wisdom cannot be divorced from the world in which we live since its purpose is to enable us to live redemptively in the world for God's glory and in his service. As far as this life is concerned we cannot be spiritual unless we are engaged in the life of the world. Why? Because our calling as God's people, the new humanity in Christ, is to bring all things into subjection to God's word (Mk 16:15; 2 Cor. 10:5). The spiritual person, or Spirit-led person, is the person who is obedient to the Great Commission and the Cultural Mandate. Our purpose in serving God here on earth is to claim the world for Christ. Dominion is a biblical principle, but without biblical wisdom there is no dominion, only domination, and as Christ made clear, we are not to pursue domination (Mt. 20:25). The Spirit-led life is a life of dominion under God's law, not a life of domination over others, and this is something that especially those who see themselves in positions of spiritual authority should remember, because spiritual domination is a snare and a temptation to many pastors and clergymen. Christ does not call teachers and pastors to bully and manipulate their flocks like little popes, nor does he give them divine authority to demand absolute obedience to their every whim and diktat. The spiritual man is not a man characterised by fear, but by boldness, power and discipline (2 Tim. 1:7). Boldness without discipline can easily turn into brashness; and this can—and often does—lead to bullying among those who aspire to be spiritual leaders in the Church. Control freaks have vandalised the Church throughout much of history, just as their counterparts in the world of politics have ruined nations. It was said of John Knox that he feared God so much that he feared no man alive—and he suffered at the hands of men himself. But the fear of God brings humility also and self-discipline. Without the fear of God and wisdom there can be no true dominion and thus no reclaiming of the world, which is Christ's inheritance, and our inheritance in him (Mt. 5:5). Our cultural mandate is to exercise dominion over the earth under God as his vicegerent, not to exercise domination over other people's lives. The former builds the kingdom of God, the latter builds mere human empires (whether of the political or the ecclesiastical variety), all of which will perish before the kingdom of God. Our focus must be Kingdom-oriented and we must build the kingdom of God with spiritual means and wage war against our enemy with spiritual weapons, i.e. in obedience to God's law (2 Cor. 10:3ff.).

Neither are we to fear Satan. Many there are whose Christian lives are almost dominated by talk of and thought about Satan, whose Churches are forever getting involved with demon deliverance and blaming everything that goes wrong in their lives on attacks from the Devil, from burning the Sunday dinner to adultery. The world for these people is infested with demons. This is

not a Christian view of the world, and in fact is more akin to
animism. The mind-set or world-view produced by this perspective is neither healthy nor biblical, indeed it is the opposite of
biblical wisdom. Satan has no power that is not given him by God.
Our lives are to be governed by our relationship to God in Christ,
by conformity to his will as revealed in his law. If we observe this
rule of spirituality we need have no fear of Satan.

The spiritual person is one who works for dominion in Christ
by applying biblical principles of wisdom and discipline in the
whole of life. As he does so he develops a Christian mind, a Christian world-and-life view, and this enables him to face those situations in life that are difficult and for which he needs guidance by
using his Christian mind in terms of biblical wisdom to determine
how he should act. This is how true spirituality is developed.

The chart on p. 111 summarises the issues discussed in this
essay and contrasts biblical spirituality with the prevailing features
of many spurious ideas of spirituality that are currently popular,
both in the Church and in the world.

To conclude: spirituality is a term much abused and misunderstood to mean many different things. Christian spirituality must
be defined biblically. If we are to develop spiritually, rather than
being led astray with every wind of spurious doctrine that blows
our way, we must seek to understand the meaning of spirituality
in terms of God's revealed word.

In terms of biblical teaching the spiritual man is: 1. a son of
God, i.e. redeemed by God's grace in Christ through faith. He is
one who has the Spirit of faith and trusts Christ for salvation. 2.
He has thoroughly changed his mind, repented, i.e. turned away
from his sin to Christ and wishes to live the whole of his life according to God's will. He is one who is being renewed in his *mind*.
3. He has turned to God's law as the divinely revealed pattern for
his life and therefore seeks to understand it and apply it to his life.
4. He is disciplining himself according to God's word, (i) by seeking to develop a Christian mind, a Christian wisdom or world-
and-life view, which will guide him through life, (ii) by seeking to
render a reasonable, a rational service to God in the whole of life,

Comparison of Biblical Spirituality with Non-biblical "Christian" and Pagan Spirituality		
Biblical Spirituality	Non-biblical "Christian" and Pagan Spirituality
—Based on public revealed truth addressed to all men	—Based on private revelations
—Rational/reasonable —Geared to understanding and applying God's word and serving God by building his kingdom	—Irrational/mystical and Gnostic—has meaning for and can be understood only by the initiated —Geared to getting in tune with the self and realising one's potential
—Engaged in the world, bringing it into subjection to Christ's law —Great Commission/Cultural Mandate	—Retreatist/pietistic —Not in the world but probably of it!
—Guidance: wisdom oriented—concerned with applying biblical principles and doctrine —Oriented to obedience to God's law and understanding his revealed word, developing a Christian mind or Christian world-view	—Guidance: by means of impressions and feelings —Antinomianism

enabling him to give a reasonable defence of the faith to those who ask it of him, and (iii) by seeking to exercise dominion in following Christ by being obedient to the Great Commission and the Cultural Mandate across the whole spectrum of life.

Now all this can be summed up in this aphorism: to be spiritual is to trust and obey God. Spirituality is not a mystical feeling, or spiritual revelations, or Gnostic insight. The one who is led by the Spirit is the one who trusts and obeys God. In order to enable us to trust and obey, the Holy Spirit renews our minds and hearts. Thus, to put it another way, the spiritual person is the one whose heart and mind have been renewed by the Holy Spirit and whose life proceeds from this renewed mind. For as a man thinks, so he is (Pr. 23:7).

9

THE CHURCH EFFEMINATE

I was once asked whether it would be correct to say that in the history of the world whole dynasties and indeed civilisations have foundered on the rock of homosexuality. My answer was that I would not put it this way. Of course I believe that homosexual practices are immoral and forbidden by God's law. However, in Rom. 1:21–32 Paul puts it this way: Men turned away from serving God to serving the creature; as a consequence God gave them over to impure passions. Homosexuality is God's judgement on a society that has turned away from God and worships the creature rather than the Creator. Spiritual apostasy is the rock upon which cultures, including our own, founder, and homosexuality is God's judgement on that apostasy. This is why homosexuality was a common practice among the pagan cultures of antiquity, indeed is a common practice among most pagan cultures, including now our own increasingly neo-pagan culture.

In short, the idea that the toleration of homosexuality is an evil that will lead to God's judgement is unbiblical because it puts the cart before the horse. The truth of the matter is that it is the other way round. The prevalence of homosexuality in a culture is a sure sign that God has already executed or is in the process of executing his wrath upon society for its apostasy. The cause of this judgement is not the immoral practices of homosexuals (immoral though homosexual acts are). The cause of the judgement is spiritual apostasy. The prevalence of homosexuality is the *effect*, not the cause of God's wrath being visited upon a society. And in a Christian (or perhaps I should say "post-Christian") society this means, inevitably, that the prevalence of homosexuality in society is God's judgement on the *Church* for her apostasy, her unfaithfulness to God, because judgement begins with the house of God (1 Pet. 4:17).

This is not a popular message with Christians. It is easy to point the finger at gross sin and immorality, but the Church is much less willing to consider her own role in the social evils that blight our age. The spiritual apostasy that led to our present condition started in the Church, and much of the debacle of modern society that Christians rightly lament can in some measure be traced to this apostasy of the Church as the root cause. And even now the Church refuses to take her responsibility for preserving society from such evil seriously and has abdicated her role as the prophetic mouthpiece of God to the nation.

Of course, this does not mean we should not challenge the gay lobby and work to establish biblical morality in our society. We must. But we must also get our priorities right, and I fear that the Church has misdiagnosed this problem and got her priorities wrong. The Church suffers from the homosexual blight as much as, perhaps more than (with the exception of the media and entertainment world), any other section of society. For most of the past century the Church has been seeking a female god to replace the God of the Bible. We have had ministers who have thought, acted and preached like women for many years now. The clergy in our age is, on the whole, characterised by effeminacy. The increasing number of homosexuals in the ministry is, I think, both a cause and effect relationship related to this and at the same time a manifestation of God's judgment on the Church. Often, of course, judgement works through cause and effect relationships, because the whole Creation is God's work; it therefore functions according to God's plan and will. The Church has become thoroughly feminised by an effeminate clergy. Ministry today is directed primarily at women, and ministers have begun to think and act like women, so that Christianity has become what someone has called "lifeboat religion"—women and children first. And the world sees this well enough.

For example, I have been told on more than one occasion by priests and ministers that when they go out visiting members of their parishes, if the man of the house comes to the door the first thing he will often say is "I'll go get the wife." Vicars and ministers are there to pamper to women and children, or so the world thinks, and this is simply because ministry in the Church is so often directed primarily to women and children, not to men. Likewise, I have been told by clergy that now that women are increasingly present in the ranks of the clergy the nature of chapter meetings etc. has changed; now these meetings of the clergy are characterised much less by doctrinal matters and discussion revolves more around "relationship" issues. In other words the meetings have been taken over by a women's agenda. I have observed the same kind of thing in church meetings. If one brings up doctrinal issues or even serious issues about the mission of the Church there is little interest. "There isn't time now. We'll deal with this another time" is the usual response, though seldom are such issues dealt with later either. But there is always enough time to consider trivial matters and in particular whether all our "relationships" need more work on them. And yet in most Churches where I have experienced this kind of attitude I have not detected serious relationship problems troubling the Church. However, there have often been and continue to be prodigious doctrinal problems and problems related to the Church's understanding of her mission in the world troubling these Churches, yet these are not even considered worthy of discussion in Church leadership meetings. Church leaders will talk endlessly about "relationships" and the like but avoid doctrinal issues like the plague because these are deemed to cause division and hinder "relationships."

Now at root I believe this is a serious problem created by the feminisation of Church leadership. The leadership agenda, which is a masculine agenda, has been replaced by a feminine agenda, which is a disaster for leadership. The Church has abandoned the God of Scripture for the cosiness of a female type of deity who does not require Church leaders to expound biblical doctrine or act with conviction according to God's word (both of which are perceived, often correctly, as causing division—Mt. 10:34ff.), but instead requires leaders simply to mother their congregations in a feminine way. This naturally produces effeminate clergymen and an effeminate Church. But this is not merely an impersonal cause and effect relationship. God works through second causes in his Creation to accomplish his will. An effeminate ministry and an effeminate Church is God's answer to the Church's determination to replace the God of Scripture with a female god; and this crusade against the God of the Bible has been, in its own way, as much a feature of evangelicalism as it has been of the outright liberalism that evangelicals claim to abominate yet so willingly imitate.

Not only is this a problem for the Church now, but because it is a problem for the Church, society at large is now feminised and effeminate. We are ruled by women and men who think and act like women. But women do not make good rulers generally. In Margaret Thatcher we had a reverse situation, a women who thought more like a man should think—but the exception does not nullify the rule. I am not making a party political point here, or endorsing any policies; because even then I believe this was all part of the judgmental situation. The world is turned upside down because men have turned it upside down by their rebellion against God. Jean-Marc Berthoud made this point well in his article "Humanism: Trust in Man—Ruin of the Nations,"[1] which I recommend in relation to this topic. We are now ruled by women and boys (Is. 3:4, 12).

But leadership is not feminine. Effeminate leaders do not rule well, either in the State or the Church. It is vital that justice is tempered with mercy. But one cannot temper mercy with justice. When mercy is put before justice societies collapse into the idiotic situation we have today where criminals are set free and innocent people are condemned. For example, punishments meted out to motorists for inadvertently driving a little over the speed limit today, even where no danger is involved,[2] are often more severe than

---

[1] *Christianity & Society*, Vol. IX, No. 2 (April 1999), pp. 24–28.

[2] I am not referring here to reckless driving that puts people's lives at risk, but to situations in which there is no danger involved. I have yet to see a police speed trap on a dangerous road or on a road where the speed limit must be kept low in

punishments meted out to thieves.[3] And a parent can be punished for spanking a naughty child today, even where such punishment is carried out in a loving and disciplined environment and there is no danger to the child. Yet one can murder one's unborn children with impunity. The State even pays for these abortions by providing them on the National Health Service.

This, I believe, is ultimately the result of the feminisation of our culture. It is often thought that feminine rule is more compassionate, more caring. This is a myth that feminist ideology has worked into the popular perceptions of reality in our culture. On the contrary, the feminist culture is a violent culture, a culture that produces abortion on demand and at the same time the demand for the banning of fox hunting. A more perverse situation is hardly imaginable. Ultimately feminism is in practice inherently violent, inherently unstable, inherently perverse, inherently unjust, because it is all these things in principle; i.e. it is a rejection of God's created order, and the consequences of such a religious commitment will always work themselves out in practice. Feminism is now working out practically the consequences of its religious vision of society (and it is a religion).

The Churches have failed to see this. They have embraced feminism vigorously, and as a consequence have become themselves a major avenue by which feminism has been able to influence our culture. The clergy were involved in feminising the faith and the Church well before the feminist movement had become so

---

order to avoid accidents involving pedestrians ("black spots"). The only ones I have seen are on roads where it is easy to trap motorists because the road obviously will take a higher speed limit than the one imposed—in other words where it is easy to stray inadvertently above the speed limit even when one is driving responsibly and with due care. This has led me to the conclusion that the real purpose of such speed traps is not to police "black spots" but simply to raise more revenue.

[3] See the interesting article by Brian Lawrence, former Deputy Training Officer for Berkshire Magistrates, "The sorry state of the criminal justice system" in *Right Now!*, issue 25 (Oct.–Dec. 1999), p. 10f. for more information on this absurd situation. He has also written a book on this subject, *They Call It Justice* (Book Guild Limited, 1999, ISBN 1-85776-372-6), which I have not seen.

self-conscious and popular. And the feminisation of our culture is
a major reason for its anarchy and violence. For instance, the result of the feminisation of society has been that men have lost
their role in many respects. Feminism has defined men into nothing more than yobbos or effeminates. These are the two alternatives for men in the feminist perspective, although this is not understood by feminists because feminism is naïve and operates not
on the basis of reason but on emotion; and this brings us again to
the problem of female leadership and rule. Emotion does not lead
or rule well. For feminists, men are incapable rulers; women should
rule. Now we have the rule of women and effeminate men. The
effect of putting the feminine virtues in the place of the masculine
virtues and the masculine virtues in the place of the feminine virtues has been to overturn the created order. As a result justice is
despised and mercy is turned into vice. Leadership is masculine,
but it needs the tempering of the feminine virtues. When feminine virtues are in leadership the masculine virtues cannot function; masculinity is made redundant. This is one of the most serious problems facing our society. Feminism has rendered masculine leadership in the Church and the nation obsolete, and we are
now reaping the spiritual and social consequences of this. Justice
is a casualty. Mercy ceases to be mercy and becomes indulgence
of the worst vices. Violence, anarchy, disorder, and a dysfunctional
society are the legacy of the feminisation of our society, because
in this order neither the masculine nor the feminine virtues can
play their proper role. The world is turned upside down. Even the
"Bible believing" Churches are numbed in their apostasy regarding this and many other matters in our society. We have an effeminate Church, and an effeminate society, and therefore God's answer has been an increasingly homosexual ministry and an increasingly homosexual society. This is God's righteous judgement
on our spiritual apostasy.

The answer is repentance: turning to God and turning away
from our rebellion against the divine order of Creation. The
Church must start this. Judgement begins with the Church (1 Pet
4:17), and repentance must also. I do not believe we will solve the

homosexual problem until we recognise its cause. It is God's judgement on the apostasy of the nation. Leading the way to that apostasy was the Church.

What I have said above is not meant to downplay the seriousness of the homosexual problem, nor its immorality. But we must recognise it as a manifestation of God's judgment, as Paul teaches so clearly in Romans chapter one. The answer lies with tackling the root cause, while not leaving undone the other things. What is said here is not meant to encourage a lessening of Christian opposition to gay rights by any means; but it is meant to encourage a wider reading of the problem, because it is in this wider reading of the problem that we detect the cause, and hopefully, the solution to the problem.

Furthermore, this issue is not an isolated one. It is all part and parcel of the repaganisation of our society, a trend in which the Church in large measure has not only acquiesced but sometimes actively encouraged by her myopic perception of the faith and her practical denial of its relevance for the whole of man's life, including his societal relationships and responsibilities. While criticism is necessary and vital in the Church's prophetic task of bringing God's word to bear upon our society, it is not enough. The Church must also throw off her own acquiescence in the practices of secular humanism and practise the covenant life of the redeemed community instead if she is to have any effect on our culture. So far, the Church, by and large, has shown herself unwilling even to contemplate the practice of this covenant life and has contented herself with mere criticism at best (though not even criticism of secular humanism or its code of immorality is to be found among many clergymen). Therefore the judgment will continue unabated until the Church once again begins living out as well as speaking forth the words of life to the society around her. Only then will she begin to manifest the kingdom of God; and only when the Church begins to manifest the kingdom of God again will our society begin to be delivered from God's judgement.

10

IDOLS FOR DESTRUCTION

On 31 August 1997 Diana, the Princess of Wales, was killed in a car crash in France. During the following week there was an astonishing outpouring of public grief that surprised everyone. People waited in queues for six or seven hours often in the rain in order to sign condolence books. Some who were interviewed on the television made it clear that even they themselves were surprised by their reaction to the news and their sense of grief. This extraordinary grief seemed excessive and even pathological to some. On the *Newsnight* television programme on the Wednesday following the accident a psychologist was brought in to analyse the phenomenon. His conclusion was that this was an unhealthy response by people who had never known Diana. People were responding to her death almost as if they had known her personally, as if they had been close friends or part of the family. The nation's infatuation with Diana was surfacing in a morbid pathological grief that seemed inexplicable.

Like many people, when I heard the news early on Sunday morning it came as something of a surprise. One does not imagine such things happening to such people. Members of the royal family are usually surrounded by body guards and their lives are planned in the most careful way to avoid any dangers such as the one that resulted in Diana's death. But the shock of the news for me was no more than one would expect on hearing of the tragic and untimely death of any well-known public figure—no more shocking than hearing the news of the untimely death of the leader of the Labour Party a few years before. *Grief* certainly did not enter into it. The public response to Diana's death seemed more astonishing to me than her death itself. What could explain this enormous outpouring of public grief? In the week leading up to her funeral this show of public feeling developed into a kind of national hysteria. Diana was being treated like some national saviour whose effect on the life of the nation had been so significant that her death was a national calamity. The *Newsnight* programme reported that some people had claimed to have seen visions and apparitions of Diana after her death. These are common phenomena in normal personal bereavement. They are understandable when the person experiencing them is a spouse, a close friend or a relative of the dead person. But for people to be grieving in this way over someone who was not personally known to them is highly unusual. It transcends the normal. The psychologist interviewed on the *Newsnight* programme stated that such delusional experiences in people not personally close to Diana would be considered clinically to be a symptom of schizophrenia.[1]

The reasons for this national grief are no doubt complex and no single explanation will explain the feelings of everyone. Some have suggested that Diana represented a kind of rebellion against the establishment that many can identify with. Another explanation that surfaced was that as a result of Diana's position as a sort of *persona non grata* in the royal family she had become an unofficial figurehead for anti-monarchy feelings in the population. There is doubtless some truth in both notions. Others have been helped by the charitable causes she represented. This latter fact certainly explains the sorrow of many. But neither this nor the other theories explain the sorrow of the masses who waited in the queues to sign the condolence books and the tremendous outpouring of grief displayed by the nation. Compared with the masses demonstrating their sense of loss at Diana's death those who were touched by her work in a personal way are few. Of course there has always been a cult of royalty in Britain, but again, it is hard to believe

---

[1] I am using here a clinical definition of schizophrenia, not the popular notion of split personality. *The Concise Oxford Dictionary* defines schizophrenia as "a mental disease [perhaps 'disorder' would be a better term here—SCP] marked by a breakdown in the relation between thoughts, feelings, and actions, frequently accompanied by delusions and retreat from social life."

that this accounts for the national sense of loss that followed Diana's death. If anything, the cult of the monarchy has been damaged by public sympathy for Diana. What then can explain this intense sense of loss for the great mass of people who experienced it?

I think there is an explanation that helps us to understand this national phenomenon. The response to Diana's death must be seen in terms much broader and greater than Diana herself or a mere sense of grief at the death of a well-known and much loved public figure. The response to Diana's death was a *religious* phenomenon.

Any State or nation needs a national focus, something that gives meaning, coherence and significance to its life and institutions. Britain is disintegrating today because it has abandoned what had previously provided that national focus, that meaning and coherence: a Christian understanding of the meaning and purpose of life, a Christian world-view. Yet the need for such a focus remains. Man cannot escape this. But without God he seeks for the meaning, coherence and significance of life in some element of the created order instead of in the God of Scripture. This is what idolatry is.

In Britain the national focus is no longer a Christian focus. It does not take account of the transcendent being of God and the salvation that he has provided for mankind in the Lord Jesus Christ. Questions concerning the ultimate meaning of existence no longer play a part in our national life. Instead the national focus is on the mundane, the economic and particularly the political. People look to the great and the famous, to the State and the party, to their hobbies or their bank balance, even their annual holiday, anything other than the God of Scripture, and there they seek ultimate meaning and significance for their lives. But these things cannot provide what they are looking for. They will always disappoint. These are gods that fail. False gods always fail. But because so much hope, trust and expectation is placed in these things, when they do fail their failure has a devastating effect on those who put their trust in them. The failure of a society's god or gods causes national calamity, grief, an overwhelming sense of loss. The loss of faith that accompanies the fall of a god has a devastating effect on both individual human beings and on society.

I think this is essentially what has happened with Diana. It explains the visions and apparitions. These are common religious phenomena. And this is how cults are born: from idols. Of course Diana is now dead, but I suspect the cult of Diana is only just being born and will grow from strength to strength. Already there has been serious discussion on the *Sunday* programme on Radio Four as to whether Diana was a saint, with one contributor earnestly contending "Of course she is." But "saint" is the wrong word entirely. Diana was an idol, a potent symbol of what it means to be rich and famous, the ultimate PC personality, the fairy tale princess. As such she epitomised what so many desire and aspire to as the ultimate achievement of human life. But when idols fail the mirage they generate for those who worship them disappears with them.

It is the absence in our society of belief in the one who alone can provide ultimate meaning, coherence and significance for the life of the nation that explains the response to Diana's death. Without God people seek for meaning in the ephemeral, in what cannot last, and thus in what must ultimately disappoint.

This happens even with Christians sometimes. I remember many years ago hearing a lady stand up in a Christian meeting and give her "testimony" to her faith in a well-known evangelical charismatic minister who had just died unexpectedly at an early age. She said her faith was shaken by his death. Why? She did not say. She could only express her shock and grief that God would permit such a thing to happen. She had made an idol of this man. Did she think God would not permit his servant to die? Obviously. Her faith was not in God but in man. When their gods fail the people are crushed in spirit. It is a personal loss to them, not because they knew the people who are so idolised personally but because those people have taken a place in their lives that only the God of Creation can fill. A real, personal relationship with the person in question is irrelevant. One can make an idol out of a piece of stone or wood. Personal interaction is not necessary. The decisive factor is the place the idol takes in one's life, the significance it has in determining the meaning of one's life. In some respects it is more difficult to idolise those whom one knows personally. Their defects get in the way. When such defects are not perceived the idol's virtues can be romantically exaggerated ad infinitum. Lack of a personal meaningful relationship with the idol is preferable. Regardless of the fact that people do not know those whom they idolise, therefore, it is a personal tragedy when they die, and it is a personal tragedy because gods are not supposed to fail or die. They are supposed to be immortal. But only the God of the Christian Scriptures is immortal. And he does not share his glory with another.

It is God alone who provides ultimate meaning, coherence and significance to the lives of human beings and societies. No one and nothing else can do this, no cause or ideology, however great, and certainly no mere human being. It is in terms of God that understanding must be sought in all things. Those who grieved over Diana, whether personal friends and family, or the masses who queued to sign the condolence books, can only find meaning for their own and Diana's life and death when they turn to God. Without such a response no lessons will be learned and no sense can be made of such tragic deaths.

It would seem that Diana was not a believer. She was dubbed by Tony Blair "The people's princess." Unfortunately her own lifestyle after the breakdown of her marriage was hardly an example to the nation. True, she worked for many good causes. But this does not excuse her. It does not excuse any man's sin. We are all guilty and stand condemned by our works. The good we do cannot atone for the evil we do. Only Christ can do that. But the royal family must give a lead to the nation, and a credible lead at that. Their high position does not excuse their dissolute behaviour; it makes the burden of their responsibility greater. From those to whom much is given, much is expected.

In this sense our present monarchy has been a failure in some important respects. Queen Elizabeth II has given her name to legislation that has legalised the murder of millions of unborn children. Doubtless some will say that she had to do this because there would have been a constitutional crisis and the monarchy would have been abolished if she had not given royal consent. But this is a poor argument. In the first place, it has not been proved, and secondly, if that *had* been the outcome, surely it would have been better to surrender the monarchy than preside over such obscene legislation. My response to such an objection is simply this: Do moral principles count for nothing against the monarchy? There is a King whose law is higher than that of Parliament and to whom even the Queen owes allegiance before all else; and indeed to whom she swore allegiance before all else when she was crowned. Preservation of the monarchy, it seems to me, surely does not take precedence over faithfulness to the coronation oath, which was taken in the sight of God and before the whole nation. Betrayal of the coronation oath is treason against God and a betrayal of the nation.

But the nation cares very little now for those principles that give meaning and coherence to our national life. Idols are in vogue today, and idols can do no wrong in the eyes of their devotees. The problem is, idols do not last. They always fail. The ephemeral, the political and the economic, the lives of the rich and the famous cannot provide meaning and purpose in life, nor can they provide meaning and purpose for a nation. And God does not tolerate idols. He brings them down. Idols are for destruction.[2]

Diana's death was a tragedy. But there are greater tragedies occurring every day in our society that fail even to get a mention in the media. It seems to me quite extraordinary from a moral point of view that the nation could mourn in this way over Diana and yet blithely ignore the holocaust of murdered unborn children since the passing of the abortion act. This shows that the

---

[2] The place for idols is hell. Jesus used the word "Gehenna" to characterise the final state of non-believers (aee Mt. 5:22, 29, 30). But Gehenna was a rubbish tip just outside Jerusalem where all the rubbish, broken idols and dead criminals were burned. The fires were continually burning in this rubbish tip—hence the Western image of hell as a place of eternal fire. It was the equivalent of today's municipal incinerator. And it was into this Gehenna that broken idols were thrown.

nation has lost its ability to reason morally, which, I suppose, is not surprising given the fact that both the use of reason and the practice of morality are at an all-time low in our society today. This situation is one that can only be explained by national apostasy and idolatry. But it is also one that portends the judgement of God upon the nation for its apostasy. There is, therefore, a cautionary tale for the nation in all this.

When a number of Jews were killed in the accidental collapse of a tower in Jerusalem Jesus asked the people: "those eighteen, upon whom the tower in Siloam fell, and slew them, think ye that they were sinners above all men that dwelt in Jerusalem?" (Lk. 13:4). Obviously they were not, and their deaths were not to be construed as personal judgement in this sense—a false conclusion to which men are too often all too ready to jump. But Jesus did not leave it there. He applied the lesson. We all stand condemned of our sin before God, and the wages of sin is death (Rom. 6:23). Therefore, said Jesus, "except ye repent, ye shall all likewise perish" (Lk. 13:5). This is a lesson that the nation needs to heed. We are, as a nation, perilously close to the end, and soon we may be cast into the fire.

11

WHAT HAPPENED TO THE PROTESTANT WORK ETHIC?

ACCORDING to Max Weber, the word *calling* is known "only to those languages influenced by the Protestant translations of the Bible"[1] The concept of a *calling*, explains Weber, "expresses the value placed upon rational activity carried on according to the rational capitalistic principle, as the fulfillment of a God-given task."[2] He also pointed out that "if we trace the history of the word through the civilized languages, it appears that neither the predominantly Catholic peoples nor those of classical antiquity have possessed any expression of similar connotation for what we know as a calling (in the sense of a life-task, a definite field in which to work), while one has existed for all predominantly Protestant peoples. It may be further shown that this is not due to any ethnical peculiarity of the languages concerned."[3] It is the concept of the *calling* that is the origin of the Protestant work ethic, which has been a decisive religious influence on the rise of capitalism in Britain and the United States over the past four centuries.

Prior to the Reformation there had been various kinds of capitalistic activity, and Weber himself emphasised that "certain important forms of capitalistic business organisation are known to be considerably older than the Reformation."[4] These forms of capitalism, however, were "predominantly of an irrational and speculative character, or directed to acquisition by force, above all acquisition of booty, whether directly in war or in the form of

---

[1] Max Weber, *General Economic History* (New Brunswick and London: Transaction Books [1927] 1981), p. 367.   [2] *Ibid.*
[3] Max Weber, *The Protestant Ethic and the Spirit of Capitalism* (London: George Allen and Unwin [1930], Counterpoint edition, 1985), p. 79.   [4] *Ibid.*, p. 91.

continuous fiscal booty by exploitation of subjects."[5] Weber gave the term "capitalistic adventurer" to those who pursued this kind of capitalistic activity. A good example of this kind of capitalistic activity was the conquest of Mexico by Hernando Cortés in the sixteenth century. Walter Ralegh and Francis Drake are good Protestant examples of the capitalistic adventurer.

The desire for profit, i.e. the acquisitive impulse, has of course characterised human activity throughout history; it is not a unique feature of Western capitalism. But the kind of capitalism that developed in Northern Europe after the Reformation and that was bequeathed to North America by the Protestant colonists was a very particular kind of outworking of the acquisitive impulse. What distinguished the latter from the kind of activity engaged in by the capitalistic adventurer was the constraints placed upon the acquisitive impulse by the moral dictates of the Protestant religion, the Protestant ethic or asceticism, to use Weber's terms. The devout Protestant was constrained by his duty to work for God in his calling, his life-task, according to the moral dictates of the Christian religion. Honesty, hard work and thrift characterised his understanding of his calling in life under God. As a result, rather than seeking the acquisition of wealth by means of irrational and speculative activities, what characterised the economic activities of devout Protestants was the *subordination* of the acquisitive impulse to the Protestant ethic. Under these religious constraints capitalistic activity could only develop by means of *economic rationalisation*, and it is this process of economic rationalisation that characterises the Protestant form capitalism described by Weber in his essay *The Protestant Ethic and the Spirit of Capitalism*. For those who laboured under the Protestant ethic economic rationalisation was the only means of economic betterment.

Thus, the Protestant doctrine of the calling along with the Protestant work ethic produced what has been called the "industrious sort of people,"[6] i.e. a culture that prioritised industrious activity based on economic rationalisation. The early settlers who

---

[5] *Ibid.*, p. 20.   [6] See Christopher Hill, *Society and Puritanism in Pre-Revolutionary England* (London: Secker and Warburg, 1964), pp. 124–144.

crossed the Atlantic from England to colonise North America were the product of this culture. With them they carried the religious impulse that created the Protestant work ethic, which was ultimately to issue in what has been called the "American dream." But the operative word here is "ultimately," because the Protestant work ethic only led to the American dream when the religious impulse of the original Protestant work ethic had been lost.

At the end of his *General Economic History* Weber claimed that the religious impulse of the early period of Western capitalism had been abandoned by the beginning of the age of iron in the nineteenth century.[7] What happened was that the Protestant work ethic was secularised, and it is the secularised version, or rather various secularised versions, of the Protestant work ethic that now motivate Western capitalism.

This has led to a reversion to pre-Reformation methods of satisfying the acquisitive impulse for many. In Britain the continuous exploitation of subjects by means of fiscal booty is now well-advanced. This is due to the predominance of socialism, which has largely replaced the religious impulse of the Christian faith in Britain, at least in terms of what we might call the national consciousness (evidenced, for example, by the sacred status of the State-run health care and education systems). Socialism is a secularised religion that aims to replace Christianity and its form of economic organisation: capitalism.

In the USA this process of secularisation has not developed in the same way that it has in Britain. The American economic dream is a secularised version of the Protestant work ethic. But because the religious impulse has gone, the possibilities of reversion to pre-Reformation methods of satisfying the acquisitive impulse are there, e.g. political exploitation of subjects by means of fiscal booty and irrational speculative forms of capitalistic adventurism. In North America it is perhaps the latter, i.e. irrational and speculative capitalism, that predominates, whereas in Britain, with her socialist State, it is continuous exploitation of subjects by means of fiscal booty that predominates (and is likely to get much worse

[7] *General Economic History*, p. 368f.

the closer we get to European political integration), though of course political exploitation is to be found in the USA and irrational and speculative capitalism is present in Britain. In this context we might note Weber's interesting comment that "where the fulfillment of the calling cannot directly be related to the highest spiritual and cultural values, or when, on the other hand, it need not be felt simply as economic compulsion, the individual generally abandons the attempt to justify it at all. In the field of its highest development, in the United States, the pursuit of wealth, stripped of its religious and ethical meaning, tends to become associated with purely mundane passions, which often actually give it the character of sport."[8]

The Protestant work ethic, when stripped of its religious impulse, becomes mere materialism, and in the vacuum left by Christianity in the West society has opened up to other religious influences, e.g. secular humanism, New Ageism, the green movement, even Islam. This will eventually produce a very different culture, since the multicultural (i.e. multi-religious) society is only a staging post on the road to the domination of society by a new religious world-view. The emptiness of the more consistently secularised version of the Protestant work ethic that now dominates the West—a form of materialism—has made this process inevitable. Most of these religious alternatives are now exerting a strong influence on the West and are very apparent in both Britain and the USA.

This is not meant to be a critique of capitalism; but it is a critique of the reduction of human life and society to the economic aspect of life. Capitalism, properly understood as private ownership of the means of economic production and distribution, is the form of economic organisation that has come nearest historically to the kind of economic organisation of society required by Christianity. But it is one aspect of society, not the whole of it. To reduce the whole of life to the economic aspect, whether on the socialist or the capitalist model, is a form of idolatry of the economic function of man's life and can only end in the demean-

[8] *The Protestant Ethic and the Spirit of Capitalism*, p. 182.

ing of human life and the political enslavement of mankind, as it has done in Britain. The answer to such idolatry, whether on the socialist or the individualistic model, is not to abandon Western capitalism, but to revivify it with the spirit that enabled it to develop so effectively in the first place, i.e. the Christian understanding of man's calling under God.

Protestantism, via its work ethic, bequeathed to North America the necessary spiritual and intellectual capital to make its economic development possible. But the religious impulse behind this form of capitalism has now largely gone, as it has in Britain, in which there were more institutional and cultural constraints hindering its unfettered development. Both nations now lay open to influences that, if triumphant, will produce forms capitalistic acquisition more akin to the irrational, speculative and exploitative forms of economic acquisition that characterised pre-Reformation economic activity. Indeed this is already happening. In Britain spiritual apostasy in the form of a reduction of human society to the economic aspect of life has produced the growth of "soft" totalitarianism supported by the ideology of secular humanism; economic activity is increasingly geared to controlling the wealth that already exists by means of political manipulation rather than the unfettered creation of wealth.

In the USA there has likewise been a process of secularisation, but this has not been dominated by socialistic ideals to the extent that it has in Britain. Whereas the ideology of socialism provided meaning for many in Britain during the twentieth century, all sorts of different ideologies have provided this in the USA. To the British, therefore, the USA seems a land of extremes and contradictions. To use religious terminology, we could perhaps say that the real difference between the two nations is that the form of idolatry that characterises the USA is more a kind of individualistic polytheism, whereas, at least until recently, the idolatry of the British nation has been more monotheistic and more focused ideologically as a result. The former produces a more "anything goes" culture of personal fulfilment, a "do your own thing," "get what you can out of life" culture, but with a greater degree of economic freedom. The latter has produced in Britain a socialistic over-regulating State that seeks to control just about everything; security is what is offered but the cost is freedom, and the security turns out to be sub-standard. Of course, these are pure types, to borrow one of Weber's phrases, and both nations have a particular mix of both these elements.

The differences may not last long though, since the phenomenal success of the culture that Hollywood is exporting around the world means that not only Britain but much of the world is now drinking deep at the trough of the secular humanistic religious idolatry that underpins the American dream. This great American export is one of the most culturally destructive forces in the modern world, since it undermines the values that made Western civilisation possible and leaves society spiritually defenceless against ideologies and religions that are alien to the religious foundations of Western culture. When the abandonment of Christianity is complete we shall lose not only the outward symbols that identify Britain as a Christian nation, but those vital Western ideals such as individual freedom, the rule of law, the concept that one is innocent until proven guilty, the belief that the strong have a duty to help the weak,—all ideals that were largely unknown to the world before Christianity was in the ascendant, and will continue to decline in the West until Christianity triumphs over all foes and becomes the foundation stone of our culture once again, providing meaning and purpose in the whole of life, including the economic organisation of society.

12

CHRISTIANITY AND
THE RULE OF LAW

The laws of national duty [to God] *now unfolded are no abstract theory. They are one main part of that law of eternal right, which is the foundation of the throne of God. Statesmen may transgress them, but cannot change them . . . Our own country, through a thousand years, from Alfred until now, has been raised to greatness as a Christian State, rendering public homage, however mingled and imperfect, to the risen Son of God. Faith in Christianity, and open honour to all the ordinances of the Christian Church, has formed the ground-work of the British Constitution.*

— T. R. Birks[1]

For over a millennium the English legal system has been informed by Christian principles of justice. Christianity has exerted a dominating influence on our legal heritage. The standards and ideals that guided the development of our law from ancient times are derived from the Bible. A great many of our legal and constitutional practices are derived either directly from the Bible (e.g. the coronation oath) or from pre-Christian practices that have been so completely transformed under the influence of Christian concepts of justice that the original pre-Christian practices from which they are derived are no longer discernable in the Christianised forms in which we know them today (e.g. oath swearing in court).[2]

---

[1] T. R. Birks, *Church and State; or, National Religion and Church Establishment, Considered with Reference to Present Conditions* (London: Hatchards, 1869), p. 327.

[2] For a more detailed account of this process of transformation and of the influence of Christianity on the development of the English legal system see Stephen C. Perks, *Christianity and Law: An Enquiry into the Influence of Christianity on the Development of English Law* (Avant Books, 1993).

This process began with the arrival of Augustine of Canterbury in 597 and continued through to the twentieth century. Both in Anglo-Saxon and Norman England the increasing influence of Christianity upon the development of our system of justice can be documented. For example, in the laws of Alfred (the earliest manuscript dates from *c.* 925) the first 48 clauses are taken from the Decalogue and the Book of the Covenant (Exodus 20:1–17 and 21:1 to 23:13), though stated in a slightly modified form to take account of contemporary Anglo-Saxon society, and followed by a exposition of the Christian use of God's law and the importance of the golden rule (Mt. 7:12).[3] This influence of the Bible on the law codes of the English kings continued and can be found in the law codes of Edward the Elder, Æthelstan, Æthelred, Cnut et al. These law codes in turn provided the basis for the compilations of English law found in a number of Norman law books.[4] It was under the influence of the clerical judges of the twelfth and thirteenth centuries that these laws and customs were transformed into the common law system.[5] Thus "Common Law was the product of a union between universal Christian laws and local customs."[6] The concepts of due process and the rule of law, the notion that guilt is individual not corporate, that a man is innocent until proven guilty and habeas corpus are all derived from a Christian understanding of justice. Our legal system presupposes a Christian world-view. The pervasive influence of Christianity on the development of Western legal systems generally has led Harold Berman to speak of Western legal science as a "secular theology" that often does not make sense to non-Christians because its theological presuppositions are not accepted.[7] It is the presuppositions of the Christian world-view that give coherence and meaning to

---

[3] The full text of Alfred's Dooms is reprinted in Stephen C. Perks, *op. cit.*

[4] See Frederick Pollock and Frederic W. Maitland, *The History of English Law Before the Time of Edward I* (Cambridge, 1898), Vol. I, pp. 97–110; see also, Stephen C. Perks, *op. cit.*, p. 37ff.   [5] Pollock and Maitland, *op. cit.*, Vol. I, p. 133.

[6] Eugen Rosenstock-Huessy, *Out of Revolution: Autobiography of Western Man* (Oxford: Berg, [1938] 1993), p. 270.

[7] Harold J. Berman, *Law and Revolution: The Formation of the Western Legal Tradition* (Cambridge, Massachusetts: Harvard University Press, 1983), p. 165.

our understanding and practice of justice and our legal system cannot properly be understood apart from those Christian presuppositions upon which it is based. Our common law was shaped under the dominating influence of the Christian religion. Thus, a basic principle of the common law was that "Any law is or of right ought to be according to the law of God." This statement is recorded in a Year Book of Henry VII's reign.[8]

Likewise in equity. The purpose of equity was to provide a remedy at law where the strict application of the common law could not provide one or where it could not provide a satisfactory remedy. It was stated that equity applied "where the law is directly in itself against the law of God or the law of Reason."[9] Equity was administered in the Court of Chancery and the Chancellor, as the keeper of the king's conscience, provided remedies according to equity and conscience. Accordingly, in 1489 the Chancellor, Cardinal Morton, stated that "every law should be in accordance with the law of God; and I know well that an executor who fraudulently misapplies the goods and does not make restitution will be damned in Hell, and to remedy this is in accordance with conscience, as I understand it."[10] The basic principle that guided the Court of Chancery was that all law must conform to reason and the law of God. Indeed, to the mediaeval clerical judges under whose influence our legal institutions and traditions first took shape there was no real distinction between the law of reason and the law of God. Reasonable law was law that conformed to God's law. Thus, Christopher St. Germain in his *Doctor and Student*, a legal treatise published in 1523 (in Latin) and 1531 (in English), stated that "When the law eternal or the *will of God* is known to His creatures by the light of natural reason, that is called the *law of reason*: and when it is showed of *heavenly revelation* . . . then it is called the *law of God*. And when it is showed unto him by *order of a Prince*, or of any other secondary governor, that hath power to set

---

[8] Cited in A. K. R. Kiralfy, *Potter's Historical Introduction to English Law* (London: Sweet and Maxwell Ltd, Fourth Edition, 1958), p. 33.   [9] *Ibid*, p. 160.

[10] Cited in Theodore T. Plucknett, *A Concise History of the Common Law* (London: Butterworth and Co. [Publishers] Ltd, 1956), p. 685f.

a law upon his subjects, then it is called the *law of man*, though originally it be *made of God*"[11] (see the diagram on p. 137).

Furthermore, we are told in the same treatise that "if any law made of men bind any person to anything that is against the said laws (the law of reason or the law of God) it is no law but corruption and manifest error."[12] Hence, traditionally our legal system and values of justice have reflected biblical law and Christian conceptions of justice. Reasonable law was law that conformed to the law of God.

This influence of the Christian religion on the evolution of our legal system has given us what we have traditionally called "the rule of law." But it is important that we understand what this Christian doctrine of the rule of law means and how it has traditionally been understood.

Chief Justice Sir Edward Coke told King James I, when the latter unconstitutionally attempted to assume the power of an absolute monarch, that "The king is under no man, save under God and the law." He was quoting Henry de Bracton (d. 1268), the "father of English jurisprudence," who had stated the dictum *Lex facit regem* ("the law makes the king"): "The king himself ought not to be subject to man but subject to God and to the law, because the law makes him king."[13] And, as we have seen, English common law maintained that the law of the land was subject to the higher moral law of God.

This concept of the rule of law, therefore, does not, at least as it has traditionally been understood and enshrined in English law, mean that rulers may do anything they please provided they merely pass a law legitimising it first. On the contrary, what the doctrine of the rule of law maintained was that the king, or the government or legislators, may *not* make any law that contradicts the higher moral law of God. This principle is still enshrined in our constitution—though rather unconstitutionally our modern legislators have ignored it and presided over the utter debasement of

---

[11] Cited in Kiralfy, *op. cit.*, p. 578f., my emphasis.   [12] Cited in *ibid.*, p. 579.
[13] *De Legibus et Consuetudinibus Angliae*, f. 5*b*, cited in O. Hood Philips, *Constitutional and Administrative Law* (London: Sweet and Maxwell, 1976), p. 33.

THE CHRISTIAN DOCTRINE OF THE RULE OF LAW
(based on Christopher Saint Germain's, *Doctor and Student*, 1523)

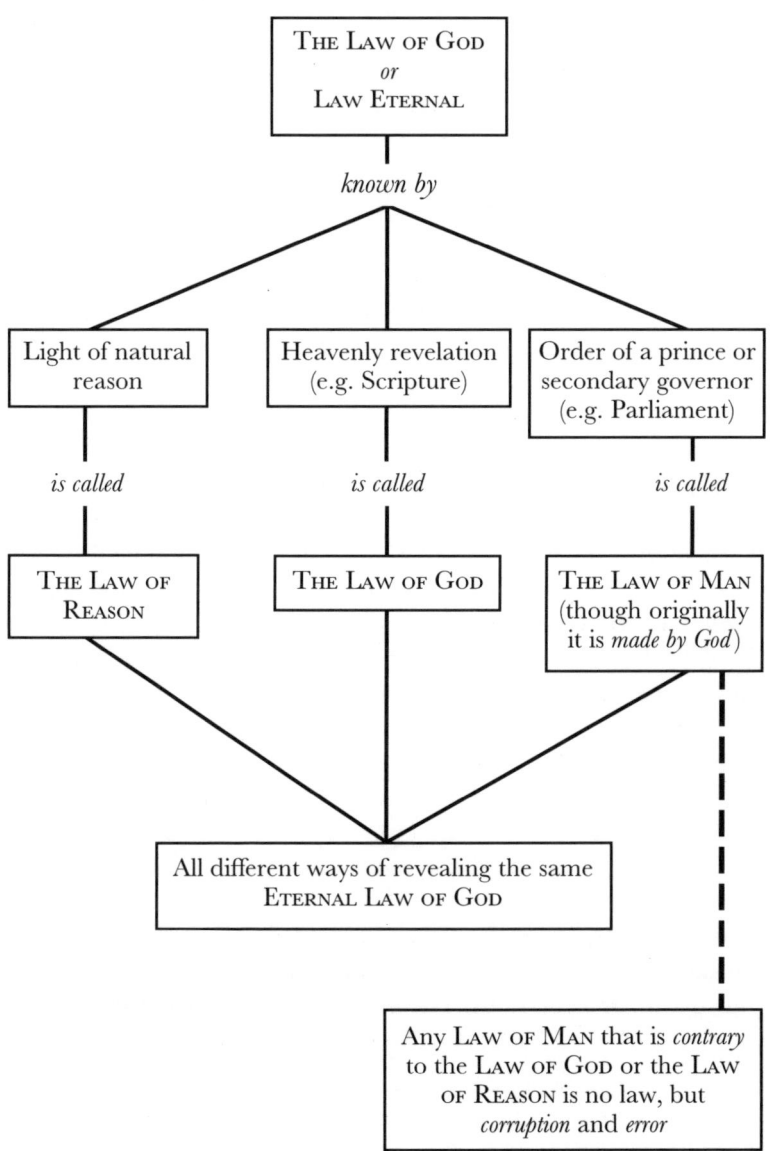

our constitutional inheritance—since in the Coronation Oath the monarch swears to "maintain the Laws of God and the true profession of the Gospel . . . and the Protestant Reformed Religion established by law."[14]

Those who make our legislation are bound absolutely, according to this doctrine of the rule of law, by the higher moral law of God. The rule of law, therefore, meant the rule of *Christian* law; and this Christian law was defined in terms of the higher law of God found in the Christian Scriptures. Justice as we understand it in the West is not something that simply hangs in the air and can be recognised by all no matter what their religion or philosophy of life. It is not a set of abstract principles to which all rational men in all ages and societies adhere. Nor is it deduced according to principles of logic and rationality by philosophers or lawyers. In a world of sin justice is not natural; it is not something to which sinners naturally aspire. Justice is the fruit of a Christian worldview and a Christian culture. It has taken centuries for our justice system to evolve. Western justice is only reasonable to Westerners because they have imbibed it as part of a Christian civilisation. Western justice is not reasonable in cultures that are based on fundamentally different religious beliefs and presuppositions. It is no accident that the highest form of justice known in history, "British justice" (i.e. the system of English common law justice that existed throughout the British Empire and North America), co-existed with the highest form of Christian civilisation known in history. This system of justice was the product of a Christian civilization.

People in Britain, by and large, do not recognise Muslim law as the kind of law they wish to see enacted in this country. Muslim "justice" is perceived here as Islamic fundamentalism and associated with terrorism—the fatwa condemning the author Salman Rushdie to death is a good example. The *Jihād* is an important part of the Muslim faith. The essence of *Jihād* is summed up in the words of the Muslim Prophet, which are recorded in a num-

[14] E. C. Ratcliff, *The Coronation Service of Her Majesty Queen Elizabeth II, with A Short Historical Introduction, Explanatory Notes and An Appendix* (London: SPCK/Cambridge University Press, 1953), p. 38.

ber of different hadiths: "I am commanded to fight against men until they bear witness that there is no God but Allāh and that Muhammad is God's messenger; only by pronouncing these words can they make their property and blood secure from me."[15]

People with a British cultural heritage will find this statement abhorrent, as they will the practical application of it, as in the case of the Rushdie fatwa for example. It is not so negatively perceived by Muslims however. This difference in perception of the character of justice is a consequence of the fact that Muslim culture is based on a different religious faith, a faith that is inimical to the Christian values and ideals that are taken for granted in the West. Many fail to realise that our own justice system has been superior to the barbarous regimes of the Muslims because it is the fruit of a Christian way of life, a Christian belief system whose principles and ideals of justice are founded on the law of God.

That foundation provided continuity for our nation for over a thousand years because the God of the Bible is a law-giving God who is the same yesterday, today and forever and thus whose law can be relied upon by man as a permanent standard of justice. The Bible, therefore, gave stability and predictability to our legal system and to our society; it gave the nation a system of justice that was reliable and sane. The abandonment of the Bible in our age is, by contrast, giving us a justice system that is not stable nor reliable and that is increasingly manifesting the kind of insanity that has begun to characterise our apostate culture generally. Principles of justice that have been established and built upon for generations are being cast aside by our legislators every time Parliament sits. And the passing of new legislation by Parliament that is based on presuppositions fundamentally alien to the religious ethic upon which our legal traditions are based seems never to cease.

This mania for new and often totally unnecessary laws is changing the character of our law and of our legal system. Common law is being superseded by statute law passed by short-sighted politicians with their eyes not on justice, but rather on the next elec-

---

[15] *Sahih Bukhari*, Vol. 1, Bk 2, no. 24; Bk 8, no. 387; Vol. 4, Bk 52, no. 196; Vol. 9, Bk 84, no. 59; *Sunan Abu-Dawud*, Bk 14, no. 2635; Bk 19, no. 3061.

tion. Legality is what matters today, not justice, and what is legal can be changed by a few politicians more concerned to maintain their power at all costs than to see the country governed properly according to Christian principles of justice. Our politicians no longer believe in a higher law to which all human law should conform. As a result legislation is today becoming the mere tool of our political masters, who will use it to sanction whatever means are necessary for them to take control of our lives and society and mould them to the pattern they judge to be appropriate. Thus, increasingly our law no longer guarantees a man's freedom under God's law; rather it is the tool that, in the hands of our State politicians, will enslave us and bring us into subjection to the all powerful predestinating State.

I want to look now at a few areas where this traditional understanding of the rule of law has been overturned and where, as a consequence, our common law heritage has been abandoned.

1.   First, *Socialism*. Our common law system of justice has suffered significantly from the creation of a socialistic Welfare State, since in order to implement the Welfare State legislation has been passed that is based on philosophical principles that are fundamentally alien to the Christian religion, which guided the formation of our legal traditions. For example, judicial independence, one of the pillars of our common law heritage, has been substantially weakened by the kind of legislation necessary to implement the Welfare State. E. C. S. Wade, in his Introduction to the 1939 edition of A. V. Dicey's *Law of the Constitution*, stated the problem clearly:

It is still accepted constitutional doctrine that the Ministers of the Crown do not tamper with the administration of justice, but Parliament indirectly has reduced the sphere of influence of judicial independence by the character of modern legislation. The abandonment of the principle of *laissez faire* has altered the nature of much of our law. A system of law, which like the common law is based on the protection of individual rights, is not readily comparable with legislation which has for its object the welfare of the public, or a large section of it, as a whole. The common law rests upon an individualistic conception of society and lacks the means of enforcing public rights as such. The socialisation of the activities of the people has meant *restriction of individual rights* by the conferment of powers of a *novel* character upon *governmental* organs.[16]

This was written over sixty years ago. The situation has become much worse since these words were written. Our society is being transformed by legislation passed in Parliament from a society ruled by law to a society ruled by politicians—i.e. a totalitarian society.

A good example of this development was the Leasehold Reform, Housing and Urban Development Act passed in 1993. Interestingly, this piece of socialist legislation was passed by a Conservative government, the Major Government, during its "back to basics" and revival of "traditional values" phase. The "traditional value" to be sacrificed by Mr Major's Conservative government on this occassion was the Eighth Commandment: "Thou shalt not steal."

The Leasehold Reform, Housing and Urban Development Act! Under this rather innocuous verbiage an act was passed that legalised theft. Private property—surely one would have thought that this particular "traditional value" would have been on even Mr Major's truncated list—has now been abolished by the Conservative Party. This act makes it possible for leaseholders to claim the "right" to purchase the freehold to their dwellings against the wishes of the freeholder. This means that the freeholder is obliged by law to surrender his property (the freehold) if a leaseholder (effectively a tenant) wishes to acquire it.

This is a law, therefore, that not only does not protect the freeholder from theft but actually abets the thief in his criminal design—I say "criminal" since this legislation contradicts our traditional Christian understanding of justice and has only been made "legal" by government decree. It is a lawless piece of legislation, contrary to the principles of justice that have underpinned our legal tradition for many centuries. Of course, it will not be too long before all private tenants will be able to demand the dubious

[16] E. C. S. Wade, "Introduction" in A. V. Dicey, *Introduction to the Study of the Law of the Constitution* (London: MacMillan and Company Ltd, Ninth Edition, 1939), p. lxxif, my emphasis.

"right" to purchase the dwellings in which they live from the rightful owners of the property.

There are, of course, many more examples of the effects of socialist legislation on our system of justice. I have picked this one out because it shows how far even Conservative governments have fallen prey to the socialist ethos of our day.

2. Second, I want to look at the *burden of proof*, particularly as it relates to corroborating evidence. There seems to be some indication that this will prove to be a greater problem the closer we get to European assimilation. It is important to note, however, that a movement away from this essential element of justice is already underway and has been for some time.

Christianity teaches that "A single witness shall not rise up against a man on account of any iniquity or any sin which he has committed; on the evidence of two or three witnesses a matter shall be confirmed" (Dt. 19:15; see also Dt. 17:6 and Num. 35:30). This principle is reaffirmed in the New Testament no less than five times (Mt. 18:15–16; John 8:17; 2 Cor. 13:1; 1 Tim. 5:19; Heb. 10:28). The requirement of multiple witnesses is necessary to protect the accused from the malice of a false witness.

What this means is that there must be sufficient evidence to put the conviction of an accused person beyond reasonable doubt. This principle is the source of the concept that a man is innocent until proven guilty. If there is insufficient evidence, the court should not convict.

This is a simple principle but it is vitally important. One would have thought it hardly needed to be reaffirmed. But unfortunately it does, because it is a principle that is now under attack. Under a Conservative government—Major's again—a Criminal Justice and Public Order Act was passed in 1994 that overturned this principle.

Much publicised at the time as the bill passed through Parliament was the clause that was popularly represented as abolishing the right to silence—though in fact what was abolished was the principle that the court should not be entitled to infer anything from a defendant's silence. This change in the law was, rightly in my judgement, abominated by many, since it strikes at the heart of the principle that the burden of proof should fall of the prosecution. The passing of this legislation removed one of the building blocks of the concept that a man is innocent until proven guilty. There is a shift of emphasis towards the defendant's having to prove his innocence. This is the thin end of the wedge. Little by little such legislation will lead to a full-blown doctrine of *guilty until proven innocent.*

However, this was not the only breach of justice contained in the Act. There were other problems in it that received far less attention in the media. The "Explanatory and Financial Memorandum" published at the time of the bill stated that the bill "abolishes the current common law requirement for judges to warn juries of the danger of convicting on the uncorroborated evidence of a complainant in a sexual offence case or of an accomplice and the corresponding requirement in summary trials."[17] The law as it stood before the passing of this Act required judges to warn juries of the danger of convicting a man in certain sexual offence cases on the sole evidence of the alleged victim or on the sole evidence of an accomplice. Convictions based on such evidence are not sound. It is unreasonable and against God's law—and it is unreasonable *because* it is against God's law—to take the word of an accomplice in a crime, or the word of the victim of an alleged sexual offence, as truth without independent corroboration. The fact that a man could be so convicted on uncorroborated evidence provided the jury was warned of the danger involved in such a conviction was bad enough. But to abolish the judge's statutory duty to warn the jury of the danger of such a conviction was to follow a bad law with a worse law.

Under the law as it then stood, however, corroboration of the evidence of a sole witness was required by statute for certain offences. Among these were certain offences covered by the Sexual Offences Act, 1956. The Criminal Justice and Public Order Act abolished in certain cases this statutory requirement that the evi-

---

[17] *Criminal Justice and Public Order Bill*, "Explanatory and Financial Memorandum," p. iii.

dence of a sole witness be "corroborated in some material particular by evidence implicating the accused."[18] These were: (*a*)
procurement of a woman by threats; (*b*) procurement of a woman
by false pretences; (*c*) administering drugs to obtain or facilitate
intercourse; (*d*) causing prostitution of women; and (*e*) procurement of a girl under age. It is now possible for a jury to convict a
man of an offence under this section solely on the evidence of a
single witness, i.e. by the testimony of the alleged victim alone.

It seems incredible that a Conservative government should
have passed such legislation. Such an action is against reason and
against the higher law of God. Sexual liaisons are a notorious
area for injustices caused by sexual jealousies and the malice of
jilted "lovers" who turn on their former partners with lies.

The abolition of the requirement of corroboration in cases
involving sexual offences, besides being the declaration of an open
season on "sexist" men by deranged feminists, was a perversion of
justice by the party that claims above all to be the "party of law
and order." It was an attack on justice and on the Christian principle that "In the mouth of two or three witnesses every matter
shall be confirmed" (2 Cor. 13:1). The principle that a man is innocent until proven guilty necessitates that the burden of proof should
fall on the prosecution. The abandonment of the requirement of
corroborating evidence is a stage on the road to the total overthrow of this important principle and the establishment of the
principle that the accused is guilty until proven innocent.

3. The third area that I want to look at is *multiculturalism*. Our
society is often proclaimed a multicultural society today. Multiculturalism is an ideal that we are constantly being encouraged to
embrace. But what does multiculturalism mean? Some think it
means a multi-racial society. I do not agree. What multiculturalism
means in essence is a multi-*religious* society.

It is not always, perhaps not often, appreciated that all law
ultimately is based on religious convictions. Consequently, there
can be no such thing as a non-religious State. All States are religious States. This is evident if we consider the simple question:

[18] *Sexual Offences Act, 1956,* 2.(2).

What is the purpose of the State? How we answer this question will reveal our fundamental religious convictions. Why? Because this question brings us inevitably to basic questions of right and wrong, and such questions are always religious questions; that is to say, the answers to such questions are always informed by one's religious convictions. Even the denial of God's existence expresses a basic religious conviction, a religious world-view, namely the idea that the world is entirely explicable in terms of itself, material processes, and has no meaning beyond these processes—which means, in effect, that mankind provides his own meaning for the existence of life, that "The world," to use Schopenhauer's words "is *my* idea." The world is understood, therefore, not in terms of the creative purpose of God, but in terms of chemical evolution or whatever intellectual idol men choose to govern their lives by. This will have significant implications for one's concept of morality generally, and thus inevitably for political ethics as well. The kind of morality produced by such a perspective, and therefore the conceptions of right and wrong in terms of which the State must act, will be different from that produced by a Christian understanding of the meaning and purpose of life. Such a perspective is just as religious as the Christian perspective. The denial of God's existence is a universal negative religious presupposition that shapes the world-view of those who embrace it. What we believe about these issues will inevitably affect our view of the function of the State.

The Christian faith teaches that chemical processes etc. do not provide valid answers to questions about the meaning of life and that if man is to have correct answers to questions of right and wrong, justice, his thinking on this subject must conform to the moral law of God set forth in the Christian Scriptures. "Here is Wisdom; This is the royal Law; These are the lively Oracles of God"—words spoken to Queen Elizabeth II at her coronation in 1953. And while being presented with the Bible she was admonished with the following words: "Our gracious Queen: to keep your Majesty ever mindful of the Law and the Gospel of God as the Rule for the whole life and government of Christian Princes, we present you with this Book, the most valuable thing that this world affords."[19] It is the acceptance of this truth that has made Western justice so much superior to the forms of justice found in un-Christianised cultures. The Western notion of justice was not plucked out of thin air by right-thinking men; it was the product of a *Christian* civilisation. All that made Western justice superior to the barbarous regimes that are to be found among societies that have not come under the influence of Christian civilisation was the result of the fact that Western justice was Christian justice. Common law was, to use the words of Eugen Rosenstock-Huessy, "the dowry of Christian baptism."[20]

It is naïve to assume that Muslims, Hindus and secular humanists will pluck the same notions of justice from thin air that modern Westerners think are the inevitable consequence of the application of pure reason. They will not. And this is because these notions of justice are not the inevitable consequence of reason—at least not in a fallen world. Rather, they are the consequence of the captivity of human reason to the word of God, the result of centuries of Christian culture and civilisation. The issue of justice is a religious issue. Hence the magistrate, who is a man created in God's image and who therefore cannot escape the religious nature of his being, must inevitably have recourse to his religious convictions as he seeks to understand and discharge the task to which he has been called. He may be quite unconscious of the way in which his religious convictions affect the work he does. That they will affect his work is inevitable.

As I have already mentioned, the Christian concept of government in our nation was the rule of law, which meant that all law must conform to the higher law of God, and this includes legislation passed by Parliament and precedent established in courts. In fact the courts of equity existed precisely to redress any discrepancy between the common law and God's law, which of course was identified with reason; the two were considered to be the same thing. What we have now is the rule of politicians; i.e. Parliament no longer deems itself accountable to the higher law of God. It can change any law it does not like and replace it with

[19] E. C. Ratcliff, *op. cit.*, p. 39.   [20] Eugen Rosenstock-Huessy, *op. cit.*, p. 271.

a new one, even if the latter totally overturns a fundamental principle of justice. This is what happened with the 1993 Leasehold Reform Act and the 1994 Criminal Justice and Public Order Act. These Acts overturned fundamental principles of our legal system. In the same way legislation has been passed that legalises the murder of unborn infants. At one time the word "abortion" was usually understood to mean a miscarriage. Unlawful killing of an unborn infant, though it was abortion, was considered a crime. Now Parliament has legalised the deliberate killing of an unborn infant through the enactment of permissive legislation.

In conclusion, it needs to be recognised that our legal system has been evolving for over a millennium. It is by no means perfect, and never has been. It is important that this process of development should continue in order that the law might meet the needs of modern life. But the law needs to evolve in terms of the religious presuppositions upon which it was originally based. The problem we face today is not that the law is evolving *per se*—that must happen if the law is to be relevant—but rather that it is evolving in terms of presuppositions that are alien to our legal and cultural heritage, on which the law itself was originally based. This will lead eventually to the overthrow of our traditional understanding of what justice is, i.e. a *Christian* conception of justice. British justice and Muslim justice are not the same by any means. A *humanistic* conception of justice is different again. But this is what is now being foisted upon us by our politicians. The values that we are losing are the Christian values that guided the development of our understanding of justice itself and hence the development of our legal system, and indeed the development of our civilisation generally.

This is all part of the process of transition from a Christian society to a neo-pagan society. The dominant philosophy today is *secular humanism*. Originally this retained many features of a Christian world-view. But slowly it has changed and is now more consistently and self-consciously pagan. All kinds of religions and philosophies are on sale in the market place of ideas today. This gets called the multicultural society. But religion is determinative of culture. Culture is largely the visible expression of religion, though it may not be self-consciously so. Our culture for a long time was Christian; it was the visible expression of the dominant religious faith. Christianity is now in drastic decline and other faiths and religions (and secular humanism *is* a religion) are offering themselves. The multicultural society is not a permanent thing. It is a society going through a transitional period in which the various religions on offer struggle for supremacy. At the moment secular humanism is dominant—*and it is secular humanism that is the source of the attack upon Christian law in our society.* Like the humanism of ancient Rome it will tolerate any religion just so long as that religion does not challenge its political supremacy. But secular humanism has unleashed a terrible monster upon society in the form of multiculturalism, which it cannot control; and secular humanism may not be the final victor. Whatever religion ultimately triumphs in this struggle will be determinative of culture. The culture of the British nation (if there still is a Britain that is—and with the European Union we cannot guarantee that) will eventually change; it will be an expression of the new religious consensus. The dominant religion will proceed to stamp its ideas upon society and determine the culture, and inevitably along with this it will stamp its own laws upon society, since law is inescapably based on the religious presuppositions that govern our understanding life and thus our understanding of justice also.

If Christianity wins, we shall go on to a new period of Christian civilisation. If secular humanism retains its hold, our law will continue to become thoroughly pagan, pragmatic, and subservient to politicians. This will be a modern version of ancient Rome, a highly totalitarian society. The State will be as god, whether it is of the right-wing or the left-wing variety, determining good and evil for itself according to its own ideas and goals without reference to the higher moral law of God. The individual will be nothing except in relation to the State. The State will provide meaning and purpose for the individual and the society of which he is, in this philosophy, an insignificant part; and the individual and society will exist to serve the State. The philosophy underpinning this kind of society has already got a very strong hold on our culture. We stand at the edge of a precipice.

THE IMPLICATIONS OF THE INFORMATION REVOLUTION FOR THE FUTURE OF THE CHRISTIAN CHURCH

§1

Who controls public opinion?

DOES the media inform and create public opinion? Or does public opinion inform the media? Or is it both at the same time? Who or what is the source of the opinions and ideology that stream forth endlessly from the media at the beginning of the twenty-first century? Who creates and controls the predominant world-view in society?

What I have to say here assumes that in the highly media oriented and largely passive societies of the Western world the *media* informs and substantially creates public opinion. It assumes, furthermore, that the media itself is informed largely by vocal and active minorities who work to influence and control society and important social institutions through the propagation of their ideology and social agenda. By the *media* I mean the television networks, radio stations, newspapers, periodicals, movies etc., all of which feature very predominantly in modern life as the source of knowledge and "truth."

This answer to the question of who controls public opinion is predicated on the seemingly self-evident fact that the majority of people in society are silent and passive. They do not want to act but are willing to be acted upon. They do not want to think for themselves. They are willing to let others do their thinking for them. They are lazy, in other words. They will suck in the endless stream of information that comes from the television and news-papers without stopping to consider how their world-view and opinions are affected by such media. Unpalatable as it may seem, I believe this is largely true of modern society.

But who influences the media, and through the media society at large? The answer to this is that those who are *motivated* and *active* are the ones who influence the media. Where society is largely passive and silent, small activist groups (small compared with the masses that constitute society that is) are able to implement their agenda in society through the influence they bring to bear upon important social institutions. The media today is a crucial factor in this process. Unless those who wish to change society are able to win the media over to their cause in a significant way their efforts will be a failure because public opinion will remain un-changed. It is through the media that the crucial softening up of public opinion takes place so that it becomes fertile ground for new ideologies and concepts of morality. Once this has been ac-complished it is much easier for such groups to influence impor-tant social institutions and those who make decisions that effect the whole of society. This may take a long time. It is grand Fabi-anism. But it works very successfully.

For example, homosexual practices could never have become a socially acceptable form of sexual behaviour in society today had they not been sanitised as a result of constant media influence on the mindset of the nation. The media has been in the forefront of this and virtually every other aspect of the sexual revolution. It constantly portrays those who oppose such practices as bigoted homophobes who have an irrational hatred of and a total lack of compassion for those who are portrayed as their innocent victims. The media has managed to argue that black is white and make it stick. It has succeeded in planting in the minds of many the idea that acceptance and toleration of such practices is the only rea-sonable, the only just, and the only compassionate attitude to those who behave in this way. This softening up of public opinion by the media was a necessary precursor to the new liberated gay culture that has blossomed in recent years. So successful was this softening up that gay couples can now flaunt their homosexuality in public and anyone who objects to or questions their "rights" to do so is deemed vicious and treated with the kind of disrespect and contempt that would be appropriate for a racist. This last point is not impertinent, since it affords a good example of how this softening up process works. Gays are frequently lumped together with blacks, women and disadvantaged minorities that are reputedly treated badly by society. This tactic associates what is defined as a crime by God's law (homosexual acts), and has been deemed by most people to be a crime throughout most of Western history, with groups whose victimisation is evil. By thus associating those who commit evils acts (homosexuals) with those who are innocent of any crime related to their victimisation or supposed victimisation (e.g. blacks and women), those who are critical of and oppose such evil acts are associated in people's minds with racists and others who oppress innocent victims. Such a blurring of the distinctions between right and wrong, good and bad, is necessary if society is to adopt the new morality. But this is to call evil good and good evil, to substitute darkness for light and light for darkness (Is. 5:20).

This total transformation of society's concept of morality has been accomplished through the media. It has been the same with socialism, though the process has been more subtle and the concentration of socialist influence has been more in the electronic and film media than the printed media, which has been more difficult for the socialists to capture, though not impossible, as became apparent with the election of the New Labour government in 1997.

§2
Conspiracy theory vs the logic of ideology

This is not meant to sound like a conspiracy theory of history (at least not in the accepted sense). Activists are motivated people who try to change society in some way. It is such groups that inform those with power and influence in the media, and through the media control society, whether they are capitalist, socialist, atheist or Christian (as we shall see, although the Church failed to do this in the twentieth century, in former centuries she did exert such influence and control through the contemporary media). But conspiracy theory posits something more insidious than this. Conspiracy theory is the idea that an elite, and usually highly placed, group of people conspire secretly to pervert the course of justice and control society for their own personal ends. While I believe that such conspiracies do exist I do not believe they have a significant effect on the course of history on the whole. I do not hold to a conspiracy theory of history.

Rather, what I am arguing is that just as the logic of an idea will work itself out in the lives of the individuals who cherish that idea, so also the logic of the dominant ideology will work itself out practically in the life of the nation, and furthermore, that it is through the media, as defined above, that these ideologies are introduced into society in modern Western nations. Ideas have consequences in other words, and this is so for societies and nations as well as for individuals. Hence, whatever ideology controls the media or is able to exert its influence through the media, will influence and control society because it will shape the mindset of the greater part of the population and will by this means create the conditions necessary for its acceptance as "truth." Once this has successfully been accomplished such ideology can function as public truth, that is to say as a form of religion. Those who refuse to accept this new orthodoxy, be it Christianity, socialism, democracy, feminism, Darwinism, gay rights etc., will be treated as heretics by the communities for which it has become public truth. Its veracity will be deemed self-evident and without need of proof. And those who deny its validity will be deemed out of touch with reality, mad, and possibly evil. This process—a form of "conversion" to use religious terminology—may be, and usually is, for the most part worked out quite unselfconsciously by society.

§3
Media status

The majority of people in Western society today receive most of their information from the media. When it comes to the formation of an individual's overall world-view the influence of the media is even greater, since it provides for most people a ready-made intellectual, social and often (especially in the case of newspapers) political perspective into which they will assimilate even the information they do not receive via the media. Since this is so for most people the media's effect on society is very great. This almost ubiquitous presence of the media in modern Western culture gives it a unique status in society.

The media does not simply present information, "the facts," or a way of interpreting those facts. It is itself now intimately bound up with creating the facts it reports. It has become an integral part of the ideology it promulgates. Politicians and their policies are made and un-made by the media. Even prime ministers and presidents are credible *as* prime ministers and presidents if they have media credibility and utilise the media to their advantage. Today in America a presidential candidate is unlikely to be elected if he has no media presence and credibility, regardless of what his policies are like (America proved the point with gusto when it elected a Hollywood actor as president). In Britain the same is increasingly true. John Major managed to get into position as prime minister despite his lack of media credibility, but his deficit in this department blighted his premiership. He, and the Conservative Party generally, faced a challenge as much from the opposition's effective media posturing in comparison with the media sleaze that dogged the Conservatives during Major's premiership, as they did from any credible *political* challenge from the left—a point that is substantially borne out by Labour's attempt to move towards the middle ground previously held by the Conservatives. (I say *media* sleaze because the Conservatives have no monopoly on political sleaze and "New" Labour could be made to look just as sleazy as the Conservatives—there's not a lot to choose between them. But Labour effectively won the media campaign over the sleaze issue.) It would not be too far off the mark to say that media presence and the likely ratings one's media performance will create are as important as one's ability as a statesman for politicians in important government posts today. Perhaps some former politicians and statesmen who are considered to have been great leaders would have little chance of meeting the criteria for office necessitated by today's ubiquitous media coverage of politics and the lives of those engaged in it. There is perhaps both good and bad in the constant media attention that politicians have to face today. Either way it is a fact of political life at the beginning of the twenty-first century.

The decisions of judges and juries are now overturned by the media's re-opening of criminal and civil cases. Television programmes such as *Rough Justice* and the like are powerful tools in the hands of the media. (This should not necessarily be taken as a criticism, simply a statement of fact.) The media reporting of the trial of O. J. Simpson in the USA became a significant issue in the trial itself and its outcome. It was every bit as much, perhaps more, a newsworthy item, and certainly had greater implications for the process of justice as a whole, than the trial itself.

Media reporting on various wars and conflicts around the world helps to make these conflicts and the plight of those involved, along with the supposed justice or injustice of the causes that fuel them, important issues that governments must be seen by the public to be dealing with in an appropriate and effective way if their credibility and therefore their prospects of re-election are not to be harmed.

Many more examples could be cited. The point is simply that the media is a powerful and important presence in modern society. It has a great deal of influence on society generally and on politicians in particular. Sometimes it uses this for good. Usually it does not. Either way, people respect the trustworthiness of the information they get from the media. They believe it (on the whole). I am speaking here of the greater part of the population. The media is authoritative on the whole for most people. "It was on the television," people say, or "It was on the radio," therefore it must be true. Similarly, there is a mystique to print. Typed text has more authority than mere word of mouth. Typeset text has more authority than typed text. People will believe something they read more readily than the gossip they hear. They will treat it with more respect and take it as truth more easily. It is more difficult to controvert printed "facts." There is something authoritative about printed matter that gossip, word of mouth, does not convey. Printed matter has something permanent and official about it. This is so even where the subject matter does not claim to be factual. Hence the influence of the novel and its power as a vehicle for articulating ideologies. The way the novels of Charles Dickens, for example, are treated almost as social histories, is a good example of the danger this fact poses. Of course, such influence can be used for good as well. This is true of television and radio programmes also. These are channels of official information in the minds of many, although those who impute such authority to these media may do so quite unselfconsciously.

There is also a sense in which the media becomes the real voice of the people or the nation in the perception of many, though again, this may be unselfconscious. People see the media as the voice of truth as opposed to the voice of official authority, i.e. government authority. The media represents, therefore, a different kind of authority. The media is often perceived as the charismatic voice of the people as opposed to the official voice of government. Hence the increasing use of media personalities as spokesmen for political parties, particularly during general elections. Of course this may be, and usually is, quite untrue, but this is the way the media is often perceived, and this is an important point that we need to remember.

In short, the media has a status and an authority that can be used either for good or bad. This is a fact of life. It will not go away if we ignore it or pretend it is not true. Like every other sphere of life the media must be captured for Christ and subjected to his Lordship. To pretend that it is not a vital strategic target in the Christian war and that Christians can ignore it is folly and will have significant consequences for the status of the Church in society. Unfortunately, this was the Church's attitude throughout most of the twentieth century in at least most Western nations. Why?

§4
The Church and the media

The Church used to control what was one of the most important forms of media in Western Christendom, in some periods of history *the* most important form of media: the pulpit. The Church no longer has any significant influence on society because it does not control any form of media that is considered important by society. The pulpit used to be considered an important authority in Western Christendom, at least following the Reformation. This influence has now passed into the hands of atheists and pagans, who have adopted alternative forms of media as a means of influencing society and bringing their ideologies to bear upon the life of the nation. The Church has, on the whole, been oblivious to what has been happening.

In the sixteenth- and seventeenth-centuries, for example, the pulpit was *the* media.[1] Kings would instruct their bishops to reinforce royal prerogatives through their direction of the clergy, and through the clergy, i.e. the pulpit, they were able to influence the people. In other words they would use the Church hierarchy to gain access to the pulpit as a means of disseminating propaganda suited to their own cause. In the time of Puritan England, for instance, Charles I ordered his bishops to instruct parish incumbents to preach the royal prerogative and the divine right of kings. Absolute monarchy was to be taught as part and parcel of God's

[1] I do not underestimate the influence of the printing press, of course, but I think as a form of popular media, in terms of the greatest influence on the lives of ordinary people, it was not as significant as the pulpit. Its influence on the literati and on the radical and activist elements of society was of course greater than the pulpit. But I am here considering the kind of media that is of greatest influence to the common man who is not part of the literati and who goes about his daily business without getting involved with such social activism.

revealed will for man. The king lost control of the media, the pulpit; then he lost his head. The pulpit was *the* media of the day; it was very powerful. Where the Puritan's did not control the official pulpit of the established Church, they established alternative pulpits as a means of communicating their message to the population. They set up lectureships, a kind of shadow pulpit, to replace the official line being promoted by Archbishop Laud et al. It is worth remembering that "gathered" Churches started originally in England as Churches within the official Church. They were subversive organisations within the official Church, not separatist Churches. There was a clear line of differentiation between the early Puritans and the separatists on this point, and even the later Puritans who were Independents, prior to the Restoration, were committed to the concept of a national, established Church. The lectureships they created as an alternative to the official pulpit, where they were denied access to it, proved to be a formidable obstacle to the king's efforts to enforce his will through the official media of the established Church. The Puritans created alternative media outlets for their message and this hamstrung the official Church's ability to control society through the church pulpit.

One way or another, either as incumbents of parish Churches or as unofficial pastors of gathered Churches using lectureships to get their message across, licensed or unlicensed as preachers, the Puritans gained influence via the media of the day: preaching. Of course, making available such an alternative ministry was costly. And it was the merchants and middle classes, among whom Puritanism was strong, that financed this alternative ministry. Had it not been for the financial backing that the Puritan movement got from these quarters it is doubtful that Puritan preachers could have had anything like the influence they did have. (Christianity does not work by magic. God uses means to accomplish his purposes in history. Even Jesus' ministry was supported by at least a few wealthy followers.) It was their ability to seize control of this important form of media or, where they could not do this, create new forms of media that were equivalent to it, that enabled the Puritans to have such an impact on the nation. The whole thing was media oriented. What they did changed the nation, and indeed the world, permanently.

Where Christians have controlled the pulpit when it was the media of the day they have informed and thereby controlled public opinion, and therefore generally controlled society. In the past people went to church to listen to preaching. It was a large part of their lives, and affected their lives considerably. It led to changed lives and as a result to a changed society. The change in the content of the preaching when Puritans took to the pulpit changed England for good and permanently. This was done not only through the official church pulpit, but through alternative pulpits such as the lectureships and the unlicensed preaching of men like John Bunyan. Despite the Restoration, this produced a permanent change that has never been reversed (though it has been badly corrupted). The Puritans were able to do this because preaching was the media of the day. And the media is very powerful. Whoever controls the media will control public opinion and society.

Even in the eighteenth and nineteenth centuries the pulpit (i.e. preaching) was still an important form of media among an increasing number of alternative forms of media. During this period preaching, especially in evangelistic campaigns and "revivals," became one of the major forms of entertainment for many people. People spent their free time attending these meetings. They went to "revival" meetings as we should perhaps go to the cinema today. There were few other forms of entertainment to compete with it, and few that could compare with the spectacular hype and bizarre antics that both preachers and their audiences got up to sometimes (and some of the sexual goings on at some of these "revival" meetings would make the couples on the back row seats in your local cinema blush). Many of the silly goings on one finds in the modern charismatic movement and in the Churches where the "Toronto Blessing" is in vogue were the common fare of these "revival" meetings. It was entertainment with a capital E.[2]

---

[2] Documentation of these bizarre and immoderate gatherings can be found in *Christian History* Vol. XIV, No. 1 (issue no 45), which ran a series of articles on these revival meetings in America.

Perhaps the destructive shift in theology in the West from the Calvinistic orthodoxy established in the creeds of the Protestant Churches to the Arminianism and antinomianism of the modern evangelical Churches can in some measure be put down to the popularity of these kinds of meetings. The old Calvinistic theology was at first represented more in the Churches and the Arminianism and antinomianism found greater room for expression in the revival meetings. As these revival meetings became a more important form of entertainment than church services the theology that came to dominate them eventually came to be seen more as genuine Christian orthodoxy. The message being preached at the revival meetings was seen as more dynamic and relevant and had a highly experiential content that had an immediate effect on the senses and appetites of those who attended them. The new theology came eventually to be linked with a "lively" faith and the old Calvinism with "dead" orthodoxy. The popularity of big name preachers, such as Wesley, and their Methodist followers, who bought into both the Arminian theology and the revival type meetings, lent credibility to this bizarre type of religion. Eventually the Arminian and antinomian theology of the revivalists became the new Christian consensus and orthodoxy.

Today Speaker's Corner is about all that is left of this form of media in Britain (certainly all that is recognised by most people as valid media of this kind). The efforts of modern day street preachers are no longer seen as valid forms of communication, let alone as valid forms of media by most people. Such methods of propagating the gospel are anachronistic and irrelevant. I am speaking here of the form of media used by Christians to get their message across to society, not the form of communication the Church should use as part of its ministry of equipping the saints for service. Obviously, preaching in the sense of the authoritative teaching of the faith to the saints is still, and always will be, an important part of the Church's ministry. But even in church, preaching, in the sense that we have come to understand the term, is no longer a form of media. Preaching, or pulpiteering as it has become, is no longer considered a form of media even by Christians who attend church, and therefore they do not listen to it as a form of media. Often it is merely something to be endured even by Church members (and given the nature of much of this preaching one can sympathise with this attitude). What is called preaching in most churches to-day is not the authoritative teaching of the Scriptures anyway. It is a solemnised (and often not so solemnised) form of what went on at the revival meetings. It bears little resemblance to the biblical ideal of preaching and teaching.[3] Much modern "preaching" is an anachronistic throwback to a form of media, and in some cases merely a pale imitation of a form of entertainment, that is no longer recognised as relevant, valid, authoritative, or even enter-taining, by society generally, or even by Christians.

This is why street preaching is so futile today, even embarrass-ing. It is anachronistic, the use of a form of media that is no longer relevant and that people no longer listen to. They listen instead to the television and radio and the newspapers. But Christians have never sought to conquer these modern forms of media in a sys-tematic and competent fashion. There is not even the desire among many Christians to control, or even use, the media as a means of influencing society. There are of course "gospel" radio stations that play second-rate "Christian" music. But this is very different; it is not a serious alternative to the media that most people listen to *as* media. The aim of these Christian radio stations is usually not to provide a serious contender for the popular media that domi-nates society, but simply to provide alternative, escapist entertain-ment programmes (e.g. Christian "pop" music) for the retreating pietists of the Christian ghetto.

The Church never kept pace with developments in the media. It therefore lost control of the media as a means of transmitting the message of God's word to society. It lost control of the media, and as a result it lost influence in society. Like the dinosaurs, the Churches have now nearly become extinct as a social force in modern society. They have become irrelevant, impotent, a joke in the eyes of society. Had they kept hold of the old truths upon

[3] See Colin Wright, "Restoring the Idea of the Throne to Christian Preach-ing" in *Christianity and Society*, Vol. v, No. 2 (April 1995), pp. 18-21.

which the faith is built instead of caving in to liberalism, and kept pace with modern developments in the media as a means of transmitting those truths to society, we might still have had a Christian culture. Instead the Church junked the timeless truth of God's word for modern liberal theology and held on for dear life to outdated forms of communication, which, in the end, have become forms of noncommunication for most people. Such a course was guaranteed to result in the failure of the Church's mission, a failure that is now so evident in Western society.

§5

Preaching and preachers

In the "Reformed" Churches things are a little different. The pulpit is still seen as central to the life of the Church by most Reformed Christians today. But even in these Churches preaching is not seen in the same way that seventeenth-century Puritans saw preaching. The "primacy of preaching" today in most Reformed Churches is a very different notion from pre-Enlightenment, pre-revival and pre-Romantic (i.e. Reformation) notions of the primacy of preaching. Neither is it seen as media, even by Christians who adhere to the primacy of preaching idea. Preaching has lost its cutting edge as media even among those groups that wish to maintain its status as central to the life of the Church. Even from a practical point of view, regardless of what theories and notions people might have of its importance, it is quite impossible for preaching to have the same status in a largely non-Christian, non-church going society that it once had in a largely Christian society in which the membership of the Church was virtually the entire population. Some still talk of the primacy of preaching, but the Church has failed to move on. The modern notion of the primacy of preaching can only have meaning where preaching is the media, or an important form of media, for society as a whole.

I do not want to be misunderstood at this point: in the life of the Church, in her educational programme and mission to the world, the biblical concepts of teaching and preaching should have a central role. I am not denying this. I think teaching and preaching are vitally important and central to the life and mission of the Church. But I am saying that preaching and teaching do not necessarily have to be done from a church pulpit in order to be valid means of communicating the gospel and the word of God either to Church members or to society generally.

In the life of the institutional Church teaching is a central activity, and preaching is central to the institutional Church's calling in the world. But the way in which this is done needs to move on with developments in the way that information is communicated generally in society if it is to remain relevant. If the Church does not move on with the times and make use of developments in information technology that society generally adopts it will lose control of the media it needs to use in order to communicate the gospel effectively. In fact this is precisely what has happened.

I am not speaking here of the message, but merely of the means of communicating that message. The *content* of the gospel does not change. Its public, official declaration must not cease. But the method of delivery, the way in which this proclamation of the word of God is presented needs to change with the times in order for the Church to be able to communicate the message as widely and as effectively as possible. The Church needs to take advantage of every means available for the transmission of the word of God to society. Not to do this is to fail to obey Scripture itself:

For though I am free from all men, I have made myself a slave to all, that I might win the more. And to the Jew I became as a Jew, that I might win Jews; to those who are under the law, as under law, though not being myself under the law, that I might win those who are under the law; to those who are without law, as without law, though not being without the law of God but under the law of Christ, that I might win those who are without law. To the weak I became weak, that I might win the weak; I have become all things to all men, that I might by *all* means save some. (1 Cor. 9:19–22)

Paul was prepared by *all* means, i.e. in every way possible, to preach the gospel to those who had not heard it. Some years ago I had a conversation with a friend who had taken up street preaching. He was a Reformed believer and his message was orthodox. I suggested to him that this method of street preaching was no longer an effective way to communicate the message of the gospel to society. Most people do not stop to listen, and those who preach in the streets are preaching to the wind most of the time (if not to raspberries). I suggested that he could reach more people who are prepared listen if he were willing to speak on the local radio. I had at the time contact with several local radio stations. I offered to put his name forward as a speaker, since on many occasions I was asked to suggest possible speakers for various programmes. The response I got was that such a method of communicating the gospel was not biblical, that the Bible commands us to preach on the streets, not on the radio, and that we must obey the Bible. But of course the Bible does not command us specifically to preach on the streets, as if this were the God-ordained method of preaching to the masses. It does give us the example of God's servants preaching on the streets, *because this was the media of their day*, the way everyone communicated their message to society, including the official messengers of kings and princes, and the Bible commands us to communicate the gospel as effectively as possible to the world. People stopped to listen to street preaching in New Testament times because this was a socially relevant method of communication. That was how people got their news. It was the media of the day. Paul and others used this method *because* it was the media of the day, not because it is inherently correct or divinely ordained. They used the method in vogue, which everyone else used. To say that what the Bible gives us is a fixed method of proclaiming the message in this way is to misread the Bible, to decontextualise it and strip it of its relevance. Would Paul or any of the apostles refuse to use the radio today when there are streets to preach on? Impossible! They would have used the most effective means available to them to get the message across to as many people as possible.

Furthermore, the "primacy of preaching" in the Reformed Churches has now been transformed into the primacy of the preacher. This is unbiblical. What counts in the eyes of many

Christians today (both "preachers" and listeners), particularly in Reformed circles is the *performance* of the preacher. For some, if the performance is not to their specifications it is not true preaching. For such it is no longer the *message* (i.e the content of the message: God's word) that the Holy Spirit uses to convince people of their sin and need for Christ, but the antics of the preacher. Thus we have the modern Reformed emphasis on preaching as "event" rather than as the communication of the word of life. If the "event" is not up to scratch and the preacher does not jump up and down like a monkey and generally make a fool of himself, the Holy Spirit cannot work. This concept of preaching admirably demonstrates the influence of existentialism and Romanticism on the Reformed Churches, despite much bravado about being true to the Reformation. It demonstrates also a perspective that differs from the charismatic movement only on details rather than basic orientation. It is the *experience* of preaching, the impression imparted to the listener by the gyrations and perspiration of the preacher that really does the job and brings the listener into contact with God. God the Holy Spirit does not work by opening the listener's mind to the truth of God's word thereby convicting him of sin and righteousness, but by moving him with emotions generated through the impressive performance of the preacher. It is not a work of conviction but of emotional experience, of arousal by egocentric oratory, and merely another form of entertainment worship. The preacher is expected to jump up and down in the pulpit, shout at his audience, cajole and harangue them and generally act like an imbecile, and, of course, the members of the congregation are then expected to act like imbeciles by complimenting the preacher on his "unction" on their way out after the service. I heard one preacher say "I've crowed like a cockerel in the pulpit to get my message across," and this was a minister who abominates charismatic worship and the Toronto blessing (animal noises are a speciality at the Toronto blessing sessions, what's his problem?). Many such preachers will tell us they are willing to make fools of themselves for Christ, as did this preacher. But of course there is a difference between being prepared to be labelled a fool by non-believers for believing the truth, and being justly called a fool by discerning men, regardless of whether they are believers. Such antics only make the gospel and the Christian faith look foolish and are in a sense blasphemous since they expose the faith to ridicule by God's enemies.

The experientialism of revivalism is what this form of preaching is all about. It is basically a charismatic perspective (Lloyd-Jones, the darling of the modern Reformed movement in Britain, demonstrated this by his adoption of charismatic theology later in life, a fact that embarrassed many of his followers, but need not, since their differences with the charismatics are really very superficial). Those Reformed worthies of the past who did not embrace this notion of preaching would go down like lead shot in many of these modern Reformed Churches, though since they are now dead they can be venerated with impunity (we can always *imagine* them preaching like they had ants in their pants). By all accounts (New Testament accounts, that is), Paul himself would have failed to come up to modern Reformed standards of preaching, since he was reputed among the Churches to have had an unimpressive personal presence (no charisma) and no oratorical skills worth mentioning. In other words he was a poor preacher in the modern sense (see 2 Cor. 10:10). His power was in his message not in his performance—few were entertained, many were converted, and many more were hopping mad after hearing him. I suspect he would have scored low in personal communication skills by modern secular humanist standards, which, unfortunately, are too often the standards used by Christians.

At the root of this notion of preaching is the unwillingness of men to use their minds in worship, a basic aspect of the great commandment as our Lord restated it (Mt. 22:37 cf. Dt. 6:5). Preaching as experience, or "event" or whatever modern-day "Reformed" people choose to call it, is simply a form of entertainment worship in which the "worshipper" is passive and in which he does not have to exert any effort (it's all done for him by the preacher, who creates this spiritual "event"). Its concession to the existentialist spirit of the age is no less real than the notion of worship embraced by the charismatic Churches. It is experiential religion. The emphasis is not on faithfully practising the precepts of the faith in one's life, and preaching is not primarily aimed at securing this effect by equipping Christians to pursue it, but rather on producing an existential experience in the listener, which, doubtless, it is hoped will produce some kind of effect in the listener's life, though what that effect should be is rather vaguely understood. But like all experiences, the "event" of preaching diminishes in its effects the further one gets from the experience. Regular attendance at church, of course, overcomes this. But when the great preacher dies and his replacement has not got the charisma to carry this sort of thing off, the Church goes into a nose dive. What held it together was not so much the truth of God's word, and the purpose of the ministry was not to equip the saints for service by imparting the wisdom of God's word in a relevant way,— i.e. in a way that is relevant to the everyday lives of the congregation—but rather the "event," the experience of the preaching. Countless examples could be given. Of course, such Churches are few and far between, and those who can only travel to their new Jerusalem every now and then live Christian lives that are a mere shadow of the lives of those who bask in the reflected glory of these super-preachers.

Unfortunately, these great Churches never seem to transform society, despite the thousands that attend or come under their ministries through cassette tape distribution etc. It does not seem to have occurred to these Christian gurus that something is missing. The cult of personality, even Christian personalities, cannot change society. For that the real thing is needed: commitment to the message of the gospel by the Church membership and a willingness to live it out in their daily lives. The preacher cannot do this for them. He can only instruct them and equip them for it. Too many are content to leave it all to the "event" of preaching (i.e. the charisma of the preacher), backed up by the mid-week prayer meeting where necessary (religion on Sundays and Wednesdays). In this sense, modern "Reformed" religion, contrary to the religion of the Reformers, emphasises sacramental grace ever bit as much as traditional Episcopal Churches, only for the modern Reformed believer the sacrament at the centre of the faith, what gives the faith its meaning and purpose and around which the Christian life revolves, is "Reformed" preaching.

This emphasis on entertainment preaching and the preacher, on preaching as a sacrament, is now what is meant by the primacy of preaching. The careful teaching and relevant application of the faith to the real issues that face most members of Christian congregations is avoided at all costs. Such teaching demands the engagement of the mind in worship on the part of the congregation, and then action, sacrifice for the cause of the Kingdom, as the congregation puts into effect what has been learned. To expect this is one sure way to get your mega-Church into a nose dive that will end with the preacher looking for a new job. So the status quo, "Reformed" preaching, is peddled endlessly instead and its recognition as true "unction" is all that is required of the Reformed believer if he is to be numbered among God's elect. At best such preaching is anachronistic. Pulpiteering is no longer in vogue. Society no longer listens. Such preaching has no real effect on society. The Reformed preacher may think he is preaching the gospel (if only to the converted), but he will only keep his job if he keeps off the congregation's toes and titillates them each week with new manifestations of "unction."

Is this, in *any* degree, really what the New Testament requires of the Church and of those who preach the gospel?

§6
Biblical preaching and teaching

The New Testament word translated as *preach* is κηρύσσω. There are three basic words in this word group that appear in the New Testament[4]: κῆρυξ, a *herald, public messenger*; κηρύσσω, *to be a herald, make proclamation as a herald* (i.e. to preach); and κήρυγμα, *what is*

---

[4] *Κηρῡκεία, the office of a herald* or *crier*, and *κήρυξις, a proclaiming, proclamation* (i.e. the act as distinct from the content), are not used in the New Testament.

proclaimed by a herald, a proclamation, public notice (i.e. preaching, both the act of proclaiming and the content of the proclamation⁵). Kittel's *Theological Dictionary of the New Testament* has some very interesting comments about these words, which I shall cite at length:

(1) Κῆρυξ. "The herald who plays so important a part in the Greek world is of little account in the NT. The word only occurs three times, and always in later writings. Jesus is never called the κῆρυξ θεοῦ ['herald (or preacher) of God'], though Paul is κῆρυξ καὶ ἀπόστολος καὶ διδάσκαλος ['herald (preacher) and messenger (apostle) and teacher'] in 2 Tm. 1:11. Cf. also 1 Tm. 2:7 and some MSS of Col. 1:23. Noah, who is regarded as God's herald in Judaism . . . is called κῆρυξ δικαιοσύνης ['preacher of righteousness'] in 2 Pt. 2:5 because by word and deed he summoned his contemporaries to repentance some 120 years before the coming flood. Noah is also described as a herald in 1 Cl., 7, 6 and 9, 4.

"How are we to explain the reserve with which the Bible views the term? In many respects κῆρυξ seems to be a very suitable word to describe the Christian preacher. It has many links with ἀπόστολος [*messenger, apostle*] and is also at many points an equivalent of εὐάγγελος [*one bringing good news*⁶]. Nevertheless, the NT manifestly avoids it. Why? The point is that it does not really fit the person of the one who proclaims the Word. For the true preacher is God or Christ Himself. Hence there is little place for the herald. The Bible is not telling us about human preachers; it is telling us about the preaching. Furthermore, the prior Greek history gives too specific a meaning to κῆρυξ. The NT knows nothing of sacral personages who are inviolable in the world [the herald was con-

---

⁵ According to Abbot-Smith κήρυγμα does not refer to the act but only to the content; it is "the substance as distinct from the act which would be expressed by κήρυξις" (G. Abbot-Smith, *A Manual Greek Lexicon of the New Testament* [Edinburgh: T. & T. Clark, Third Edition, 1986], p. 246). Other scholars, e.g. Kittel and Thayer, include both the act and the content in the meaning of the term, the former being included on the basis of texts such as Mt. 12:41; Lk. 11:32; 1 Cor. 2:4; Tit. 1:3; and 2 Tim 14:17, none of which seem to be conclusive, and on the basis classical Greek usage.

⁶ A εὐάγγελος can also be a sacral messenger, one who declares an oracle (see Gerhard Kittel, ed., *Theological Dictionary of the New Testament* [Grand Rapids, Michigan: Eerdmans, 1964], Vol. II, p. 711).

sidered inviolable; he was not to be harmed or mistreated by those to whom he came and to lay hands on him was a great offence— SCP]. The messengers of Jesus are like sheep delivered up to wolves (Mt. 10:16). As the Lord was persecuted, so His servants will be persecuted (Jn. 15:20). The servants of Christ are, as it were, dedicated to death (Rev. 12:11). But the message does not perish with the one who proclaims it. The message is irresistible (2 Tm. 2:9). It takes its victorious course through the world (2 Th. 3:1). Hence κηρύσσειν is more important than the κῆρυξ in the NT."[7]

(2) *Κηρύσσω.* "When we to-day speak of the proclaiming of God's Word by men, we almost necessarily think of preaching, and with few exceptions Luther always used this word (*predigen*) in translation of κηρύσσειν. The NT is more dynamic and varied in its modes of expression than we are today." Friedrich, the author of this article in Kittel's *Theological Dictionary*, cites twenty-eight different terms and phrases besides the κηρύσσω word group that the New Testament uses to convey the idea of proclaiming the word of God, and concludes: "Naturally there are differences between these verbs. But our almost exclusive use of 'preach' for all of them is a sign, not merely of poverty of vocabulary, but of loss of something which was a living reality in primitive Christianity."[8]

Furthermore, and of significance for the argument of this essay, "Even if we disregard the other terms, and restrict ourselves to 'preach' in translation of κηρύσσειν, the word *is not a strict equivalent of what the NT means by κηρύσσειν.* κηρύσσειν does not mean the delivery of a learned and edifying or hortatory discourse in well-chosen words and a pleasant voice. It is the declaration of an event. Its true sense is 'to proclaim'. And it is because κηρύσσειν has this sense that we may understand why, like εὐαγγέλιον [*good news*] and εὐαγγελίζεσθαι [*to announce good news*] . . . it does not occur in the Johannine writings except at Rev. 5:2. John prefers μαρτυρεῖν [*to bear witness, testify*]. From the standpoint of his eschatology μαρτυρεῖν is better adapted than the dramatic and efficacious herald's cry to describe witness to that 'which was from the beginning, which we

---

[7] Gerhard Friedrich, "κῆρυξ (ἱεροκῆρυξ), κηρύσσω, κήρυγμα, προκηρύσσω" in *ibid.*, Vol. III, p. 696.   [8] *Ibid.*, p. 703.

have heard, which we have seen with our eyes, which we have looked upon, and our hands have handled' (1 Jn. 1:1; cf. Jn. 3:11; 15:27). It is in keeping with the content of Jn. and Hb. that κηρύσσειν is not used. We find it 9 times in Mt., 14 in Mk., 9 in Lk., 8 in Ac. (with another 4 in D at Ac. 1:2; 16:14; 17:15 and 19:14), 17 in Paul, another 2 in Past[oral Epistles], once in 1 Pt. and once in Rev. The verb occurs 61 (65) times in all in the NT. If we compare these figures with those for κῆρυξ and κήρυγμα, we are led already to some conclusions as to the theological significance of the terms. Emphasis does not attach to the κήρυγμα, as though Christianity contained something decisively new in content—a new doctrine, or a new view of God, or a new cultus. The decisive thing is the action, the proclamation itself. For it accomplishes that which was expected by the OT prophets. The divine intervention takes place through the proclamation. Hence the proclamation itself is the new thing. Through it the βασιλεία τοῦ θεοῦ ['kingdom of God'] comes."[9]

(3) *Κήρυγμα.* "At Mt. 12:41 par. Lk. 11:32 κήρυγμα has been correctly rendered *cohortatio* [*encouragement*], *exhortatio* [*exhortation*], *praedicatio* [*proclamation*]. The preaching of Jonah was followed by the repentance of the Ninevites. At 1 C. 2:4 κήρυγμα is the act of proclaiming. Christian preaching does not persuade the hearers by beautiful or clever words—otherwise it would only be a matter of words. Preaching does more. It takes place in the Spirit and in power. It is thus efficacious. In the short Markan ending, however, the reference of κήρυγμα is to content: τὸ ἱερὸς καὶ ἄφθαρτον κήρυγμα τῆς αἰωνίου σωτηρίας ['the sacred and imperishable proclamation of eternal salvation']. The sacred and incorruptible *kerygma* is in some sense a doctrine which treats of eternal salvation. Yet this does not exclude the possibility that the message which thus treats of salvation, or proclaims it, may also effect it. This is at least the meaning in 1 C. 1:21: The foolish message of Jesus crucified saves those who believe. At 1 C. 15:14 the resurrection of Jesus from the dead is the content of the *kerygma*. At R. 16:25, too, the reference is to the message with a very definite content. The gos-

[9] *Ibid.*, p. 703f. my italics.

pel of Paul is identical with that which Jesus Himself preached during His earthly life.

"In Tt. 1:3 κήρυγμα is *actus praedicandi* ['the act of proclaiming']. By preaching is manifested the λόγος [word] which brings to man the eternal life that was promised . . . The κήρυγμα is the mode in which the divine Logos comes to us."[10]

What is clear from all this is that there is no office of preacher or herald (κῆρυξ) in the New Testament Church. It is the apostles, evangelists, prophets, pastors and teachers who preach the word of God (Eph. 4:11f.). The term *preacher* or *herald* (κῆρυξ) occurs only three times, and the herald had no official status in the Church. There is no *office* of preacher in the New Testament Church. The officers of the Church who engage in preaching are the apostles, evangelists, prophets, pastors and teachers. The activity of preaching, the proclamation of God's word, however, is very important. But κηρύσσω (*to preach*) is nowhere in the New Testament used to denote *the discharge of the office of a herald.*[11] It means *to publish, proclaim openly*, and refers to the public proclamation of the gospel and matters pertaining to it. It is the proclamation that is of primary importance, the publishing of the gospel, not the style or method of the preacher, nor the context in which it is done, all of which are secondary matters that must be geared to making the proclamation of the word as effective as possible.

Nevertheless, preaching is only one means among many of communicating the gospel to the world. What is of primary importance in the New Testament is that the message, the word of God, is proclaimed and made known somehow. Street preaching was an important form of official media in New Testament times. It is to be expected that the apostles would take their message out onto the streets and proclaim it openly. This was the way news and important information was made know to people. Not to have done this would have been to fail to make use of one of the most effective means available for spreading the message of good news to the world.

[10] *Ibid.*, p. 715f.   [11] *Ibid.*, p. 716. Even in classical Greek it is rarely used to mean this (*ibid.*, p. 697).

The open and clear proclamation of the word of God must never cease. It is the means God has ordained by which the word of life is transmitted to those who are being saved. In this sense, *preaching* must never cease. The authoritative proclamation of the word of God is central to the calling of the Church. But the method of doing this is not the primary consideration. That the message is proclaimed as effectively as possible somehow is the important point. This means that all forms of media open to the Church in her task of proclaiming the gospel are valid. The Church is not tied in specifically to a particular method of preaching. Neither are we told in the New Testament that in proclaiming the word of God (preaching) one must preach from a pulpit, preach in a particular way or style, that one must not sit but stand and use one's whole body (Lloyd-Jonesism), that one must have an introduction and three points, that one must be as animated and as agitated as possible, that one must shout at and harangue those listening, and that one must always wear a shirt and tie or suit. To stress such things is Pharisaism. The emphasis in the New Testament is rather on communicating the truth of God's word as effectively as possible, and all other things are to be subordinated to this goal. All possible means open to the Church of communicating the gospel are valid. Preaching in the sense of what the minister does in the pulpit each Sunday is one such means, but there are other means and methods open to the Church, and in emphasising one or other of these methods the Church should take into consideration the effectiveness of the means used. This may mean abandoning some traditional means of communicating the gospel to the non-believing world in favour of methods that are more culturally relevant and therefore more effective in contemporary society.

Furthermore, preaching in the New Testament is *not* what is understood as preaching in most church services today, i.e. an exposition or homily from the pulpit. It is rather *the simple declaration of the pure word of God*. It was important that a κῆρυξ (a herald or preacher) did not embellish or exaggerate his master's message or enter into negotiations with those to whom he was sent. His duty was to declare the message simply and plainly, to deliver it exactly as he heard it from his master.[12] Reading or directly quoting Scripture is the purest form of preaching. All explanations and exegesis of the text are a move away from biblical preaching. Exposition and exegesis do not fit the New Testament category of preaching. Preaching in the New Testament is the simple declaration of the pure word of God. We have no New Testament examples of preaching that are not the plain proclamation of the undiluted word of God. Exegesis is not preaching. Neither is exposition.

Of course, exegesis and exposition are activities of central importance to the purpose and task of the Church ministry. Exegesis and exposition is the task of the *teacher*, which *is* an office in the New Testament Church. The term *exegesis* comes from the Greek word ἐξηγέομαι, meaning *to reveal, interpret, narrate, unfold in teaching*,[13] which is used in the New Testament. But in the New Testament preaching is the proclamation of the message of the gospel simply and purely. It is not exegesis in the modern Reformed sense; it is not expository preaching in other words, but the formal proclamation of the gospel. It is declaration not exposition.

Lest there should be any misunderstanding, let me make it clear that I believe exegesis and exposition of Scripture are vitally important and central to the ministry of the Church. In fact, such teaching is what should happen each Sunday in the church service. Exegesis of Scripture is the function of the teacher and a primary aspect of the Church's ministry to the saints. The office of teacher is fundamental and vital to the life of the institutional Church. But such exposition and exegesis of Scripture for the purpose of equipping the saints for service (Eph. 4:11–12) is very different from what passes for preaching in most churches today and is to be distinguished from the formal proclamation of the gospel (preaching) required of the Church in the New Testament.

This is why I believe the notion of the primacy of preaching in modern Reformed Churches is seriously astray from the biblical ideal. It is a notion, indeed an ideology, that has taken on a life of its own quite independent of any real connection with what the

---

[12] *Ibid.*, p. 687f.   [13] Ἐξηγέομαι means (1) *to be a leader*, (2) *to show the way*, then (3) *to prescribe the form of words* or *set forth in language*, and (4) *to explain, interpret, reveal*.

New Testament sets forth as either teaching (exegesis) or preaching (proclamation). It has become the primacy of the preacher, and in Reformed circles this wayward notion of preaching has become an end in itself rather than a means of communicating the gospel. What is of importance in this ideology of preaching is the sermon itself, preaching as an art form, the preacher's performance and the audience's experience of the event, i.e. the impressions and emotions such preaching arouses in them. These ideas are openly promoted and encouraged in popular Reformed manuals on preaching and preachers. It is all about the cultivation of an art form geared to creating the right existential experience in the audience, and as in most modern art forms, following the Romantics, the performance of the artist is what is considered of paramount importance.[14]

The Church must return to the biblical ideal if it is to communicate the gospel effectively. It must seek to communicate the gospel to the world by the most effective means possible. There is no mileage in trying to get people into church by titillating them with prancing pulpiteers. Even if this succeeds in getting people into the church in the short term (which is increasingly unlikely due to its decline both as a form of media and entertainment), it will achieve very little in the long term. Any revival in the Church's fortunes as a result of such endeavours will come to an end when the preacher leaves for better pastures, or drops dead. The Church must be built on a surer foundation, the foundation of the teaching of the apostles and prophets, the word of God (Eph. 2:20).

Conclusion

Why all this talk about preaching when the subject is the media and the Church's future? Because it is necessary to deal with a misconception before we can get back to the correct conception of the task before the Church.

[14] D. M. Lloyd-Jones' book *Preaching and Preachers* (London: Hodder and Stoughton, 1971) is perhaps one of the more influential and popular manuals on

From the time that preaching in the modern sense ceased to be a major form of media in Western society, Christians have not had the financial strength to control the media; certainly they did not have the financial strength in the twentieth century. The Church lost control of the media and never invested in the new forms of media that took the place of preaching in society. Now the Church cannot afford to be a significant player in the modern media world. But if we are to rebuilt society effectively as a *Christian* society we need to think and act strategically. If we are to proclaim Christ to the world effectively we need access to the media.

At the beginning of the twenty-first century, however,—and this is the important point—the media is again undergoing vast changes. New developments are taking shape in computer technology that will change the shape of the media in the twenty-first century. This new computer technology will be the media of the future, and this technology is now coming within financial reach of most Churches, even within reach of most individuals. These developments are taking place at an exponential rate. The Church must be ready, willing and able to take advantage of the opportunities this new technology brings. It will likely be the mass media for the next century. If Christians do not seize the day the Church may decline for another century. Entrenched, old-fashioned attitudes will not help us. We cannot relax and hope that people will start coming to church again to listen to "great preaching." People no longer listen. We are commanded to go out into all the world and preach the gospel (Mk 16:15), not to wait until the world comes into the church.

It is vitally important that people come under the ministry of God's word if they are to be saved and society is to be Christian

---

preaching as an art form in Reformed circles. It is a classic statement of the position. It is doubtful Lloyd-Jones' intellectual criteria would have allowed most of the disciples to matriculate into Jesus' training programme. Jesus himself, and Paul, who doubtless would have fitted Lloyd-Jones' intellectual criteria, would have failed the Doctor's test miserably on preaching skills since they both, as was the custom, sat down to preach (Mt. 5:1; 23:2; 26:55; Lk. 4:20ff.; Jn 8:2; Acts 16:13 cf. 13:14–16), a major defect according to the Lloyd-Jones school of preaching.

once again. But listening to traditional pulpit preaching in church services is not the only means of bringing people under the ministry of God's word, and perhaps in future it will not be the main or most effective means of doing so. We must use the new media to communicate the word of God to the world. It is the truth of God's word that convicts, that the Holy Spirit uses to bring men to faith. Therefore men can only be saved as they are brought into contact with this word. If we are to do this effectively we must use the most culturally relevant means of communication available. By all means we must communicate the word of God to the world. It is the proclamation of that word that saves men, societies and nations. While the Church prizes and worships irrelevant and extra-biblical notions of preaching and the preachers who thrive on such misconceptions, rather than the effective communication of God's word, she will fail to proclaim the gospel. Indeed such failure is precisely what much so-called "great preaching" has brought us. The emphasis has moved away from God's word and its requirements on our lives to men and their ideas and often what prevails as "preaching" is no more than the cult of personality.

The battle for the rebuilding of Christian society and culture will be fought on two fronts in the twenty-first century: education and the media. These two fronts are two fronts of the same battle field, and they are coming closer together all the time now. The battle for society will not be won in the church; most people don't go to church any more. The Church must go into the world with the gospel. The battle for society will be won when the Church goes out into the world, which is precisely what Christ commanded (Mk 16:15). The battle for society used to be won in the pulpit, many generations ago. But those days have gone. Then the membership of the Church was society. Not any more. We must take the timeless truth of God's word into the twenty-first century, using the means, the media, that people now look to for their information, news and general world-view. If the Church does not take to the field and engage in the battle there are plenty of other religions and ideologies that will. The Muslims and secular humanists are more active and aggressive today than the Church in proclaiming their teachings and world-view and in claiming the lives of individuals and society.

I believe that the New Testament supports this understanding of the Church's task, because that is precisely what the apostles and prophets did in terms of their contemporary culture. They used the media available and relevant to their age and culture. So must we.

This means that Christians must wake up to reality and stop living in the past. We must seize on the new technological developments in media and information technology and use them effectively to bring the message of God's word to a world desperately in need of it. For the Church not to do this is to fail in her Great Commission to go into all the world and preach the gospel to the whole Creation.

14

THE CHURCH AS
A COMMUNITY OF FAITH

And in those days, when the number of the disciples was multiplied, there arose a murmuring of the Grecians against the Hebrews, because their widows were neglected in the daily ministration. Then the twelve called the multitude of the disciples unto them, and said, It is not reason that we should leave the word of God, and serve tables. Wherefore, brethren, look ye out among you seven men of honest report, full of the Holy Ghost and wisdom, whom ye may appoint over this business. But we will give ourselves continually to prayer, and to the ministry of the word. And the saying pleased the whole multitude: and they chose Stephen, a man full of faith and of the Holy Ghost, and Philip, and Prochorus, and Nicanor, and Timon, and Parmenas, and Nicolas a proselyte of Antioch: Whom they set before the apsotles: and when they had prayed, they laid their hands of them. (Acts 6:1–6)

When the unclean spirit is gone out of a man, he walketh through dry places, seeking rest, and findeth none. Then he saith, I will return unto my house from whence I came out; and when he is come, he findeth it empty, swept, and garnished. Then goeth he, and taketh with himself seven other spirits more wicked than himself, and they enter in and dwell there: and the last state of that man is worse than the first. Even so shall it be unto this wicked generation. (Mt. 12:43–45 cf. Lk 11:24–26)

THERE is in Britain today a discernible decline of the Christian faith. This problem is not new. It goes back at least to the beginning of the twentieth century and probably the root causes go back as far as the Enlightenment. But it is only now that we are beginning to see where the abandonment of Christianity as the prevailing world-view of society will take us. There is a settled, almost institutionalised, antipathy to the Christian faith in Britain today. One can see this at many levels: politically, in the type of legislation that is being passed and the social engineering that is increasingly taking place; in family life, where the Christian family is now not only considered old-fashioned but actually in a minority (childless marriages and one parents families are now more numerous than are heterosexual two-parent families); in the kind of education that is provided in the State schooling system and indeed for the most part in the private schooling system; and in the media, which in many ways has been in the vanguard of promoting the permissive society and the overthrow of Christian morality. And along with this there is a tolerance for almost everything the sets itself up in opposition to the Christian faith. Political correctness has created an ethos in which people no longer feel that they have the liberty to speak freely about many issues that are of grave concern for the future of the British nation. A good example of this last point was the attempt by the British government at the end of 2001 to introduce a "religious hate law" that would have effectively outlawed Christian evangelism, which already suffers badly at the hands of the authorities. The fascist State now looms large on the British landscape. To put this another way, we could say that the British nation is now well-advanced on the road to re-paganisation.

I suspect that this phenomenon is more widespread than Britain however. I think it is a Western problem, and may very well be a world-wide problem. It seems that at the beginning of the twenty-first century there is a world-wide decline of the Christian faith. And the Churches on the whole have been unable to do anything realistic about this situation. After two official "decades of evangelism" the Church in Britain is still in decline. Furthermore, the Church has been hijacked and stripped of her role in society by the secular humanist State, though it has to be admitted that the Church did not really put up much of a struggle against this and has even condoned it by promoting socialist ideology as a "Christian" model for social organisation. Why people should take the Church or her message seriously given the fact that she has abdicated her responsibilities so willingly to the secular humanist State seems not to have crossed the minds of our Church leaders. Add to this the fact that the Church is virtually destitute of any prophetic message to the nation any more and it is not really surprising that the Church is so irrelevant to the lives of most people. The salt has thoroughly lost its saltiness.

Finding the correct answer to this dilemma is the most pressing problem facing the Church in Britain today, though for the most part the real nature of the problem is not even recognised by Christians. How to get more people into church on Sundays and bolster the already ineffective and irrelevant institutional Church seems to be the main consideration of Christians, not how to change the *nation*. How to disciple the *nation* to Christ is not on the Church's agenda at all today. The nearest that Christians get to this usually is snatching brands from the fire, saved souls, who are then left to waste their lives as if they had never turned to Christ. Yet Christ's Great Commission to his Church was the command to disciple the *nations*, not to snatch brands from the fire. I dare say that the Great Commission has never been so neglected by the Church in Britain as it is today and probably in the West generally. Given this fact we must surely see the Church's decline as the inevitable consequence of her own short-sightedness.

If the Church is to recover from this decline she must identify the cause and rectify the defect. What I have to say here is an attempt to identify this problem and propose the biblical solution to it.

The Bible gives us a picture of the Christian Church as a community of faith—a community with all the problems that beset human society in a fallen world. The picture of the Church given us in the New Testament is not a cosy ideal, an unrealistic pretend community. That is often what the Church tries to create by refusing to face the real issues that confront her. But the Church as presented in the pages of Scripture is a real community functioning redemptively in a fallen world. This is why I chose the reading from Acts 6:1–6. What we have here is a real community dealing with real issues in a biblical manner. The Church of the New

Testament was not perfect by any means. Just look at them, arguing and complaining about who gets the most food. The issue was *welfare*. Oh yes, that thorny old issue that the modern Church has now neatly sidestepped by handing it all over to the State!

But what did the apostles do about this? Well, they recognised first of all that it was a responsibility of the Church. They did not say, "Hum! This is not a spiritual issue, we must give ourselves to preaching the word and prayer, tell them to go and get some State handouts." They said "We must give ourselves to the word and prayer, so we shall appoint some appropriate people in the Church to deal with the problem" (v. 2). They dealt with the problem as a community of faith. They recognised it was a problem for the *Church* to deal with as a community.

Second, they did not relegate the issue to the "non-spiritual" issues box. They recognised that this was a spiritual issue needing to be dealt with by people who were full of the Spirit and wise (v. 3), i.e. by people who were able to deal with the situation in terms of biblical wisdom—in other words in terms of a Christian worldview. There was no dualistic split in their thinking. Indeed, such a dualism was not part of biblical culture and would not have been part of the culture of the Jews at this time. Manual labour was not viewed by the Jews in the same way it was viewed by the Greeks, who considered it demeaning. For the Jews of the first century manual labour was considered God-honouring work every bit as much as intellectual labour such as teaching. So there was no spiritual/secular split in the apostles' thinking as there is in much of the Western world today. They recognised that the Church lives in the real world and has to deal with the problems of the real world, and has to minister to the real needs of the body of Christ. Spirituality was not seen as a preoccupation with some other-worldly dimension, unrelated to the everyday concerns of this world, but rather as the proper attitude to this everyday world, an obedient attitude that dedicates this everyday world to Christ and seeks to live for his glory and honour in it.

So we see here that the Christian Church in the New Testament inhabited the real world, and dealt practically with the real

issues of everyday life that faced the Christian community. And
the New Testament Church was prepared to provide help and
guidance to people so that they could live out their faith in this
world. The Church was a community of people living *as* a community, with all the everyday concerns that a community faces.
The life of faith in Christ is not a form of escape from the real
world in any sense, but rather the proper dedication of this mundane life, in all its details and practicalities, to Christ. What makes
our actions spiritual is our attitude, not the nature of the job we
are doing.

Now the problem is that the Church does not often function
this way in Western society, at least in modern times. The Church
is seen largely as an institution, the main purpose of which is to
provide for cultic activity, e.g. worship services, baptisms, funerals
etc. By the term "cultic" here I am not referring to some form of
weird sect or religion. The word is incorrectly used of such groups.
The term "cultus" or "cult" refers to the system of ritual worship
that takes place in church services and meetings. The Church in
the Western world is defined largely in terms of the public Christian cultus, i.e. the system of ritual worship used in church services. The cultus is the paradigm that gives meaning to the Church
for most people in the Western world, most Christians included.

The New Testament, however, does not give us this kind of
paradigm for understanding the Christian Church and her function in the kingdom of God. It gives us no liturgies, no formulas
for cultic activity, nor does it in any other way specify what the
public Christian cultus should be like. Yes, it does give us principles for how we are to behave towards each other when we meet
together. It tells us that we are to worship and pray together, and
the institutional Church has the duty to provide for the teaching,
edification and equipment of the saints for the work of the Kingdom. But this is a far cry from the highly cultic formulas of the
modern Church. Where then did the Church get this cultic paradigm from?

The answer to this question is that the Church got the cultic
paradigm of Church activity from the ritual worship of the Tem-

ple cultus of the Old Testament. Now, I want to make myself clear at this point. I am not saying that the Church has merely imitated the sacrificial rituals of the Old Testament Temple. This is clearly not the case. There are no blood sacrifices in the ritual worship of the Christian Church. What I am saying is that the kind of paradigm that underpinned the Temple worship, i.e. ritual cultic activity, has been used as the paradigm for understanding and structuring Church activity. And many of the features of this type of worship have been incorporated into the Church, including the Old Testament concept of priesthood, altars, special clothing etc. Nor is this something that is only relevant to Episcopal Churches. In varying degrees it also structures Protestant Free Church activity.

But is this the correct paradigm for understanding the Church and her role in the kingdom of God? I do not believe it is. The New Testament talks of apostles, prophets, evangelists, pastors and teachers (Eph. 4:11) as offices in the Church. However, these offices were *not* part of the Old Testament Temple cultus. The Temple cultus terminated in Christ, to whom it pointed. In fact, the central features of the ministry of the offices of the institutional Church in the New Testament are the word of God and prayer (Acts 6:4). Proclaiming the word of God and teaching the faith is central to the work of the institutional Church. This does not come from the Temple. The Priests were not primarily ministers and teachers of the word. The Old Testament model for ministry of the word is the prophet, not the priest. It is the prophet who calls the nation to God's word as the principle around which society should structure its life.

Now, I am not denying the fact that there is an institutional aspect to the Church's life, nor am I saying that there is no place for ritual at all or that there should be no public Christian cultus. There must always be an expression of corporate public worship in the Church's life and this will inevitably constitute some form of cultus. I am not denying the validity of the public Christian cultus therefore. But I am saying that this should not provide the paradigm for our understanding of the function of the Church, nor should it define the Church. But because it often does define the Church, I am saying that the balance is wrong, that the cultus has been elevated, at the expense of other priorities, to a status that is not validated by the New Testament. The New Testament presents the Church as a community of faith acting in the whole of life, one aspect of which is corporate worship, the public cultus. The focus of the New Testament is not on the cultic activity of the Church, but on the kingdom of God, which functions across the whole spectrum of human life and society. I am not denying the validity of the Christian cultus therefore, but I am saying that it has been misunderstood and incorrectly modelled on the paradigm of the Temple cultus and that the Church has been incorrectly defined by such cultic activity rather than as a community of people sharing the same faith and structuring their lives and community around God's word. As a result we have much ritual (much that is not necessary) but little real community, which I think characterised the New Testament Church far more than it does modern Western Churches. There is much conformity in the ritualised modern Churches of the West. But this conformity exists alongside a serious lack of community. This model is seriously astray.

In previous centuries, when close community life was more a feature of society generally, this defect was not so obvious. Indeed, there may not have been the same defect because the Christian world-view was dominant and Western societies were largely made up of Christian communities. This is no longer the case today. The communities that make up our society are not Christian, and the prevailing world-view is not Christian. On top of this, community generally is breaking down—certainly *Christian* community has largely gone.

But the Church has not recognised the problem. She has carried on as if the world has not changed. As a result the Church and her message have become increasingly irrelevant to the real world and its problems. When society and community were generally Christian, the Church's infatuation with ritual perhaps did not seem so irrelevant. Today this is no longer the case. The

Church, on the whole, at least in Britain, does not address the real world with a decisive message for the world. It merely peddles hell-fire insurance.

For example, in most of the Churches to which I have belonged the membership has come from a wide catchment area around the Church, but few members have actually lived in the community in which the Church meets (where the building is). Even Churches planted with the specific intention of being a mission to the community in which the building is located seldom have had memberships that are drawn mostly from the community that the Church supposedly serves. There are two problems with this: first, the Church is not really part of the community it claims to be serving and so does not have a real presence there, only a few meetings each week that mean nothing very much to the local community anyway. The Church's mission is thus something of a pretence. Second, the members of the Church, who come to the meetings from far and wide, do not themselves constitute a real community of faith, which is the leaven needed to affect the dough, i.e. the mission community, because they cannot. They live too far apart to constitute or function as a community.

What happens in this kind of situation is that the Church becomes a mere cult, and the faith becomes merely a personal worship hobby for those who attend the meetings. But this situation cannot facilitate the true mission of the Church. At best the message proclaimed will be some form of hell fire insurance, i.e. the faith will be restricted to the question "What happens at death?" Christ is held out as a means of escaping hell-fire. But this is a truncated view of salvation, and because of this an unbiblical one.

If the Church is to be an alternative community that will act as leaven in society, she must function as a true *community* of *faith*. This, I suggest, is the true paradigm for the Christian Church given us in the Bible. The ritual cultus is not a biblical model for the life of the Church. The Temple has gone. The ritual paradigm is the wrong paradigm for understanding the Christian Church. I am not saying there is no institutional Church nor that there should be no public Christian cultus, nor that there is no place whatsoever for ritual in the worship meetings of the Church. But I am saying that this should not define the Church, that the Church is primarily a community of faith, and that although teaching of the word and prayer etc. are vital to the life and growth of the Church in the faith, unless the Church is a *community* of faith she ceases to be a Church. Great preaching halls and great preachers do not constitute the Church on their own; a Church is a community of believers living out the faith *as* a community of faith.

Well, this is all well and good, but what should a Church be like on the model that I am suggesting? What difference would it make practically? The whole point is that the congregation, the people of God, should function as a *community* bound together by God's word not only when they are worshipping corporately in church meetings held specifically for praise, prayer, teaching etc., but also in all the other aspects of community life. Here are a few examples. They are not meant to be exhaustive, but they do attempt to identify some of the more important areas that are presently neglected on the whole.

First, the New Testament gives us an important model in Acts 6:1–6. As we have seen, this passage shows how the Church responded to a very specific and practical need. Servants were appointed to provide for those in need. This was how the Church dealt with a *welfare* issue. Welfare is a function of the Church. Not that the Church is the primary agency for welfare. The Bible teaches that the family is the primary agency of welfare. But because the Church also is a family, the family of God, she has a duty to those who are needy and without help from their families (1 Tim 5:1–16). The Church functions as an extended family. She must act as a true community. There is also an important welfare function for the Church as part of her mission to the non-believing world.

Second, another aspect of community life is work, our vocations and businesses. The Jews have often shown us a good example here. They have often functioned as a community of faith far better than Christians have, especially in an unsympathetic environment, but even where the environment has not been unsympathetic. They look after their own, especially in terms of business and work life. They have often shown a better understanding of what it means to belong to a community of faith. Of course, this may often have been the result of persecution, and they do not seem to have the same commitment to evangelism that Christianity has, and this has a tendency to produce a ghetto mentality, which is not something we should imitate at all. Nevertheless, I think a case can be made for the creation of a Christian work environment and business environment that is open and outward looking, providing an example to the world of how the faith should affect our work and business life. This is especially relevant now because it seems to me that business ethics are virtually at a point of collapse in Britain. Christian ethics and a Christian understanding of one's calling played an important part in the development of the economies of the Western world. The prevalence of the Christian world-view and its code of ethics was important in providing society with a stable foundation for the development of the free market order in particular and a free society generally. Christian ethics have now been cast aside and both society generally and economic and business activity in particular is reverting to forms of economic activity that are often little better than fancy forms of piracy. Business ethics seems to have all but collapsed.

Now of course, the Bible does not say that we may only trade with other Christians or use the services of other Christians, and I am definitely not arguing for this in any way. In fact, as things stand often Christian business activity is no different from non-Christian business activity; indeed, Christians in Britain have a poor reputation as businessmen and employers on the whole, which does a very great disservice to the gospel. But it ought not to be this way. It ought to be the case that Christians provide leadership to the non-believing world here as elsewhere. Christian businesses and employers ought to provide both a good witness to the gospel and form part of the Christian community. There is no reason why the wider Christian community should not generate its own economy in many ways. This does not mean that Christians would refuse to deal or trade with non-believers or that Christians would never use business services provided by non-believers. But the consensus created by a significant part of the business and economic community's following the Christian ethic in the way it operates and co-operates as part of the Christian community, and the way it ministers to both the Christian community and the non-believing community would be a very significant witness to the faith and help to create, maintain and promote the growth of the Christian community of faith, which is the leaven that should affect the whole of society. This also is part of our calling to disciple the *nation*.

Furthermore, we must recognise also that the Bible does tell us that we are not to be unequally yoked (2 Cor. 6:14), and this applies to the sphere of business as much as it does to any other area of human life.

Third, the education of children is a vitally important aspect of the Christian life. How does the Church expect to maintain her influence upon society when she is sending her children to be educated by secular humanists *as* secular humanists? This is truly one of the most scandalous of all the failures of the modern Church. The schooling system in Britain had its origins in the private Christian schools and charity schools that were created by a Christian society in the discharge of its Christian responsibilities. This system was largely hijacked by the State, which, when it had taken control of it, proceeded to secularise it so that now virtually all traces of the Christian faith have been expunged from the system. And it seems that Christians on the whole are happy to send their children to these secular schools.

This seems to me to be standing the gospel on its head. In all missionary situations Christians accept that the children of Christian missionaries should be educated as Christians and that the children of those to whom the missionaries are ministering should also be educated as Christians. The idea of permitting a pagan community to educate the children of missionaries who are ministering the gospel to that community, so that their children learn to live a non-Christian way of life, is absurd and would be condemned by any Christian Church. And so the establishing of Christian schools in the mission field is seen as quite necessary, even essential, to the success of the mission. And yet, when one turns to the home mission, in a society that is now thoroughly secularised and almost as pagan in its own way as any foreign mission field, precisely the opposite happens: the children of Christians are sent to be educated by secular humanists and atheists.

Rather than secular humanists educating Christian children, Christians should be establishing schools for educating the children of non-believers. The situation faced by the Churches in the Western nations today is a *mission* situation. The provision of Christian education for Christian children is vital and essential for the progress of the gospel in the Western nations. The Church cannot hope to survive without this, and it is an abdication of responsibility for Christians to send their children to secular schools. But beyond this, the Church also has an opportunity to provide Christian education for non-believers. The nations of the West are *mission fields*. How has the Church failed to see this? It is vital that this should be remedied. I would go so far as to say that this is the most important issue facing the Church today in terms of her responsibility to her own children and her wider mission to the world.

Fourth, in a similar way the provision of Christian hospitals and medical services is an essential aspect of the Church's mission, and has always been seen as such in previous centuries. Christ commanded us, emphatically, to preach the gospel *and* heal the sick (Mt. 10:7–8; Lk 9:2; 10:9). Wherever the gospel has been preached throughout the world the healing of the sick and the establishing of hospitals has gone along hand in hand with it. And the hospital system in Britain was a result of this process. The secular State did not set up a health service, nor did it initiate a hospital building programme in order to create the National Health Service. Rather, it took over, hijacked, the existing health care system, which was the product of a Christian society. The whole concept of hospitals in Britain had its origin in the mission of the Church to heal the sick. Now that the State has taken over this area of life the Christian values that once built the hospitals and guided their work are being systematically stripped from the National Health Service, just as the Christian values that once underpinned education have been stripped from the education system.

The Church must see her mission in this broader context of life as the ministry of the whole word of God to the whole person in the whole community, rather than as confined primarily to ritual worship, the cultus. Just think of the influence that the gospel would have if people in our communities were to look to the Church for help for the problems of life instead of to the secular State. What if the Church rather than the State dispensed welfare to the needy according to Christian work ethics in our society? What if, instead of children being sent to secular humanist school to be taught that the world and all things in it are autonomous and have no relation to God or his word, and that at best the Christian faith is a private matter, people sent their children to be educated at Christians schools, to be taught how to structure their lives and society around God's word? What if people worked for Christian companies pursing Christian ethics, and did business with Christian businesses that operated on the basis of Christian ethics, instead of secular business ethics, which increasingly resembles piracy in all but name? What if, instead of looking to the secular State, the sick in our society were to look to the Church for healing and were to go to Christian hospitals and medical practices when they were ill? What if, when people became Christians and joined the Church they became part of a real community that lived *as* a community of faith in all areas of life? Would not all this be a much more real and meaningful expression of the Christian message of salvation in our communities? Do you think that the Church and the Christian faith would be as it is today, without influence and relevance in society? Of course not. God's name would be honoured in our nation, hallowed, just as we pray in the Lord's Prayer, "Hallowed be thy name. Thy kingdom come, thy will be done on earth as it is in heaven." And the kings of the earth would kiss the Son (Ps. 2).

The Church will not fulfil the Great Commission until she sees her mission in these broad terms. If Christians were to act in a concerted way in society as a community of faith with a mission in these four areas—welfare, education, medical services and business—it would have a transformational effect upon the nation. It would be a relevant, practical witness to the faith and a demonstration of the Church's commitment to building the kingdom of God in society.

Political lobbying will not achieve this. Stopping good laws from being abolished and bad laws from being passed will not accomplish anything anywhere near as effective as this kind of activity will. We cannot expect politicians to do what we are not prepared to do as Churches. Of course, I am not saying we should not try to stop good laws from being abolished or bad laws from being passed. But unless lobbying and political action takes place in the wider context of the Church's mission in all these areas of life it will achieve nothing of permanent value. Unless Christians are prepared to make the sacrifices for the faith that this wider mission will involve, they will not conquer the world. Christianity is useless to the world as a mere cult, a personal devotion hobby. The purpose of the Christian faith is to glorify God by changing the world and bringing all nations under the discipline of Jesus Christ. Nothing less than this is commanded in the Great Commission.

A word of warning here. Jesus told us that when an unclean spirit leaves a man and finds no place to rest, it returns to the house from which it came, and finding it cleaned and swept, takes seven other devils with it, so that the latter state of the man is worse than the former. This is very pertinent to the Christian community and the attempt by Christians to get the evils they perceive in society remedied by government programmes. Many Christians are lazy. They are prepared to support lobbying organisations that will try to coerce the government to do for them what they should be doing for themselves. This is an abdication of responsibility. It is not that lobbying of government is wrong as such, i.e. when it is done for the right reasons. But often Christians will lobby for State education to be cleaned up and made Christian. Why? So that they do not have to fulfil their own responsibilities to provide a Christian education for their children. The same goes for welfare and health care and other spheres of life. So what will happen if the Church is successful in her lobbying? What if she manages to keep a good law on the statute books or prevent a bad law from being enacted? The Church may have cast out the devil and swept the house, i.e. society, only to find that the devil returns with seven more worse devils, so that the latter condition of society is worse than the former.

This is no idle speculation. It is what is happening all the time in Britain. The lobbying of government is quite popular, and often *initially* successful, but the clean house always gets re-occupied by seven more deadly devils, so that more lobbying is then required, and more funds to finance the lobbying. But the real work of providing alternative Christian education, Christian hospitals and medical services, Christian welfare, a Christian presence in the spheres of business and economics etc., gets neglected for the most part. The house, that is to say the nation, does not get re-occupied by the Christian Spirit. So the devils come back. Lobbying and political action, without the ongoing work of Christian mission across the whole of life and society, discipling the nation in other words, will achieve nothing in the long term, and the latter condition will be worse than the former. We cannot use government to do those things that we should be doing ourselves. The aim of reform of government should be to get it doing those things it should be doing, not giving lazy Christians an easy time. And if we succeed in cleaning up the house by political means but fail to replace the devil with a Christian presence, the vacuum will be filled by seven worse devils, who will use the political system to their own advantage. Wherever the Church leaves a vacuum in this way, thinking that such areas are religiously neutral, this is what happens, because there are no areas of religious neutrality. Christ is Lord of all and claims ownership of all. As Abraham Kuyper said, "There is not a single inch of the whole terrain of our human existence over which Christ . . . does not proclaim 'Mine!'"

The Church needs to understand this broad mission to the world. Without engaging in these areas the decline of the Christian faith will not be halted. These are things that the Church has always done as part of her mission in times past anyway. This is nothing new. I am not asking anyone to consider doing anything that the Church has not always in previous centuries seen as part of her mission to the unbelieving world. The creation of a Christian society, Christians schools, Christians hospitals, the pursuit of Christian work ethics etc. has always in the past been seen as essential to the Church's mission. It is the Great Commission, after all. Why has the Church stopped believing these things and pursuing this agenda?

The greatest part of the Christian life of faith is not spent in church engaging in ritual worship; rather it is spent in the world, in the mission field. Unless we seek to make this world a Christian world, a world that structures its life around God's word, our worship services will amount little more than personal worship hobbies, cults practised in a ghetto. We are not called to be a ghetto, but to disciple the *nations*. If we are to do this we must start living as a real *community* of faith that will act like leaven in society, transforming the nation into a Christian society. This will mean for most of us a great deal of upheaval both in our attitudes and thinking, and in our practical lives. But there is no alternative that does not amount to neglect of the Great Commission, in other words *disobedience*. How long do you think God is going to put up with a disobedient Church? Time is running out for Britain, perhaps for the West generally. Does not judgement begin at the house of God? (1 Pet. 4:17).

15

CORRUPTION

How is the faithful city become a harlot! it was full of judgement; righteous-
ness lodged in it; but now murderers. Thy silver is become dross, they wine
mixed with water. Thy princes are rebellious, and companions of thieves: every
one loveth gifts, and followeth after rewards: they judge not the fatherless, nei-
ther doth the cause of the widow come unto them. Therefore saith the Lord, the
LORD of hosts, the might One of Israel, Ah, I will ease me of mine adversar-
ies, and avenge me of mine enemies: And I will turn my hand upon thee, and
purely purge away thy dross, and take away all thy tin: And I will restore thy
judges as at the first, and thy counsellors as at the beginning: afterwards thou
shalt be called, The city of righteousness, the faithful city.

(Isaiah 1:21–26)

IN this passage of Scripture Isaiah describes the state of corruption and immorality into which the people of Jerusalem had fallen,
and he contrasts this deplorably fallen state with the glory of Jerusalem's former days. Jerusalem was the city of David, and of Solomon, the most famous of all judges. Solomon's administration of
justice, his judgement, had been a legend in his lifetimes. The queen
of Sheba came to visit Solomon in Jerusalem because she had
heard of his reputation, and she marvelled at the wisdom of Solomon in the righteous judgements that he made (1 Kg. 10:1–13).
The case of the disputed child is the most famous of Solomon's
judgements (1 Kg. 3:16–28). But Solomon's wisdom was a gift from
God. Solomon prayed: "Give therefore thy servant an understanding heart to judge thy people, that I may discern between good
and bad: for who is able to judge this thy so great a people?" (1 Kg.
3:9). And God answered Solomon:

Because thou hast asked this thing, and hast not asked for thyself long life; neither hast asked riches for thyself, nor hast asked the life of thine enemies; but hast asked for thyself understanding to discern judgement; behold, I have done according to thy words: lo, I have given thee a wise and an understanding heart; so that there was none like thee before thee, neither after thee shall any arise like unto thee. And I have also given thee that which thou hast not asked, both riches and honour: so that there shall not be any among the kings like unto thee all thy days. And if thou wilt walk in my ways, to keep my statutes and my commandments, as thy father David did walk, then I will lengthen thy days (1 Kg. 3:11–14).

The ability to judge wisely, therefore, was God's gift to Solomon because as king of Israel he sought not his own glory or wealth, but rather wisdom from God to rule, i.e. to judge the people, wisely. And this is the way that it should always be with rulers. Rule, kingship, presidency etc., is not a business enterprise entered into for one's own benefit, in order to accumulate wealth and gain power. Rather, it is *service*, a ministry. The ruler is to serve God by dispensing justice according to biblical wisdom, according to the law of God. The ruler is a *servant* of God in this (Rom. 13:4). In the law of God the ruler is specifically forbidden to use his office in order to accumulate wealth and power for himself and is instead commanded to look to God's law for wisdom to judge (i.e. to rule) the people properly (Dt. 17:16–20)

Furthermore, the Bible has much to say not only about the *office* of the ruler, i.e. the purpose or function of the ruler (e.g. in the case of the political ruler or magistrate this is the public administration of justice or judgement), but also about the *character* of rule, the *nature* of the kind of rule that God expects of those who exercise authority over others. This is what Jesus taught us about those who rule:

But Jesus called them unto him and said, Ye know that the princes of the Gentiles exercise dominion over them, and they that are great exercise authority upon them. But it shall not be so among you: but whoever will be great among you, let him be your minister [i.e. servant]: and whoever will be chief among you, let him be your servant (Mt. 20:25–27).

Jesus was not speaking here only about Church leaders. He is speaking about all rule and authority, about the very nature of *Christian* rule in whatever sphere that rule is exercised. The AV's translation here is less than adequate. The word translated "minister" (διάκονος) means "servant," but the word translated "servant" (δοῦλος) means "slave," hardly the kind of connotations that one normally associates with those who hold high office either in State or Church. The Christian doctrine of government is the very antithesis of the doctrine and practice of government espoused by and found in the world. The ruler is to be a *servant* and a *slave* to those over whom he has authority. He is to see his ministry as a sacred trust, and himself as answerable to God.

Solomon, when he ascended the throne and began his ministry as king of Israel, epitomised this Christian or biblical doctrine of rule. As a result he became the most famous judge of his age, indeed the most famous judge of any age, as Scripture foretold that we would (1 Kg. 3:12).

But just look what happened. The city of Jerusalem, she who was full of justice,—righteousness once lodged in her—had fallen into a state of utter corruption. And this fall began in Solomon's own lifetime; indeed, Solomon himself caused the people to fall by his own example. He erected idols and shrines to false gods for his foreign wives and worshipped Ashtoreth, the goddess of the Zidonians and Milcom, the abominable idol of the Ammonites (1 Kg. 11:1–14). He turned away in his old age from the principles that had guided him in his youth. And in turning away from God and disobeying his law in this way he led the nation into ruin. In the two hundred years or so from the time of Solomon to the time of Isaiah the nation of Israel steadily but surely declined until the nation was plunged into a cycle of religious and moral corruption that turned everything upside down. The rulers and religious leaders alike turned their back on God, corrupted his worship and abandoned his law, and the people followed them in their unrighteousness. And this is the very state of affairs that Isaiah describes.

This situation was a *social* problem. It was not just that a few of the leaders of the nation or a minority of people were un-righteous in their dealings with others. No, what Isaiah describes is the apostasy of the whole nation. This was a society-wide prob-lem, a cultural apostasy. Listen to how Isaiah describes the situa-tion:

Thy silver is become dross, thy wine mixed with water: thy princes are rebellious, and companions of thieves: every one loveth gifts [i.e. bribes], and followeth after rewards: they judge not the fatherless, neither doth the cause of the widow come unto them. (v. 22–23)

Here we see the whole corrupt state of society described. First of all economic corruption is described; second, political corruption; and third, the unrighteous and corrupt attitudes and actions of the people generally in their chasing after bribes and their neglect of the poor, weak and needy members of society. Isaiah compares Jerusalem to a harlot, a prostitute, and he tells us that murder has replaced righteousness as the ethos of the community. What a terrible fall! The faithful city had become utterly corrupt. Let us look more closely now at what this corruption consisted of.

　　1. First, there was economic corruption: "Thy silver is be-come dross, thy wine mixed with water" (v. 22). What Isaiah refers to here first of all is the *debasement of money*.[1] The practice of debas-ing silver was a process in which silver was mixed with base met-als, e.g. tin, and the resulting alloy passed off as pure silver in the marketplace. Those who received this debased silver in exchange for goods and services would be unaware that what was being exchanged for their goods and services was only partly silver. Some-one might agree to deliver a certain consignment of wine for a shekel of silver, for example, but receive instead of pure silver a shekel of debased silver, an alloy consisting of part silver and part tin. In this case he will receive only part of the payment, but he is unaware, at least at first, of the fact that he has been short changed, cheated by his customer. Thus, by debasing their silver in this way

---

[1] See G. North, *An Introduction to Christian Economics* (The Craig Press, 1973), p. 3ff. and *passim*. The rabbis understood this verse as referring to the charging of interest (see Exodus Rabbah, XXXI, 4).

those who practised this sort of economic corruption could obtain goods and services by deception, paying less than the price asked for without those with whom they were dealing being aware that they were being cheated.

But of course this kind of corruption can only go on for so long before people begin to get wise to what is happening. And when they realise what is happening they start taking steps themselves to deceive those who are trying to cheat them by making payment with debased money. What will happen when the wine merchant eventually finds out that those with whom he is dealing are cheating him? What will he do? Well, Isaiah tells us here. He will start diluting his wine with water. He will start cheating as well. And so corruption spreads through the whole economy. No one can trust the market and everyone is "on the take," trying to get the better of his neighbour.

Now, what Isaiah describes here, the debasement of currency, is very common, and has been throughout most of history. Indeed, debasement of currency has been, and continues to be, a common practice of banks and governments the world over. And the consequences are devastating for the economy. It is the debasement of currency that usually causes inflation. When banks and governments engage in this sort of thing they ruin their nation's economy and impoverish the people. But bankers and members of governments themselves usually benefit at the expense of the rest of society. This is a form of corruption, and the Bible condemns it in no uncertain terms. When governments act in this way, or permit or license others (for example banks) to act in this way, they are not serving God by administering justice, which is their true calling under God; rather, they are serving themselves by defrauding others.[2] This brings us, therefore, to the second part of Isaiah's description of the moral corruption of Jerusalem.

2. Second, Isaiah tells us that the rulers of Jerusalem are rebellious—i.e. that they have turned away from God and rebelled

[2] For a more detailed explanation of this see Stephen C. Perks, *The Political Economy of A Christian Society* (Taunton: The Kuyper Foundation, 2001), pp. 68–74, Chapter Four, "The Banking System," pp. 99–145, and *passim*.

against his word—and "companions of thieves; every one loveth gifts [i.e. bribes], and followeth after rewards" (v. 23). The very calling and duty of the rulers, namely the administration of justice, is turned into an opportunity to act corruptly, to pervert justice in return for a bribe, to plunder those who seek justice. Why? So that rulers can live in luxury on their ill-gotten gains, and all under the pretence of being judges and serving the people. Political corruption had got hold of Jerusalem.

Now, not much has changed since the days of Isaiah. This kind of political corruption still goes on and is rife in many parts of the world. The political office is prostituted and used as a means of personal aggrandisement for those in power. Those who gain political power use their position to better themselves or the group to which they belong; but they never tire of telling us that everything they do is a selfless act of service on the behalf of others. Yet politicians themselves always do very well out of their "service." They love the power to push other people around, and the wealth that political power so often brings with it. But how many of these politicians see this office as a calling to serve God by obeying his law and administering justice according to his word? Very few. Political corruption is a great snare to those who rule, and it is, I am tempted to say, almost the prevailing condition of politics, and has been throughout most of history. Yet such corruption is condemned by God in the severest terms. Politicians are not supposed to rule in order to benefit themselves. God commands them to repent of their sins just as he calls all men everywhere to repent of their sins (Acts 17:30), and he demands that they rule justly according to his word.

However, we must make a further point here. Although this political corruption is so widespread in varying degrees that it seems almost that politics is inevitably linked with the corruption of power, Isaiah does not condemn the *office* of ruler, he condemns the corruption of the office. It is not politics *per se* that is at fault when political corruption prevails. There is nothing unholy or sinful about the calling and office of the ruler. Therefore politics is not an area that Christians should shy away from because it seems to be so contaminated by the world. Rather the reverse is true. Politics, like every other area of life, must be redeemed by Christ, and this inevitably means that Christians must get involved with the political process, not in order that they might secure wealth and power for themselves by participating in the corruption of the political office as the world does, but so that justice might be done and God's law prevail in society. Christians must show an example to the world of how politicians should behave. They should pursue justice and refuse to take bribes. They must seek political office not for rewards, not for their own personal aggrandisement, but in order to serve God and the people he has given them to rule over. It is the wicked and rebellious hearts of rulers who seek only their own benefit from political office that Isaiah condemns, not the political office itself, which is a God-ordained institution that must be valued as essential to the good order of social.

3. Third, this corruption is not limited to the rulers. We have already seen how this corruption has taken root in the market-place. Of course, the "every one" of whom Isaiah speaks refers in the first place to the princes; i.e. every prince loves a bribe and chases after rewards. It is not just a few bad apples, but the whole of the ruling class who have degenerated to this level of corruption. But this does not happen in isolation from the rest of society. It has consequences for the whole of society. It is not only the princes, the ruling class, who have fallen into this state of immorality and corruption. Isaiah's strictures apply equally to the rest of society. For example, who is doing the bribing? Not the rulers. They are benefiting from this bribery and corruption of course. But they are not the only ones. Those who pervert the course of justice by bribing the judges also benefit. Corruption spreads like a disease across the whole of society. Politicians seldom keep it to themselves. By their own corruption of the political office they foster a climate or ethos of corruption within society generally, and so corruption spreads and permeates the whole of society.

This has very serious and damaging effects on society. For example, it hinders rational economic development and this leads to the withdrawal of investment. This point is especially relevant to the poor countries of the Third World. Foreign aid, while it does have a legitimate role in certain circumstances, cannot create a wealthy society. It can only alleviate a crisis. Where it is used outside a crisis situation, it actually hinders and sets back the development of a viable market economy that will enable a country to become economically independent. Aid does not do the job that investment does, and it is investment that is needed for economic growth. Aid is irrational from the economic point of view, though of course not from the humanitarian point of view, *provided* it is correctly targeted. But where aid is not correctly targeted it fosters economic servitude and this is extremely harmful for the economy and thus for the whole nation. This is particularly true of government to government aid. Aid will not create a prosperous economy. The free market, however, when it is permitted to operate on the basis of just and moral principles—i.e. when the State fulfils its proper function of enforcing justice according to Christian standards—will provide the investment needed where those with the economic initiative necessary to develop the economy are permitted to do so. This is the only stable and sure way to economic prosperity.[3]

But what happens when corruption and bribery get hold of a nation? Those with capital will not invest. If they have invested in such a society this investment will be withdrawn the more corrupt society becomes because corruption hinders economic rationalisation. Corruption, when it gets a hold on society, makes the development of a rational economy impossible. Investment dries up because investors will only tolerate so much corruption, and not necessarily because they have high moral principles either, but merely because the prevalence of corruption in society is *economically* disastrous. If investors can find a better return on their capital elsewhere, therefore, they will withdraw their investments and invest in economies that are not in the process of being ruined by corruption. Economic growth is thus severely hindered by the prevalence of corruption in the economy. And the State cannot effectively replace private enterprise in the economy. It is not pos-

[3] For a more detailed consideration of this point see *ibid.*, pp. 14–22.

sible for the State merely to take the place of private enterprise
when the latter abandons a country because of the prevalence of
corruption. Nationalised industries do not create economic growth,
i.e. they do not lead to a growth in the creation of wealth. Rather,
they make such growth more difficult. There has never been in
history an economically successful socialist government. *All* socialist economic experiments have failed or are failing. Socialism
does not ultimately share out the wealth in society; it merely shares
out the poverty. Economic equality is in one sense the ultimate
end of socialism; but it is not an equality of wealth. Socialism
merely ensures that ultimately all men are equally poor, except of
course the politicians, who use their power for personal aggrandisement at the expense of the people.

And when corrupt governments have frightened all investment
away from the country, and plundered their own people, ruining
the economy in the process, what will become of the weak and
helpless in society? They will be forgotten. Therefore,

4. Fourth, where corruption gets hold of a society, where everyone loves a bribe and chases after rewards, society deteriorates
economically and the weakest members of society are the ones
who suffer most. Those who do not have the political muscle and
economic power to help themselves or who are not able to play
the game of corruption and bribery in order provide for themselves are shoved to the bottom of the social heap. And this is
what Isaiah says "they judge not the fatherless, neither doth the
cause of the widow come unto them" (v. 23). The helpless, for
example orphans and widows, are the ones who suffer most.

This is not acceptable to God. He will not permit this situation to continue indefinitely. He commands us to care for the weak
and the needy amongst us: "pure religion and undefiled before
God and the Father is this, to visit the fatherless and widows in
their affliction" (Js. 1:27). Our responsibility to care for the weak
and the needy means not only that we must give them help in
their need, in their hour of crisis, but that society should maintain
a just economic order in which the weak and the needy are not
forced into hardship and poverty because the economic order is

based on corruption and bribery, on the ability of those who are strong to exploit unjustly those who are weak.

Bribery and corruption are great enemies of prosperity. People think they are getting wealthier when they engage in corruption and bribery, when they take "back-handers," but ultimately this is an illusion. Why? Because corruption destroys the values and virtues that make economic progress possible, namely honesty, hard work and thrift. Without these virtues of honesty, hard work and thrift no society can prosper, and it is precisely these virtues that corruption destroys.

A society in the grip of this kind of corruption is in a seriously dangerous situation. If the corruption is not dealt with society will collapse into anarchy, and history teaches clearly that anarchy is usually followed by harsh totalitarian rule. And so it was most of the time in antiquity. Likewise in the modern world where the light of the gospel of Jesus Christ has not been lit or where it has been extinguished. Either anarchy with abject poverty prevails, a situation in which economic progress is often shunned[4]; or totalitarian rule, dictatorship and oppression of society by a powerful political elite, again with poverty for the masses, becomes the order of the day.

Only Christianity can end these problems, by creating a different outlook, a different set of values that makes the rule of law and helping one's neighbour the prevailing ethos of society, rather than corruption and the unjust exploitation of the weak. History bears this out. Only where the Christian world-view has become dominant have these problems been overcome in sufficient measure to facilitate the development of rational economic growth and thus significant social amelioration across the *whole* of society.

But what happens when a Christian country, or a nation that claims to be Christian, or has been in the past Christian, turns away from God's law to corruption and bribery? How does God deal with apostate nations? Isaiah tells us here:

---

[4] See the comments on the Lovedu in Helmut Schoeck, *Envy, A Theory of Social Behaviour* (London: Secker and Warburg, 1969), pp. 39–41.

Therefore saith the Lord, the LORD of hosts, the mighty One of Israel, Ah, I will ease me of mine adversaries, and avenge me of mine enemies: and I will turn my hand upon thee, and purely purge away all thy tin: and I will restore thy judges as at the first, and thy counsellors as at the beginning: afterwards thou shalt be called, The city of righteousness, the faithful city. (vv. 24–26)

In these verses Isaiah tells the people that God will restore their judges as at the first, that righteousness shall be restored and the city saved from its corruption. In this God shows his mercy. But mark well the means by which this salvation is to be accomplished. God accomplished this by means of a "purging" or *smelting* away of the dross (v. 25). There is no smelting without *fire*. In order for the impurities in a metal to be removed, smelted away, the metal has to be heated up to a great temperature, so that the dross can be floated off. And this is how the Lord says he will remove the tin, the dross, the corruption, from Jerusalem. The Lord will avenge himself of his enemies by purging Jerusalem as the impurities of metal are purged away. He will turn his hand against those who have turned bribery and corruption into a virtue. He will turn against those who are companions of thieves, against those who love bribes and chase after rewards. He will turn against those who cheat their neighbours in the marketplace, and he will turn his hand against those rulers who abuse their positions of power and authority.

This process of purging away the sin and corruption of the people is a process of testing by *fire*, a process of removing the slag, the dross, of the nation by heating up the temperature until the pure silver is separated from the impurities that have debased it. When a nation gets into the state of apostasy described by Isaiah in this passage of Scripture the only way to remove the corruption and restore justice and righteousness is through fire, that is to say, through the judgement of the Lord against his enemies. In this process of judgement the bad is cleared away, destroyed, so that righteousness can flourish once again. But the silver is heated up to the same temperature as the dross. The whole lump of alloy has to be subject to the fire. Only when the whole piece of metal,

silver and tin mixed together, is heated to the required temperature is the dross able to be smelted off. Therefore the whole nation
must go through this process of testing by fire, this process of judgement. Israel was eventually led away captive to Babylon, and the
people had to suffer under the hand of those who conquered them.
My point is simply this, that this process of testing by fire, of judgement by which the impurities are removed from society, is not a
pleasant experience for *anyone* in society. Nothing less than national
calamity is often the means by which God accomplishes his purpose in purging apostate nations of the evil and corruption that
have come to characterise their cultures. It has to be this way,
otherwise how would the evil be removed? Purging, smelting away
the dross, whether from silver or from nations, has to be accomplished by *fire*.

Now, I do not want anyone to think that I am here pointing
my finger at Africa only. This message of Isaiah is highly pertinent
to the UK and other Western nations as well. As the proverb says,
"If the hat fits, wear it"! The point is that wherever we are, and
wherever we live, we need to heed the message and learn the lesson before it is too late and our nation gets thrown into the smelting fire. If you are a corrupt person who takes bribes, if you cheat
your neighbour in the marketplace, if you abuse the power and
authority you have been given over others for your own personal
gain, or if you are a politician involved in corruption at the highest level, your only hope is to repent, i.e. turn away from your sin
to faith in Christ, seeking his forgiveness of your sins through his
sacrificial death on the cross. Christ is the only hope for you and
for your society. And turning to him in faith means turning away
from corruption, from chasing after rewards; it means no longer
accepting bribes or asking for "back-handers"; and it means helping those who are weak and downtrodden, helping your neighbours. We must put justice and mercy first. God requires this of us
all, politicians included, since it is the duty of the political office to
ensure that justice prevails in society. The plea of the widow and
the orphan must come before us and we must not put our own
personal gain before the justice due to others. We must seek to live

righteous lives, i.e. lives dedicated to justice and mercy. This is not a private message to the devout only. It is God's message to the whole nation. The gospel is a public truth addressed to all men and all nations *as* nations.

If we do this, if we repent, God will restore our judges, and our counsellors, and our cities will be called cities of righteousness, faithful cities. Repent while there is time. Yes, God's kingdom will be established—nothing is more certain in history than this fact. The Lord of hosts will accomplish this. God's kingdom will be established even in Britain and Zambia, but unless our nations repent of their sins, the process by which God will establish his kingdom will be through the smelting fires of his wrath against all the ungodliness and unrighteousness of men *and* nations, who refuse to submit to Jesus Christ in humble faith and in obedience to his word.

16

SODOM AND GOMORRAH

IT is commonly assumed that Sodom was judged by God and destroyed because of the homosexual sin that was prevalent in the city. The very term "sodomy" refers to the sexual perversion perpetrated by the men of Sodom. Yet, although this terrible sin was indeed practised by the people of Sodom and is condemned in the Scriptures as an abomination (Lev. 18:22), an act of sexual chaos, the truth is that the Bible nowhere gives the prevalence of this sin as the reason for the destruction of Sodom and Gomorrah. In Gen. 18:20–21 we are told merely that "The LORD said: Because the cry of Sodom and Gomorrah is great, and because their sin is very grievous; I will go down and see whether they have done altogether according to the cry of it, which is come unto me." And in Gen. 19:13 we are told that God would destroy the place because "the cry of them is waxen great before the face of the LORD." The fact that the angels whom God sent to assess the condition of Sodom immediately came up against the insatiable homosexual lust of the men of the city is then assumed to be the reason for the destruction of Sodom. This is perhaps an understandable reading of the text taken on its own. But like all texts of Scripture, it should not be taken on its own. We must interpret Scripture with Scripture, and it is when we do this that the whole sorry story of Sodom takes on a new meaning.

In Romans chapter one Paul clearly sets out the course of human apostasy and its inevitable conclusion. He tells us there that the whole of created reality bears witness to the glory of God. But men refuse to accept this. They deny the God of Creation and seek to find the meaning and purpose of life somewhere else. But the only place that men can turn for such meaning beside

God is the created order itself. Therefore they elevate some aspect of this created order to the level of an ultimate principle of explanation. In other words they place some aspect of the created order in the place of God and seek to explain the meaning and purpose of life in terms of that which takes the place of God. This is what idolatry is. It matters little whether such idolatry is of the gross superstitious kind, or the more pseudo-intellectual kind such as evolution; the basic principle is the same, namely the belief that the cause, meaning and purpose of the whole cosmos is to be found in the created order itself. This is so for all forms of paganism as well as modern apostate philosophy and science, since the gods of the ancient and pagan worlds were themselves aspects of the cosmos itself, which was considered eternal. The gods that the pagans believed had shaped the world were further up the chain of being, to be sure, but they were essentially still part of the same substance, the same reality as mankind and all other things. This world is all there is. There is no totally transcendent being who created the cosmos out of nothing. Therefore the meaning of the cosmos is to be found in itself.

As a result of this idolatry, this search for meaning in the created order itself rather than in the one who created it out of nothing, men became fools and exchanged the truth of God for a lie (Rom. 1:25). Therefore God gave men up to their own sin, to their own degraded passions, i.e. the lust for homosexual relations, fornication, wickedness, covetousness, maliciousness, envy, murder, deceitfulness etc. (Rom. 1:26ff.).

The prevalence of homosexual sin in society, therefore, is not the cause of God's judgement upon men for their sin. Rather, it *is* the judgement of God upon men for their sin. The very fact that society is afflicted with this sin of sexual chaos points to the judgement of God upon society for its idolatry and apostasy. Homosexual practices were common in the world of ancient paganism, and it seems that this pattern is repeated wherever society is in the grip of idolatry and apostasy. The blight of homosexuality upon society is God's judgement against men for their idolatry, an expression of his wrath, not what initially provokes that wrath. The homosexualised culture is the end product of a society that has abandoned the God of Scripture and turned to idolatry in order to find the meaning and purpose of existence, and therefore the consequence of men being given up to their sin, to their own desire to be free of God and his will for their lives.

If as Christians we wish to see our society free of the blight of homosexuality, therefore, we must seek to understand the causes of God's judgement upon the nation. Merely remonstrating about the evils of homosexuality will achieve nothing (though this does not mean we should not disapprove, and declare our disapproval, of such sin.) We must seek to understand what led to such a judgement being visited upon our society. The cause will be found in the nation's spiritual apostasy from God, not in the gay bars of the homosexual underworld. And the remedy will be found in the repentance of the nation for that spiritual apostasy, not in the passing of laws proscribing homosexual activity. Of course this does not mean that we should not have laws proscribing homosexual activity. Homosexual acts are crimes in the Bible and our own legislation should reflect this fact. But merely re-criminalising homosexuals acts without seeking to remedy the national apostasy that led to God's visiting this terrible judgement upon our society will not on its own solve the problem. We must take seriously the argument of Paul in the first chapter of Romans. Shutting our eyes to the truth he there expounds will not help us.

What light can the story of Sodom and Gomorrah shed on our situation. A great deal in fact. The Scriptures are given us that we might learn and understand God's will for our lives and for our societies and nations, because as Jesus commanded, we are to disciple all nations to Christ, i.e. teach them to live in conformity with the will of Christ as revealed in his word, the Bible. That is our Great Commission from Christ himself (Mt. 28:18–20. cf. 5:17–20).

What then was the reason for Sodom and Gomorrah's destruction? What was their sin? We are told quite explicitly by Ezekiel that the sin of Sodom was fourfold, namely pride, excess, idleness and neglect of the poor and needy (Ez. 16:49). And to this is then added that the people of Sodom were "haughty" and "committed abominations" before the Lord (v. 50). Furthermore, we are told that the sins of Jerusalem were greater than those of Sodom and Gomorrah, and Isaiah likens Jerusalem to Sodom, saying to the rulers of Jerusalem, "Here the word of the LORD, ye rulers of Sodom; and give ear unto the law of our God, ye people of Gomorrah . . . Wash you, make you clean; put away the evil of your doings from before mine eyes; cease to do evil; Learn to do well; seek judgement [i.e. justice], relieve the oppressed, judge the fatherless, plead for the widow" (Is. 1:10, 16–17)—i.e. make sure justice prevails and that the orphan and the widow are not oppressed in their affliction. In these Scriptures the sins of Jerusalem and those of Sodom, against which the comparison is made, are not exclusively sexual sins, e.g. the perversion of homosexuality, but the sins of pride, excess, idleness, injustice perpetrated against and a lack of regard for those in society who are least able to defend themselves against oppression, e.g. the poor and needy, orphans and widows.

Now it is clear that modern Western society, including Britain, is afflicted with the plague of homosexuality. The comparison with Sodom is therefore pertinent. But the comparison is not limited to this sexual sin, as is clear from Paul's listing of many other sins that plague an idolatrous culture. The pride and arrogance of modern Western society in its rejection of God and his word, the satisfaction with which it trusts in its own wisdom, and the ridiculing contempt in which it holds the law of God,—and such ridicule and contempt for God's law is even to be found in the Church—is as heinous in the sight of God as the pride of Sodom, for which it was destroyed. The excess of bread, the satiety, to which reference is made by Ezekiel is explained in the book of Proverbs: "Remove far from me vanity and lies: give me neither poverty nor riches; feed me with food convenient for me: Lest I be full, and deny thee, and say, Who is the LORD? Or lest I be poor, and steal, and take the name of my God in vain" (Pr. 30:8–9). There is nothing sinful in riches *per se*, and prosperity is not a sin. Indeed God promised prosperity to his people if they would obey his law (Dt. 28). We are told that the Lord takes pleasure in the prosperity of his people (Ps. 35:27). But the problem with the sinful human heart is that it tends to forget who the author of that prosperity is. Men congratulate themselves and refuse to give the glory to God. They come to trust themselves and believe they have no need to turn to God. What has God done for them? Their own industry has brought them the wealth they enjoy. It is their hard work that has led to their prosperity, not the grace and gift of God. And so God is forgotten. Men trust in their own power. Both of these sins, pride and excess, condemned by Ezekiel as sins that brought the judgement of God upon Sodom, are characteristic sins of modern Western society. We should do well, therefore, to heed the lesson that the story of Sodom provides.

Next is mentioned by Ezekiel the sin of idleness. At this point it would be difficult and erroneous to say that this sin is characteristic of Western society generally, though doubtless it is characteristic of some elements within Western society (see below). The Protestant work ethic has had a significant influence in the Protestant nations in this regard. But it has not been retained in its original form. Instead this ideal has been secularised, emptied of its Christian meaning, so that it exists now more as an idol, a symbol of materialistic gain for its own ends. In this sense it is part and parcel of the culture of excess that characterises modern Protestant nations. British people, for example, on the whole work a good deal longer than most other Europeans. Indeed, the long working hours demanded by many professions has led to these professions being called "totalitarian"—and there is some truth to this because this has been achieved at the expense of other important and God-ordained social institutions, e.g. family life. But for most people the goal and purpose of work is not the glory of God. It is the excess of material benefits, the pursuit of leisure, stripped of all constraint by the moral law of God. The meaning of life is reduced to the mere satisfaction of human appetites: *excess!* The net product of human industry thus does not contribute to the glory of God and the building of his kingdom on earth. Instead it contributes to the culture of excess in which individual self-satisfaction is exalted as the highest human ideal, the chief aim of man. In this self-centred culture those virtues and social institutions that are necessary for the preservation and amelioration of human society in terms of God's will for mankind are forgotten and lost.

Take for example the Christian ideal of the family. In Britain now the traditional ideal of the family is in the minority. There are now more childless and one parent families than there are heterosexual two parent families. A marriage is judged to be successful or unsuccessful on the basis of what each partner can get out of it. If one party decides that the marriage is no longer offering him the best satisfaction of his wants and desires, and someone else is found who can offer more or make him happier, the marriage can be dissolved easily. Indeed marriage is being abandoned altogether by many as an unnecessary bind. The plight of children traumatised by the loss of one of the parents when a marriage breaks up is seen as a secondary issue and divorce is justified by all kinds of specious rationalisation. But the consequences are usually devastating and long-lasting. It is much harder for the children of broken homes to make successful and lasting marital relationships when they become adults than those who have had a happy and stable family background. This is in part at least what Scripture means when it says that the sins of the fathers are visited on the children to the third and fourth generation (Ex. 34:7). It will take generations for our society to escape the socially destructive effects of the divorce culture that is now developing in our nation. As a result of the abandonment of stable family life society has become dysfunctional. The Christian ideal of the family is the foundation of a well-ordered society. If the family becomes dysfunctional society as a whole will become dysfunctional. And this is just what we are seeing increasingly.

But what about the sin of disregard for the poor and needy? Of all the sins listed by Ezekiel this is the one that most provoked God to anger in the Old Testament. The people of Israel are condemned for this time and again. Relief of the oppressed, the rendering of justice due to the poor and care for the needy were more important to God, and therefore constituted a more pure expression of true religion, than all the sacrifices and ceremonies of the Temple cultus (Is. 1:11–17 cf. James 1:27). Surely this sin cannot be imputed to modern Britain with its high cost welfare State. The poor are provided for more than adequately in this system, are they not?

Unfortunately, the answer to this question is not so simple. There is of course a sense in which the answer to this question is yes. But there is also an important sense in which such an answer would miss the point and fail almost totally to take account of the issues that the Bible sets before us.

It is so often thought that the welfare State is the best method of providing justice for the poor and needy because it ensures that there is an ongoing wealth redistribution programme run by the State. In Britain on the whole it is believed that this is how a caring society should behave, how it should provide for the poor. And it is believed by many Christians that State redistribution of wealth, i.e. the welfare State, in some form at least, is the closest approximation to, indeed the very incarnation of the Christian ideal of caring for the poor and needy that is set forth in Scripture as essential to the practice of true religion.

But it is precisely this notion that I want to challenge. The welfare society is not a caring society. It is a society that has abdicated its responsibility to care for the needy to the anonymous State. And the welfare State simply does not work, not only on the level of delivering real help for the poor, but in the way that it attempts to deliver that help. Indeed, in the very pursuit of this anonymous welfare State the function of the State, namely the public administration of justice, what the Bible calls doing judgement, is compromised, and the failure of the rulers to do justice is as severely condemned in Scripture as disregard for the poor. In fact it is the very failure to deliver justice that is condemned in the Bible as oppression of the poor. Such injustice may affect all classes in society of course, but those who are least able to defend themselves against it are the poor and needy, the orphan and the widow, i.e. those without economic power. For such people injustice is also oppression because they have no means of defending themselves against it. The redress for such oppression, the Bible tells us repeatedly, is the pursuit of justice: "seek judgement, relieve the oppressed, judge the fatherless, plead for the widow" (Is. 1:17). But in Scripture the *magistrate* is never given the responsibility of establishing a welfare State or of pursuing enforced wealth redistribution programmes within society. Why? Because such practices are *un*just, and it is *justice* that the Bible commands. In other words, two wrongs do not make a right. We may not overturn the justice due to one person in an attempt to secure the justice due to another. It is the job of the State to do judgement, justice, and it is the job of society at large, individuals, families and communities, to care for those who are genuinely in need. The responsibility of the State to provide justice may not be abdicated in order to usurp the responsibilities of individuals and families, nor may the responsibilities of individuals and families be abdicated to the State.

Yet this is precisely what has happened in our socialist welfare State. In this process justice has been turned on it head. The guilty are set free to pursue their reign of terror and violence in society, which is held accountable for the evil that criminals do, while the innocent are continually oppressed economically to provide for the lazy. Society is constantly fed the lie that "poverty causes crime," and this mantra is deemed to justify the continuous wealth redistribution programmes that constitute the fraudulent virtue known as "social justice." But such a system does not merely fail to do justice—i.e. righteousness (in the Bible justice and righteousness mean the same thing). Neither does it help the genuinely poor, i.e. the *deserving* poor. It merely creates an indolent underclass who are able to live off the sweat of others and enjoy their lifestyle of idleness and irresponsibility as a "human right" because it is supported by a perverse and politically correct human rights industry funded by its victims, the tax-payer. The result is a kind of perverse slave society, but one in which all the usual norms of slavery are stood on their heads. It is not the rulers and the middles classes who live off the slave labour of the underclass but rather the underclass that lives off the benefits provided by taxation of those who create the wealth in society. Those who work labour at least two days each week (probably more) in order to pay the taxes that fund the government agencies that provide this iniquitous system of hand-outs to the new leisured class in our society. The suggestion that the idle beneficiaries of this system should be made to do some work in return for their keep will bring down the wrath of our politically correct and tax-funded human rights industry. In this sense, therefore, there is in our society a significant measure of the sin of idleness condemned by Ezekiel as one of the causes of Sodom's destruction. The welfare State has overturned the basic principle of biblical work ethics, namely that if a man *will* not work, neither should he eat (2 Thess. 3:10).

The welfare State is at the heart of our national decline. It is not merely that the State-run welfare system is experiencing the adverse effects of the de-Christianisation of our culture along with other institutions. The welfare State is itself a substantial cause of this deterioration of our culture, which is at heart a process of de-Christianisation of society. It is not the only cause. But it is a major contributing factor in our decline. For example, the welfare State is responsible in large measure for the decline of the Christian ideal of family life, for the loss of the responsibility of parents for their children, and particularly for the loss of the father's headship of his family, which has been transferred to the anonymous welfare State. Here again we see the loss of those virtues that create and sustain family life because responsibility is abdicated to the State. Such abdication of responsibility is not the characteristic of a caring society at all. The welfare State is an expression of a people's desire to rid themselves of the virtues that characterise a caring society.

For example, the welfare State has to be funded by taxation. Taxation on the scale necessary to maintain the welfare State confiscates the resources that the family needs in order to care for its own members properly, let alone for others who need help. Such a system plunders the family's financial resources to such an extent that the majority of families become dependent on the State in some measure. This in itself weakens the family, which is foundational to the whole structure of society. Indeed it makes the Christian family obsolete. The family is replaced by the ever bountiful State—bountiful to those who are its dependants that is, not to those who have to fund the tax bill for the irresponsible lifestyle of those who are dependants of the State. Increasingly the State takes the place of the family. Families that are taxed to pay for all the services that the State provides from a supposedly amoral, religiously neutral perspective are not able to provide for those in need in terms of Christian principles. (Of course such neutrality is impossible and the supposed amorality is immorality from the Christian perspective—witness the abandonment of Christian ethics in the spheres of education and health care, e.g. the crusade to abolish Clause 28 in schools and the growth of the abortion industry in the NHS).

The practice of the Christian faith is intimately bound up with care for the poor and healing of the sick: "Pure religion and undefiled before God and the Father is this, To visit the fatherless and widows in their affliction, and to keep himself unspotted from the world" (James 1:27). We are commanded not only to preach the gospel of the Kingdom but to heal the sick also (Mt. 10:7–8; Lk. 9:2, 10:9). But care for the poor and healing of the sick that disregards God's will for the individual, the family and society at large is not really care at all, nor is it healing. It is idolatry, and idolatry enslaves men rather than freeing them. Welfare and health care that is stripped of all reference to God's will for man is ultimately cruel.

What then is the answer to this situation? Christian work ethics must be brought back into our care for the poor. Christian charity should not be divorced from Christian work ethics. The separation of charity from Christian work ethics is the legacy of our godless State welfare system, which is, as a result, subject to massive abuse. The provision of welfare, education, health care etc. in our society must be restored to those God-ordained institutions responsible for these things—the family, the individual, and the Church, which can apply the biblical principles necessary for these spheres of life to function in a godly way. The amelioration of our society requires the practice of the Christian virtues. Such is not facilitated by State funding and organisation of welfare. Rather the reverse is true. State welfare has a deleterious effect on the practice of the Christian virtues and therefore on the practice and influence of the faith in society. We must begin replacing the welfare State mentality with a Christian understanding of what it means to be a caring society, i.e. with a perspective that links care for the needy with Christian work ethics, because both are essential to man's well-being. Christian ethics must also be restored to the practice of medicine. This means not only that abortion, euthanasia etc. must be opposed and made illegal, but that the model of human nature that is used in the diagnosis and treatment of illness should be a Christian one, that we should start with an understanding of man as God's image bearer and vicegerent and work from these principles in seeking to heal men. These developments will not take place in the godless welfare and health care programmes run by the modern secular State. Christians and Churches must, therefore, begin their own welfare and health care programmes that function in terms of Christian ethics, a Christian model of man as created in God's image and a Christian model of the social order that God requires of our society.

The welfare State is not a system of justice, and therefore it is not consistent with righteousness. It is a denial of the righteousness that God demands of individuals and of society because it negates the responsibilities required of the individual, the family and the community, thereby rendering virtue obsolete. Thus in the Church, for example, virtue has been replaced by "piety." The good Christian is the one who behaves piously, not the one who practises the Christian virtues, since these are largely now obsolete in our society. The State has usurped our duty to act virtuously. It cares for the poor and needy on our behalf, provides education for our children and health care for the sick, takes in the orphans and provides hand outs for widows—all of which were at one time functions of the individual and the family, and where these were unable to provide, the Church. But that was when this nation was a Christian nation. We no longer look to God for these things any more. The all-powerful State has taken the place of God. It is our new religion. Our idolatry is virtually complete. The State has claimed for itself a position and an importance in our lives and society that belongs rightfully to God. But unlike the Christian God, it cannot deliver what it promises. The growth of the State has gone hand in hand with the decline of the Christian faith, increasing breakdown of order in society and the growth of the culture of irresponsibility and crime described above.

The godless, indulgent, proud and immoral culture in which we live is a modern Sodom and Gomorrah. And the judgement of God is already upon us. Our society has been given up to its own sin. The plague of homosexuality and the pervasive immorality and crime in our society are testimony to that fact. It is time that the Church woke up to the reality of the situation and faced up to the spiritual apostasy that has provoked God to pour out his wrath on our society. Instead a kind of deadening slumber has fallen upon the Church. What will it take to waken the Church out of this deep sleep, to impress upon her once again the high calling of the Great Commission and the social and political responsibilities that this commission entails? I do not know the answer to this question. But whatever it is, it will most likely be, given the current state of our nation, a rude awakening.

17

PROTESTANTISM AND SCIENCE

[Reviews of Peter Harrison's *The Bible, Protestantism and the Rise of Natural Science* (Cambridge University Press, 1998, ISBN 0-521-59196-1) and Alfred W. Crosby's *The Measure of Reality: Quantification and Western Society 1250–1600* (Cambridge University Press, 1997, ISBN 0-521-63990-5)]

THERE have been many attempts to explain the rise of the highly developed scientific culture of the Western world since the Reformation that link this development with the religious changes produced by the Reformation itself. There have been perhaps as many attempts to explain this development that do not link it directly to the religious changes produced by the Reformation. Harrison's book falls into the former category, Crosby's into the latter.

Harrison's fundamental thesis is that the change of hermeneutic method of reading the Bible produced by the Reformation, namely, from a highly allegorical to a "literal" reading, led to the demystification or de-allegorising of the natural word, replacing Western society's view of the natural world as a system of symbols, the ultimate purpose of which is to point to the higher spiritual meaning of life, with a mechanical model of nature.

Behind this change was the understanding that God has revealed himself to mankind in two books: the book of Scripture and the book of nature (i.e. the created order). Prior to the Reformation both these books were read allegorically. The physical phenomena of nature were explained in terms of what they signified or pointed to, not in terms of causation and how they function in the world. After the Reformation both the book of Scripture and the book of nature were beginning to be read "literally." The Re-

formers' insistence on a "literal" rather than an allegorical reading of the book of Scripture led unwittingly, but inevitably, to a
"literal" rather than an allegorical reading of the book of nature,
and it was the abandonment of the allegorical reading of the book
of nature that produced the modern scientific world-view, i.e. a
reading of the phenomena of nature in terms of causation and
their function in the world rather than their spiritual significance.
By overturning the symbolic world-view of the Middle Ages the
Reformers facilitated the development of modern natural science;
i.e. they freed the study of the natural world from a system of
interpretation that assigned meaning to objects as allegorically
pointing to higher realities that are not related to the specific functions of those objects in the natural world. The following lengthy
quotation from Harrison's introduction explains this:

"The emergence of 'proper' natural history . . . was not simply the result of stripping away unwanted and extraneous symbolic elements, leaving a core of pure and unadulterated science.
Rather a new conception of the world, itself premised on a particular view of the meaning of the texts, was to drive a wedge
between words and things, restricting the allocation of meanings
to the former. Only then was a genuine science of nature . . .
gradually able to occupy the territory vacated by the humanities,
ordering the objects of nature according to new systematising principles. The new conception of the order of nature was made possible . . . by the collapse of the allegorical interpretation of texts,
for a denial of the legitimacy of allegory is in essence a denial of
the capacity of things to act as signs. The demise of allegory, in
turn, was due largely to the efforts of Protestant reformers, who in
their search for an unambiguous religious authority, insisted that
the book of scripture be interpreted only in its literal, historical
sense. This insistence on the primacy of the literal sense had the
unforeseen consequence of cutting short a potentially endless chain
of reference, in which word refers to object, and objet refers to
other objects. The literalist mentality of the reformers thus gave a
determinate meaning to the text of scripture, and at the same
time precluded the possibility of assigning meanings to natural

objects. Literalism means that only words refer; the things of nature do not. In this way the study of the natural world was liberated from the specifically religious concern of biblical interpretation, and the sphere of nature was opened up to new ordering principles. The mathematical and taxonomic categories imposed by Galileo and Ray on physical objects and living things represent an attempt to reconfigure a natural world which had been evacuated of order and meaning. It is commonly supposed that when in the early modern period individuals began to look at the world in a different way, they could no longer believe what they read in the Bible. In this book I shall suggest that the reverse is the case: that when in the sixteenth century people began to read the Bible in a different way, they found themselves forced to jettison traditional conceptions of the world. The Bible—its contents, the controversies it generated, its varying fortunes as an authority, and most importantly, the new way in which it was read by Protestants—played a central role in the emergence of natural science in the seventeenth century" (p. 4f.).

Harrison makes it clear in his introduction, however, that this link between the development of modern science and Protestantism is not a direct one. He argues for "an indirect, even diffuse, influence of Protestantism on the development of modern science" (p. 8). Although he acknowledges a wide range of factors contributing to the scientific revolution, the specific agent he identifies in his study as the most important of these is the Protestant hermeneutic, i.e. the stress on the "literal" reading of the text.

Harrison traces the mediaeval allegorical hermeneutic to Origen. "Despite the considerable suspicion with which Origen's theological writings were viewed during the Middle Ages, he exerted an enormous influence on medieval thinkers through his methods of interpretation. The approach of medieval thinkers to both world and text derive ultimately from Origen" (p. 16). He then quotes the following passage from Origen's commentary on the Song of Songs:

"Paul the apostle teaches us that the invisible things of God are understood by means of the things that are visible, and that the things that are not seen are beheld through their relationship and likeness to things seen. He thus shows that this visible world teaches us about that which is invisible, and that this earthly scene contains certain patterns of things heavenly. Thus it is to be possible for us to mount up from things below to things above, and to perceive and understand from the things we see on earth the things that belong to heaven. On the pattern of these the Creator gave to His creatures on earth a certain likeness to these, so that thus their great diversity might be more easily deduced and understood" (cited on p. 16).

Physical objects symbolise spiritual realities. This symbolic method was also used to read Scripture. Although allegory had been used prior to Origen by the Church it was Origen who raised this method to the level of a science (p. 18).

By the time of Anselm, however, there was beginning to be a renewed emphasis on the physical. Anselm's doctrine of the atonement changed the older pay-off to the Devil theory, a transaction between two spiritual beings, for a theory that placed greater stress on the physical incarnation. As a result the physical world took centre stage in God's redemptive activity. This new emphasis on the physical in religious concerns also had implications for the mass. According to Harrison "Official recognition of this new emphasis came at the Lateran council of 1215, when transubstantiation became official Catholic dogma, and with the observation of the feast of Corpus Christi, commanded by Urban IV in 1264" (p. 37). This new emphasis also led, however, to a new emphasis on the human senses. Knowledge was understood to come through the senses, i.e. through bodily organs, not through ideas placed in the mind and illuminated by God. Thus Bernard of Clairvaux (1090–1153) stated that "there is no access open to us, except through the body, to those things whereby we live in happiness . . . The spiritual creature, therefore, which we are, must necessarily have a body, without which, indeed, it can by no means obtain that knowledge which is the only means of attaining to those things, to know which constitutes blessedness" (cited on p. 37).

This led by various routes to the rediscovery of nature. Harrison gives the following definition of nature and natural science: "The idea of nature is that of a particular ordering of natural objects, and the study of nature the systematic investigation of that order. These, in turn, require new theoretical conceptions, absent from the intellectual traditions which the eleventh century had inherited from late antiquity. Such conceptions were the products of new schools and new books" (p. 39). Understanding nature was a matter of relating the parts of nature to the whole. "As a single passage of scripture might be made to bear the meaning of the whole, so discrete material objets were seen to be reflections of the whole. A speck of dust, observed Robert Grosseteste, 'is an image of the whole universe' and 'a mirror of the creator'. The model which medieval thinkers were to rely upon to establish such connections in nature was thus the ancient idea of microcosm-macrocosm, a conception employed in biblical exegesis, but one which, as Plato had intimated in the *Timaeus*, could be applied to the world" (p. 47f.). Harrison attributes some importance to the influence of Plato's *Timaeus*. Although mediaeval exegetes were familiar with the microcosm-macrocosm idea in the interpretation of texts, "From their encounter with Plato's *Timaeus*, they now learnt that the microcosm-macrocosm relation could be redeployed in the natural world" (p. 49). One important way in which this idea was employed was by comparing the human body as the microcosm to the whole natural order as the macrocosm.

Nevertheless, one cannot help wondering whether this method of description and explanation got a little out of hand in the theorising of some. According to Ambrose Pare, a sixteenth-century surgeon, "Just as in the big world [i.e. the macrocosm] there are two great lights, to wit, the sun and the moon, so there are in the human body two eyes which illuminate it, which [microcosm] is composed of four elements, as in the big world in which winds, thunder, earthquakes, rain, dew, vapors, exhalations, hail, eclipses, floods, sterility, fertility, stones, mountains, fruits, and several divers species of animals occur; the same thing also happens in the small world which is the human body. An example of winds: they can be observed to be enclosed in windy apostemas and in the bowels of those who have windy colic; and similarly in some women whose belly one can hear rumbling in such a way that it seems there is a colony of frogs there; the which [winds] upon issuing from the seat make noises like cannons being fired. And although the artillery piece is aimed towards the ground, nevertheless the cannon smoke always hits the nose of the cannoneer and those who are near him" (cited on p. 51).

The Reformers also played a role in shaping the reformation of learning. "If the techniques of textual criticism pioneered by the humanists had played a role in precipitating a revolution in religious matters, now the Protestant Reformation, through its challenge to traditional authorities, was to assist in the reformation of learning" (p. 101). In liberating the individual to read and interpret the Scriptures for himself the Reformation also gave an impetus to the same freedom of interpretation in the book of nature. Ancient authorities could no longer maintain their credibility by virtue of their position as accepted tradition. Many in the seventeenth-century called attention to the perceived link between the Reformation of religion and the reformation of learning. "In 1605, Francis Bacon had observed that 'in the age of ourselves and our Fathers, when it pleased God to call the Church of Rome to account for their degenerate manners and ceremonies, and sundry doctrines obnoxious and framed to uphold the same abuses; at one and the same time it was ordained by the Divine Providence, that there should attend withal a renovation and a new spring of all other knowledge'" (p. 103).

However, problems soon arose with the new learning, in their own way no less serious than the old learning. According to Harrison: "It is frequently assumed that accommodation was a defensive strategy which preserved biblical authority by showing how particular passages of scripture could be reconciled with contemporary scientific theory: accommodation replaced allegory as a means of reconciling scripture to other authorities. From another perspective, however, it might be said that scientific theories could actually become a way of discerning hidden meanings of particular passages of scripture—meanings which had hitherto been obscured because the words which expressed them had been accommodated to the capacities of more primitive minds" (p. 136). Thus, Francis Bacon claimed that an understanding of the book of nature was the key to understanding Scripture (Harrison references *Advancement of Learning*, I.VI.16 for this). Likewise Robert Boyle stated that "God has made some knowledge of his created book, both conducive to belief, and necessary to the understanding of the written one" (p. 136).

But it is the development of this kind of thinking that has led to many of the Church's problems today. Whereas the Christian must insist that the book of nature is interpreted through the book of Scripture, i.e. that we understand the world around us by looking at it through the spectacles of the Bible, today the scientific community insists on reading the book of Scripture through the spectacles of the book of nature. And the Church in large measure has bought into this idea. The result has been the loss of the Bible as an authoritative text. It has been privatised and credited with authority mainly as an existential revelation, i.e. it has become the word of God for individuals in their particular circumstances. But it has lost the status of a book that proclaims an authoritative public truth. The desire for intellectual respectability in a secular scientific environment has largely driven this failure among many modern Christians. The result, inevitably, however, is that the scientific world is interpreting the book of nature with the wrong theory, and the consequence for the Church is that this erroneous theory has also been used to interpret the Bible. Whereas the Reformers' biblical hermeneutic led to a re-reading of the natural world, following the Enlightenment the reverse has happened. The book of nature is now used to interpret the book of Scripture.

The purpose of developing a Christian world-view in our day must be to address this problem decisively. Its aim must be to restore the proper order. But this proper order is not an allegorical reading of the book of nature—we have no desire to cast off the many blessings of science, which are certainly the true children of a Christian civilisation. But certainly the book of nature, if it is to be correctly interpreted, and therefore developed and used for the glory of God and the betterment of mankind and the natural world itself, must be subjected to the Creator's authoritative interpretation of its meaning; i.e. the book of nature must be read through the spectacles of the book of Scripture. Only then shall we find its true meaning. This is the problem that Christian philosophy must address in our day; it is an essential task to be accomplished if we are to speak intelligently about the faith to the modern world. Why?

The scientific world-view that developed following the Reformation replaced a world of meaning with a world of purpose (i.e. causation). As a result modern Western man lost meaning, something that he cannot live without. So he seeks meaning in the created order, i.e. he idolises some aspect of the created order in an attempt to find meaning. Secular science has created a spiritual vacuum for Western man and he has responded by seeking the meaning of life in science itself. The Church, because of its accommodation to secular science, has likewise been unable to fill this vacuum, except with pious platitudes, and this has produced an under-nourished and feeble Church. It is not that the scientific search for purpose, i.e. causation, is in any way illegitimate in itself. The problem is that the search for the meaning of human life, the cosmos and everything in it, has been *reduced* to the scientific task. Meaning has been reduced to causation, scientifically understood. This is a form of idolatry, since it seeks to explain the meaning of reality without reference to the God who created it. It is also immensely dissatisfying spiritually, as the modern age is proving only too well. Many are now looking to alternative idols to provide meaning for their lives. The Church, in her stupor, has failed to recognise the situation and address the issues.

The problem is clear from what Harrison says on p. 195f. "More caution was required for the prosecution of the advantages of the book of nature over the book of scripture. One ground for superiority which suggested itself to seventeenth-century minds was that nature was a universal text which, unlike scripture, had been accessible at all times, in all places, to all peoples: nature was, in the words of Thomas Browne, 'a Universal and publick Manuscript . . . The vulgar and illiterate were also able to comprehend the theology of the book of nature, while the subtleties of scriptural doctrines were likely to escape them."

But of course this is precisely incorrect. In the state of sin the book of nature is *not* more accessible to all. Only when man, in subjection to God's word, sees nature rightly through the spectacles of the Bible, does he interpret it correctly. When men have tried to read the book of nature without using the spectacles of God's word to interpret it, they have embraced the grossest forms of superstition and idolatry and groped around in utter darkness and ignorance, worshipping the creature rather than the Creator. And along with this, instead of exercising dominion over the natural world, men found themselves in bondage to the world around them, governed by their fear of the natural world and the spirits they believed were responsible for controlling it (animism). It has only been the freeing of man from this animistic religion born of reading nature without reference to the word of God—now resurrected in New Age thinking—that has enabled Western society to climb out of such darkness and ignorance. But this is a liberty that man owes to the Christian faith alone. The scientific revolution was born out of a Christian cultural matrix; it led to man's greater dominion over the world. Nature religion, i.e. reading the book of nature without reference to the word of God, did not achieve this; it held mankind in a debilitating bondage to animism. Secular humanism, and the liberalism of the Church in its accommodation to this secular humanism, has now inverted the proper order that produced the scientific revolution. The Bible is read through the book of nature. As a result our culture, and the Church as well, is returning to the ignorance and darkness that characterised the world before the rise of Christian civilisation. The modern ecology and New Age movements, feminism, Jungian psychology etc., embraced by the Church often as much as by the world, are part and parcel of this process of reversion, this rebirth of paganism. The secularisation of science and the accommodation of the

Church to that process of secularisation is partly responsible for this development.

That scientists were to be the new priests of this secular religion of natural science is clear from Harrison's quotations on p. 198. He writes: "Reformers in religion and science alike were to insist that the true function of a priest was not the performance of ritual acts with symbolic objects, but the exposition of some authoritative text and the communication to others of information. The text given to students of nature to expound was the world itself. The image of natural philosophers as priests expounding a wordless text struck a chord with a number of seventeenth-century writers. Henry More spoke of the universe as 'the temple of God'. Fellow Platonist John Smith agreed that the world was 'God's temple'. Robert Boyle exploited the same image. 'I esteem the world a temple,' he wrote, and 'if the world be a temple, man sure must be the priest'. Natural philosophy, Boyle goes on to say, is 'reasonable worship ($\lambda o\gamma\iota\kappa\acute{\eta}$ $\lambda a\tau\rho\epsilon\acute{\iota}a$) of God . . . and discovering to others the perfections of God displayed in the creatures is a more acceptable act of religion, than the burning of sacrifices'. The study of nature, he concluded, is 'the first act of religion, and equally obliging in all religions'. The book of nature and those natural philosophers who interpreted it thus assumed part of the role previously played by the sacraments and the ordained priesthood" (p. 198f.).

But in the fallen state, the state of sin, man does not read the book of nature correctly. God, in his mercy, has given mankind the Scriptures to correct this misreading. Harrison quotes Richard Baxter to this effect: "The pious Richard Baxter allowed that 'the world is God's book, which he set man at first to read'. Robert South, too, wrote of Adam, that 'He had no catechism but the creation, needed no study but reflection, read no book but the volume of the world'. Yet, for neither of these writers was there any suggestion that nature was an adequate source of saving knowledge of God. On the contrary, it was the human failure to discern truths in the volume of nature which necessitated the more direct revelation now to be found in the pages of scripture" (p. 202). It was the entrance of sin into the human heart that led to man's perversion of the meaning of the book of nature. Only the correcting lenses of Scripture can put his vision right.

Harrison shows how the Reformation hermeneutic for reading Scripture had positive ameliorating effects in human culture: "The Christian doctrine of creation had always held that the natural world had a purpose, a purpose related to human welfare. However, up until the modern period, that purpose had encompassed both spiritual and material aspects of human existence. When the world could no longer be interpreted for its transcendental meanings, it was actively exploited solely for its material utility. Equally importantly, however, the central canonical text of the Western tradition contains a narrative which, when interpreted in its historical sense, presents the image of a human individual who knows and controls nature, and who directly exercises a divine grant of dominion. The recognition that the paradise of knowledge enjoyed by our first parents was an historical reality, combined with the acceptance of the command 'have dominion' in its full literal sense, provided a vital impetus to the seventeenth-century quest to know and master the world. Only when the story of creation was divested of its symbolic elements could God's commands to Adam be related to worldly activities. If the Garden of Eden were but a lofty allegory, as Philo, Origen and Hugh of St Victor, had suggested, there would be little point in attempting to re-establish paradise on earth. If God's command to Adam to tend the garden had primarily symbolic significance, as Augustine had believed, then the idea that man was to re-establish paradise through gardening and agriculture would simply not have presented itself so strongly to the seventeenth-century mind. If dominion over the animals was thought to be an oblique reference to mastery of the passions . . . then Baconian notions of reproducing the effects of nature through knowledge of efficient causes would never have been allied with the necessary religious motivations. If the command to be 'fruitful and multiply, and fill the earth' was taken to refer to the cultivation of virtues or 'fruits of the spirit', then there would be no onus on the human race to colonise under-utilised lands. If the Fall were not an historical, but a cosmic event in which souls fell into bodies, then its consequences would be difficult to reverse in the present life. Now that Genesis was regarded primarily as historical narrative, however, the divine imperatives it contained could be read unequivocally" (p. 206f.).

Thus the Reformational reading of the Creation and Fall as historical events indirectly helped to stimulate scientific advancement and progress for the Western world. But Harrison does not leave it here. There is another interpretation of the effect of the Reformers' "literal" interpretation of Scripture, namely that it led to religious bigotry and hostility towards the sciences (see page 276). Harrison argues against this idea. He writes that "the seventeenth-century dispute was more to do with the rights of individuals to make their own determinations about how the books of nature and scripture were to be read. Galileo himself adopted a literal approach to scripture, albeit one which allowed for a certain amount of 'accommodation' on the part of the biblical authors. The mistaken premise of this version of history [the one that sees the Reformation hermeneutic as a hindrance to scientific development—SCP] is the assumption that to read the Bible literally is to consider the Bible to be literally true" (p. 267f.). According to Harrison "the triumph of the literal approach to scripture opened up for the first time in the history of biblical interpretation the real possibility that parts of the Bible could be false" (268). He argues that it was the desire to secure the truth of every word of Scripture that led to the adoption of the allegorical and tropological hermeneutics in the first place. By adopting this approach mediaeval scholars could reconcile the biblical texts with themselves and other authorities. With the abandonment of the allegorical method, "the text of scripture was for the first time exposed to the assaults of history and science" (*ibid.*). Thus, Harrison concludes that "While the Protestants' insistence that passages of scripture be given a determinate meaning proceeded from the purest of religious motives, they were inadvertently setting in train a process which would ultimately result in the undermining of that biblical authority which they so adamantly promoted" (*ibid.*).

What are we to make of this? First, we need to consider the meaning of the term "literal." I have used the word "literal" above in quotation marks. Some explanation of this is needed. The Reformers' stress on the "literal" interpretation of Scripture must be understood in its historical context. This point needs to be made because modern evangelicalism and fundamentalism has a doctrine of literalism that does not quite correspond with that of the Reformers. The literal reading as understood by the Reformers should be defined against the highly symbolic allegorical reading of Scripture prevalent in the mediaeval era and before, and the corresponding allegorical reading of the book of nature. According to Harrison "Over all, evidence from medieval commentaries supports Chenu's assertion that throughout the Middle Ages systematic allegorising had universally destroyed the literal text of scripture" (p. 111). But the "literal" reading is the *natural* or *plain* meaning, the meaning of the text without its being subjected to layer upon layer of allegory and trope. This does not mean a literalistic interpretation. The idea of a literal meaning must be understood against the backdrop of centuries of allegorising that obscured the plain meaning of the text. It was the plain or natural meaning of the text that was understood by the term "literal meaning." In contrast to the allegorical interpretation the Reformers championed this "literal" interpretation. As Harrison correctly states, their intention was "to deny the indeterminacy of meaning of canonical texts, and thus to insist that each passage of scripture had but a single, fixed meaning" (p. *ibid.*). This point is extremely important. "Protestant exegetes were to use a variety of terms to express this approach—literal sense, grammatical sense, historical sense, plain sense. It was always possible that such an approach would lead to a situation where the single sense of some biblical passage was not, strictly, its literal sense, as for example in the parables of Jesus, or the prophesies of Revelation. Protestant 'literalism' thus needs to be broadly conceived as an assertion which usually, though not invariably, will lie with the literal sense" (*ibid.*).

The term "literal meaning" is not a propitious one for us today however. The modern evangelical fundamentalist emphasis on a literal reading has lost this context. It repeats the verbiage but no longer understands the context and therefore the real meaning of the terminology. As a result the language of the Bible is often not allowed to function in the way it was intended to function because the text is forced into a literalistic straight-jacket, even where apocalyptic and poetic language is used, thus distorting the meaning the text just as much as mediaeval theologians distorted the text by their allegorical reading of non-allegorical types of biblical literature. In other words, the kind of literalism espoused by modern evangelical fundamentalism does not often get at the plain meaning of the text; indeed often the result of such a literalistic approach is nonsense, not the correct sense. Repeating the Reformation dictum that the literal sense is the correct sense will not save evangelicals and fundamentalists from such error. Decontextualised shibboleths from past ages do not help the cause of truth in our own age. The only way to avoid such errors is study and understanding, namely the use of the mind in God's service, a task that modern evangelical fundamentalism, with its heavy accent on anti-intellectualism, has shown itself unwilling to embrace. The Reformers' use of the term "literal meaning" and the modern evangelical fundamentalists' use of the same term are not exactly equivalent. The cultural context must be taken into account in this matter. In fact much Reformed exegesis of Scripture could not be classed as literal in the modern evangelical fundamentalist sense. But neither is it allegorical in the mediaeval sense.

Second, however, we must also consider whether the seed of modern evangelical fundamentalist literalism was not present in some degree in the Reformers' literal method. Can the Bible really be read in a mono-hermeneutical fashion, whether literally or allegorically? Does not Scripture actually use a very wide range of types of literature? Of course the Reformers recognised this in their exposition of Scripture, though not all to the same degree (one is reminded of Luther's insistence on the literal meaning of "this is my body") and not necessarily in a self-conscious way. The purpose of hermeneutics is to get at the *meaning* of the text. To adopt a literalist approach at the outset is equally as unsatisfactory as adopting an allegorical approach. In our interpretation of Scripture we must pay careful attention to the kind of language that is being used. It is no better to read the Bible only in a literalistic way than it is to read the complete works of Milton in a literalistic way. He wrote both prose and poetry. We must respect both types of language and read appropriately if we are to understand him properly. Likewise with Scripture, except that Scripture is more complicated in places because it uses forms of literature, such as apocalyptic, that are very unfamiliar to the Western mind.

Third, in a section entitled "Learning the language of nature" Harrison points out that the language of science is mathematics. "The nature of physical objects became insignificant in accounts of their behaviour. Order was to be imposed on the objects of nature, not through an understanding of their essential qualities, but through the discovery of the laws which they obeyed. These laws were external to their natures, and were demonstrable mathematically . . . The identification of mathematics as a language of nature was the final stage in the imposition of the new ordering principles to which physical objets were subject. It represents, on the one hand, the last stage in the evacuation of meaning from the natural world, and on the other the triumph of mathematical physics—the most conspicuous feature of the scientific achievement of the seventeenth century" (p. 262). But mathematics is not the ideal language that many hoped it would be. It does not explain everything. Indeed it does not explain at all; it merely describes. It is unable to provide mankind with the meaning he desires. Hence the futility of reading the Bible as a scientific text, since the Bible speaks about meaning; it gives us the history and meaning of the Creation, Fall and Redemption. Mathematics, science, cannot do this. Science is an *abstraction* from the whole, a partial truth; it describes an aspect of reality. Valid in its own sphere though it is, it cannot provide mankind with meaning. Thus, Harrison writes, "The seventeenth century quest for a language of nature, a real character, a universal language—signifies an awareness of the absence of ordering principles in nature. They are not merely attempts to revisit the encyclopaedic knowledge of an Adam, who through literal readings of Genesis had been reborn in the seventeenth-century imagination as polymath and scientist, but also to repair the gulf between words and things, a division which for the seventeenth century was the legacy of the Fall and Babel. Mathematics, it must be said, fulfilled only some of the functions of the ideal language. It did not penetrate to essences, it did not grasp natures, it did not provide meanings, it seemingly failed to grasp the full significance of living things . . . At the very beginning of the medieval period, the book of nature was written in symbols which were laden with various meanings, but which were not related to each other in any systematic way. Nature was a vast lexicon in which objects were given meanings, but grammatical and syntactic linkages between the elements of the language were completely absent. By the end of the seventeenth century the wheel has come full circle. Natural objects have been stripped of their intrinsic meanings, and even their qualities and essences are gone. In the physics of Descartes and Newton simple natural objects are denuded of all but basic quantitative properties" (p. 263f.).

And yet man seeks meaning above all. He cannot live without it. The idolatry of science and mathematics has not provided that meaning. Science deals with physical causation. i.e. it describes second causes. The Bible cannot be read scientifically in this way. It speaks of the meaning of life, of Creation, Fall, Redemption. Modern scientific man thinks the truth can be found only in mathematics. A good example of this was Bertrand Russell, who wrote: "I came to philosophy through mathematics, or rather through the wish to find some reason to believe in the truth of mathematics. From early youth, I had an ardent desire to believe that there can be such a thing as knowledge, combined with a great difficulty in accepting much that passes as knowledge. It seemed clear that the best chance of finding indubitable truth would be in pure mathematics . . ." (B. R. Russell, "Logical Atomism" in A. J. Ayer, ed., *Logical Positivism* [The Free Press of Glencoe, 1959], p. 31). Then modern scientific man, convinced that only mathematics can describe reality and show us the truth, comes to the Bible, which does not use mathematics, the language of science, to proclaim the words of life. In his disgust modern man throws up his arms and walks away from the Bible cursing it because it does not bow to his idol and demands instead that he bend the knee to God and humbly confess his sin, his need for Jesus Christ and his reliance on God's revealed word if he is to know the truth about the world in which he lives and seeks to understand. But he will not accept that the Bible speaks truth, that it speaks about God's action in history, because it does not accommodate itself to his idolatry of the created order, namely the belief that science, mathematics, is the infallible source of all truth.

It is this idolatry of science, the search for the meaning of the cosmos within itself, that is the source of so much of modern man's inability to believe the Bible to be historically true. The Bible is not deemed to be historically true because it does not speak the language of modern scientific idolatry. The answer for modern man is not the abandonment of science, however, or of the language of science, mathematics; it is, rather, his submission, and the submission of all human thought, including science and mathematics, to the word of God.

Harrison's book is an immensely stimulating and informative read. It throws up questions that the Church needs to think hard about and deal with. It is highly recommended.

Crosby's book seeks to describe the effects of the rise of a highly developed sense of quantification on Western culture. The book covers many fields of learning and art from the development of measured music notation and form to double entry bookkeeping, algebra, cartography, perspective in art, the invention of the clock etc. He shows how the quantification of time and space and the development of mathematics affected the developing perception of reality in the later mediaeval and Renaissance periods. He argues that it was the quantification of reality that led to the new (i.e. modern) model of the cosmos. During this period "Western Europeans evolved a new way, more purely visual and quantitative than the old, of perceiving time, space, and material environment" (p. 227). The book is a description of how this change of perception happened and how it affected the various fields of study and art. He does not attempt to penetrate to a religious or any other kind of motive at work during this period of change. Nevertheless, the book is fascinating and well-worth reading for the number of examples he gives of how our modern perception of reality differs from that of the ages prior to the Renaissance.

For example, prior to the development of modern mathematical ideas of quantification during this period an emphasis on precise numbering was not common—and not always easily achieved until the introduction of Hindu-Arabic numerals. The introduction of zero into the Western counting system was a revolution, but for some time the old Roman numbering system was used in conjunction with the Hindu-Arabic numerals. "Sometimes Europeans would adopt Hindu-Arabic numeral place value and the zero, but express them with Roman capitals, a particularly confusing compromise. IVOII is (and how would you ever know unless told?) 1502: that is, I in the thousands slot, V in the hundreds slot, none in the tens slot, and II in the digits slot. The painter Dirk Bouts placed on his alter at Louvain the number MCCCC4XVII, which designates—what? My guess would be 1447. What is yours?" (p. 115).

Of significance is the fact that in the mediaeval period rough estimates rather than exact numbers were widely accepted as accurate enough for many purposes. "Recipes for making glass, chalices, organs, and other things included very few numbers: 'a bit more' and 'a medium-sized piece' were precise enough . . . Medieval Europeans used numbers for effect, not for accuracy" (p. 40f.). To give someone's age as 90 when he was 87 or 93 was deemed accurate enough. This shows how we must be careful not to read books written at a time prior to the rise of modern scientific exactitude with the same kind of assumptions about mathematical criteria that we should adopt in reading a modern text. Such anachronistic reading of Scripture, for example, has led many to doubt the historical veracity of Scripture and its divine inspiration. But the problem is not with Scripture; rather, it is with the use of anachronistic criteria to determine the meaning of Scripture. Are not many of the problems modern "scientific" pedants claim to experience in reading the Bible really problems created by their own anachronistic insistence on reading the text of the Bible in the same way one would read a post-Enlightenment text on science? In other words, are they not really problems created by their own idolatry of a particular aspect of the created order, an abstraction from the whole, which blinkers them from seeing the whole picture?

There are a number of places in Crosby's book that throw further light on Harrison's book. For example, Crosby refers to the resurgence of Neoplatonism at the time of the Renaissance under the influence of men such as Nicholas of Cusa, who tried to find God by squaring the circle, Leon Battista Alberti and Piero della Francesca. "Fincino [*sic*], his colleagues, and their like across Italy provided the intellectual milieu for a revival of the Platonic faith that numbers 'have the power of leading us toward reality' and that 'geometry is knowledge of the eternally existent'" (p. 179). He also quotes Galileo: "Philosophy is written in this grand book, the universe, which stands continually open to our gaze, but the book cannot be understood unless one first learns to comprehend the language and read the letters in which it is composed. It is written in the language of mathematics, and its characters are triangles, circles, and other geometric figures without which it is humanly impossible to understand a single word of it; without these, one wanders about in a dark labyrinth" (p. 240). Precisely wrong! Philosophy is the love of wisdom, and wisdom cannot be achieved merely by means of the technology of numbers because wisdom is not written in the language of numbers. Man's search for wisdom and knowledge in the language of mathematics is vain (cf. the quotation from Bertrand Russell above). Wisdom seeks the answer to the question Why? not the question How? Science seeks, properly, to answer the question How? but fails miserably to provide any kind of answer to the question Why? Only wisdom can provide the answer to the question Why? And wisdom begins with the knowledge of the Lord (Pr. 9:10). It is in the word of God, revealed to men in terms of propositional truth, that men find

wisdom (Pr. 2:6). The search for the universal language in mathematics was and is a complete failure because its premiss is at heart
the rejection of God's revealed word as the final answer to the
deepest questions that man asks about life and meaning.

Crosby's book is full of interesting details. On the section on
the invention of the escapement, for example, we read: "Some of
the most spectacular clocks ever made were constructed within
the first few generations after the invention of the escapement.
The famous Strasbourg clock, begun in 1352 and finished two years
later, told the hours and included an automated astrolabe, a per-
petual calendar, a carillon that played hymns, statues of the Vir-
gin with Christ child and three worshipping Magi, a mechanical
rooster that crowed and flapped its wings, and a tablet showing
the correlation between the zodiac and the parts of the body, indi-
cating the proper times for bloodletting. To say that the city clock
told the time and to say no more would be like saying that its
cathedral's stained-glass windows admitted light and saying no
more" (p. 85).

Both Harrison's and Crosby's books make for fascinating reading, for very different reasons. The information they provide on
the emergence of modern Western culture is very valuable for
anyone who wishes to understand the religious crisis of the modern age.

18

MISCONSTRUING
FEDERAL THEOLOGY

[A review of David A. Weir's *The Origins of the Federal Theology in Sixteenth-Century Reformation Thought* (Oxford: The Clarendon Press, 1990, ISBN 0-19-826690-1)]

I am seldom as engrossed after reading the first few pages of a book as I was upon first picking up this fascinating book. From an historical point of view I found this book very informative and useful, and highly stimulating. Unfortunately there are some serious errors in it which tend to vitiate the author's thesis and this makes the book disappointing ultimately. In the Introduction Weir states the subject matter clearly on the first page:

"In the past century there has been much discussion of the sixteenth- and seventeenth-century concept of covenant and what relation it has to Protestant dogmatics. One of the basic theological shifts in those centuries was the manner in which Reformed Protestant theologians of northern Europe divided biblical times. Whereas John Calvin (1509–64), in his *Institutes of the Christian Religion*, spoke of an Old Covenant which extended from after the Fall to Christ and then of a New Covenant which extended from Christ to the Day of Judgement, the Westminster Confession of Faith, written eighty years later, spoke of a covenant of works and a covenant of grace. There were basic differences between these two concepts, differences which affected the way Calvinists thought and acted."

The purpose of this book is to trace out the origin and early development of the federal theology that led to this shift of emphasis among Reformed theologians, which was later given the stamp of orthodoxy by the divines of the Westminster Assembly, and to show some of the far-reaching implications that it had for Puritan theology and thought, particularly with regard to the Puritan understanding of the Church-State relationship.

The distinctive feature of federal theology is the prelapsarian covenant, or covenant of works between God and Adam as the federal head of the race, established before the Fall. Zacharias Ursinus was the first Reformed theologian to postulate this idea. Before Ursinus Reformed covenant theology had dealt exclusively with the postlapsarian world and the covenant of grace. From Ursinus on, however, there was a shift among Reformed theologians from an old covenant/new covenant distinction to a distinction between the covenant of works and the covenant of grace, i.e. between the prelapsarian and postlapsarian covenants.

According to Weir there were two stages in the growth of the federal theology: "the first in 1561–3, as Ursinus first proposes the idea; the second in 1584–90, when the idea becomes accepted and becomes integrated into the theological thinking of Reformed systematic theologians" (p. 36). Four theologians especially played an important role in the spread of federal theology: Caspar Olevianus, Thomas Cartwright, Dudley Fenner and Franciscus Junius. After 1590 the prelapsarian covenant idea becomes so widespread that it is no longer possible to establish connections between theologians using it.

Weir states that there is much confusion about what is meant by "federal theology," "covenant theology" and the "covenant idea," which has led some "to trace the origins of the shift from a postlapsarian covenant schema to a prelapsarian/postlapsarian covenant schema to earlier periods in history than can be warranted" (p. 3). Having noted W. Adams Brown's distinction between the covenant idea and the covenant theology Weir goes on to explain these three terms:

"The covenant idea is a common inheritance of the Judaeo-Christian tradition found in the Bible. In recent decades the meaning of covenant has been expanded to include a much richer Near Eastern conception of commitment. Covenant theology grows out of the covenant idea. Covenant theology is a theological system in which the covenant forms the basic framework and acts as the controlling idea in that theological system. Almost all Christian theologians ultimately practice some form of covenant theology, in that they must somehow distinguish themselves as Christians and not as believers under the Old Testament dispensation. Martin Luther, for instance, saw this distinction in terms of Law and Gospel. John Calvin described it in terms of Old Testament and New Testament. The federal theology is a specific type of covenant theology, in that the covenant holds together every detail of the theological system, and is characterized by a prelapsarian and postlapsarian covenant schema centred around the first Adam and the second Adam, who is Jesus Christ" (p. 3).

Thus, "'The federal theology', in this book, refers to the doctrine that God, immediately after creating Adam, made a covenant with Adam before his Fall into sin" (p. 3). Furthermore, as Weir writes: "part of the covenant before the Fall involves the giving of the moral law, the decalogue, to Adam, and laying it on his heart; in his perfect estate Adam knew the moral law perfectly and obeyed it perfectly" (p. 4). Finally, "this covenant was binding upon all men at all times in all places, both before and after the Fall, by virtue of their descent from Adam. If Adam had not fallen, his children would have been obligated to keep the prelapsarian covenant" (p. 4). As we shall see, there are some problems here with Weir's understanding of the covenant of works in federal theology.

Weir quotes extensively from the Westminster Confession of Faith, which at a later date (1647) set forth the federal theology schema in a clear manner. He then sums up the federal theology of the Confession: "Thus we see that the classical distinctions between the Old Testament and the New Testament (and the Mosaic Old Covenant and the Christian New Covenant) are subsumed under one covenant, the postlapsarian covenant of grace, and that the new element in Calvinist thinking is that of the prelapsarian covenant of works. In the federal schema the covenant of grace now consists of Jesus Christ, the covenant-keeper, keeping and fulfilling the prelapsarian covenant of works as the second Adam. Christ takes Adam's place as the obedient God-man and fulfils the prelapsarian covenant where Adam failed. This was known as the active obedience of Christ. Furthermore, Christ takes upon himself the punishment, anger, and wrath of God which Adam deserves for his disobedience, even though Christ was sinless. This was known as the passive obedience of Christ. This gracious work of redemption was then applied to the elect of God's sovereign choice" (p.5).

Weir then makes the following important comment: "The postlapsarian covenant of grace is really therefore the prelapsarian covenant of works in disguise, but a new Adam (Christ) was needed to keep the covenant which God had established with man at the beginning of the world. Once the prelapsarian covenant of works is established it can never be broken [i.e. abrogated—SCP]." Thus, in the federal theology the substance of the prelapsarian covenant (made with Adam, the first man and federal head of humanity) and the postlapsarian covenant (made with Christ as the Mediator and federal head and representative of his people) is the same; but whereas Adam fell and broke the covenant, plunging the whole race into condemnation, Christ, the last Adam, fulfils the covenant perfectly and redeems God's elect—who through faith are members of the new race, the family of God by the adoption in Christ— by his active and passive obedience, i.e. his substitutionary life and propitiatory death on their behalf. Just as the whole race fell in Adam, that is to say because of the covenant solidarity between the members of Adam's race, so likewise the Christian is redeemed because in Christ he is united covenantally with the one who has fulfilled the law perfectly as his representative and federal head and discharged the debt that he owed but could never have paid. Christians are saved *in Christ*, i.e. because of the covenant solidarity between Christ and his people: "As in Adam all die, even so in Christ shall all be made alive" (1 Cor. 15:22).

Next Weir considers some of the implications of this federal theology, and in particular its implications for a post-mediaeval Christian doctrine of the State:

"The first aspect of the federal theological system that we should notice is that the prelapsarian covenant of works binds all men, before and after the Fall. . . Each man and women will stand before the judgement seat of Christ on the basis of whether or not he or she has obeyed the covenant of works. While because of Adam's Fall no one can be totally obedient to its stipulations, nevertheless each man is bound to them. The ramifications of this are extremely important. Through the idea of all men being required to obey the covenant of works through Adam versus some men enjoying the covenant of grace through Christ, one now had a potential basis for the State: the State, being the government of all men, could be founded on the covenant of works and the law of God, whereas the Church could be founded on the covenant of grace. The State could be entrusted with enforcing the law of God" (p. 5f.).

This is not strictly correct however. It is only the abiding validity of the *law*, its jurisdiction over all men, believer and non-believer alike, not the covenant of works, which in Puritan theology provides the moral basis for the State. As we shall see, Weir here fundamentally misunderstands and misconstrues an important element in early Reformed and Puritan theology by identifying the covenant of works as coterminous with the law.

Weir notes next that the federal theology, because it treats man as a legal creature from the beginning, God's law being written on the heart of man in the state of perfection, reinforced Calvinistic antipathy towards antinomianism. "The final aspect which we should note about the covenant of works," the author continues, "is that it becomes, in some sense, the primary covenant that God has made with man. The Adamic relationship of perfection in Eden takes on greater weight than the Abrahamic relationship of grace. Grace is, as it were, a remedy to correct creation's fall into sin. The eschatological importance of the covenant of works thus becomes significant: man is being restored, after the Day of Judgement, to the relationship which he enjoyed with God prior to the Fall—with some differences. The federal theologians thus interpreted Jeremiah 31:31–4 as, in some sense, a return to the covenantal state of Eden, when the law of God will be written on the hearts of the redeemed elect" (p. 6f.).

In an important note Weir observes that "J. F. Veninga, in 'Covenant Theology and Ethics in the Thought of John Calvin and John Preston', is less than accurate when he tries to explain the ethical consequences of the federal theology: 'with man's sin, the covenant of works becomes obsolete, although the obligatory ethic associated with it continues its validity as the standard of conduct for the regenerate' (p. 203). He goes on to maintain that the theology of Calvin and the federal theology are virtually the same" (note 17, p. 39). This, argues Weir, is incorrect: "What Veninga fails to realize is (*a*) the significance of the fact that Calvin never taught the idea of a prelapsarian covenant or covenant of works; and (*b*) that the federal theologians believed that the covenant of works was binding upon all men—regenerate and unregenerate—after the Fall, and that they are obligated to keep it, whether they are members of the Church or not. Such a mandate affects an ethical system drastically" (*ibid.*, p. 40).

But neither is Weir correct here. In federal theology the covenant of works remains binding upon all members of Adam's race outside of Christ, but not upon believers, who stand in a totally new covenant relation to God. In fact Veninga is much nearer the truth since some Reformed theologians maintain that the covenant of works was disannulled at the Fall and set aside (cf. Robert Shaw's *Exposition of the Confession of Faith*, p. 193). And in some sense it might be argued that the covenant of works was disannulled since man's communion with God has been broken by sin and man cannot now in that state of sin enjoy the benefits of that covenant fellowship with God, nor can he by his works merit God's favour. Yet in another sense the covenant of works is clearly not disannulled, since as a sinner man is subject to the covenant sanction, which remains in force for all of Adam's posterity unless and until through faith they are united with Christ in a new covenant relationship with God by means of grace. Thus, it is more correct to say that the covenant of works remains in force after the Fall but that man's relationship with God and his legal standing under the covenant of works has been altered by the entrance of sin. As a sinner man stands convicted of transgressing the covenant and is thus subject to the sentence of God's law, i.e. the covenant sanction: death. In Christ, however, that sentence has been discharged fully for the elect by Christ's sacrificial death on the cross and the believer is thus delivered from the guilt and condemnation of Adam's original sin as well as all personal sins and restored to covenant fellowship with God.

The covenant of works thus consists of three parts: life, i.e. fellowship with God (the promise), man's obedience (the condition), and the sanction for disobedience (death). To this most though not all Reformed theologians have added the reward of eternal life for obedience (see The Sum of Saving Knowledge, I.II but cf. Westminster Confession of Faith, XIX.I in which eternal life is not mentioned). This latter is an inference from Scripture, however, not an explicit statement. Disobedience has rendered the promise unattainable. Yet man is still bound by the covenant sanction. Furthermore, it is clear from Scripture that all three elements of the covenant of works remain in force formally after the Fall, since life is promised to those who fulfil the condition, i.e. perfect obedience to the law (Lev. 18:5, Rom. 10:5, Gal. 3:12), though in fact no one of Adam's fallen race is capable of fulfilling that condition on account of his being born in sin and thus by nature inclined to rebel against God. Christ, however, was born sinless and fulfilled the condition as the federal head and representative of God's elect, the new race, as well as suffering the penalty for their transgressions, thereby discharging their debt and accomplishing in himself their redemption. In doing this, however, Christ has brought the believer into a new covenant realtionship with God based not on works but grace operating through faith.

Thus, most Puritans and Reformed theologians considered the covenant of works to be binding on men outside of Christ. Those who are in Christ, i.e. under the covenant of grace, however, are no longer under the covenant of works. Thomas Brooks writes, "*there are but two famous covenants that we must abide by*. In one of them all men and women in the world must of necessity be found—

either in the covenant of grace or the covenant of works . . . No man can be under both these covenants" (*Works* vol. 5, p. 303; quotations from Puritan writings to this effect could be multiplied). Of course the *law* remains binding upon believers as a rule of life (Westminster Confession of Faith, XIX.VI). Furthermore, the believer, under the covenant of grace, is redeemed in Christ in order that he might walk in the good works that God has ordained for man before the creation of the world (Eph. 2:10); but to say that the covenant of works remains binding on regenerate believers is to use a terminology that is not found in federal theology, since under the covenant of works man must be justified by his own works righteousness, and this is incompatible with the believer's justification on the basis of Christ's righteousness alone. Whether and to what extent the use of the terminology of a covenant of works is valid or useful in describing man's continuing duty to obey God's law will depend upon what precisely is meant by it, but it is not the usage of the federal theologians or Puritans. Such terminology would, moreover, seem to be fraught with problems and at the very least likely to be severely misunderstood.

It would have been helpful if Weir had given citations from primary sources to support his argument, but unfortunately these are conspicuously absent on this point. However, among some federal theologians there were differences over the point to some degree with regard to the Mosaic covenant. John Owen, for example, did not view the Mosaic covenant as a dispensation of the covenant of grace as did most Reformed theologians from Calvin on, but rather as a particular temporary covenant in which the covenant of works was renewed, but in which there was relief provided against the believer's inability to yield perfect obedience (*An Exposition of the Epistle to the Hebrews* [Goold edition], vol. II, p. 389, and vol. VI, pp. 77, 86). According to Sinclair B. Ferguson, for Owen "The *substance* of the covenant of works was renewed in the Sinaitic covenant, but the *form* of that renewal was changed. It was now given to a people that were under the covenant of grace (though not yet in the new covenant). The substance of the covenant of works is God's will for man *as man*, and in that sense unalterable" (*John Owen on the Christian Life* [Banner of Truth, 1987], p. 53). But this is still a long way from Weir's claim that the covenant of works binds the non-believer and believer alike.

In spite of his statement that "part of the covenant before the Fall involves the giving of the moral law " (p. 4) Weir does not subsequently seem to distinguish between the law and the covenant of works and confuses the binding validity of the former as a rule of life for all men, even believers, with the idea that all men, including believers, are under a covenant of works. In the federal theology of the Westminster Assembly the law binds man, as God's creature, to God's moral standards of perfection, but obedience to that law did not in itself merit eternal life until God entered into covenant with Adam and promised eternal life on condition of obedience. According to The Sum of Saving Knowledge, (I.II) the covenant of works is the contract in which God promised eternal life on condition of obedience and is distinguishable from the duty to render perfect obedience to God's law, which binds all men regardless of any promise on God's part. As far as I understand Weir here he has erroneously identified the law with the covenant of works, treating the two as coterminous. But this is incorrect. The law is relevant to both covenants, but in the covenant of works it appears as a rule of life *and* as a means of justification and merit, whereas in the covenant of grace it appears as a rule of life only, justification being through faith in Christ.

This does raise, however, a very interesting and important question. As we have seen Weir notes that the federal theology strongly reinforced Calvinistic antipathy towards antinomianism and its extreme logical conclusion: libertinism (p. 6). Calvin was of course strongly against such antinomianism. But later Puritan theonomy was much more self-conscious and consistent on this point than Calvin and the early Reformers. Why? The logic of Weir's argument would lead us to conclude that it was the development federal theology that made the difference. Weir gives as an example of this change, especially as it was worked out in the doctrine of the State, the change in the interpretation of the fourth commandment that occurred between Calvin and later Puritanism. "Most federal theologians came to the conclusion that all people, both members and non-members of the Church, must keep the sabbath, and that this commandment should be enforced by the State . . . The sabbath issue rises to the forefront concurrently with the rise of the federal theology between 1590 and 1640, and it seems that extreme Sabbatarianism had its roots in the federal theology" (p. 6).

Weir here assumes that because the two rose to prominence at the same time they were linked. This is not so however, or at least it has not been shown to be so by Weir. Two points need to be made here: first, it is not logically necessary to conclude that federal theology commits one to Sabbatarianism even if it could be shown that there was an historical link, since Sabbatarianism can be critiqued even from within a federal theology framework. Indeed, I would argue that Sabbatarianism, as distinct from sabbath keeping however, is necessarily problematic for a consistently developed federal theology since it ties certain ceremonial elements of the Mosaic dispensation to the creation ordinance thus blurring the distinction between the pre- and postlapsarian covenants. This discussion is beyond Weir's point however. Secondly, as already noted, the Puritans did not see the covenant of works as binding on believers. They did, however, see the moral law as binding on all, and also the equity of the Mosaic judicial law as binding upon society. It was not their doctrine of the prelapsarian covenant of works that led to Sabbatarianism, therefore, but their particular interpretation of the fourth commandment along with their belief that the equity of the Mosaic judicial law still bound the civil magistrate. Weir attributes too much importance to the prelapsarian covenant of works generally and particularly in his understanding of the Puritan doctrine of the State. We must look for the rationale for Puritan Sabbatarianism and theonomy in something other than the prelapsarian covenant of works therefore. Puritan theonomy and the Puritan doctrine of the civil magistrate find their basis in the Puritan understanding of the abiding validity of God's law quite apart from the doctrine of the prelapsarian covenant of works.

Weir maintains that the federal theology schema of biblical history has extensive implications. Some of these have not yet been explored but most came to fruition in the seventeenth century. One implication Weir touches on relates to the doctrine of creation: "As a consequence of this transformation of thought, there is a shift in the importance of certain *loci* of scripture. The doctrine of creation, and the relationship between Adam and Christ, took on greater importance. While exegetes continued to discuss the importance of the covenants with Noah, Abraham, Moses, and David (as aspects of the postlapsarian covenant of grace), there was now a place for a doctrine of nature and a theology of creation: creation and redemption each had its proper place. Christianity spoke both to the areas of the created world and to the areas of grace and redemption. The federal theologian now had the potential for a basic world view which includes 'nature' and 'grace'. According to this schema most men live only under nature, but the redeemed live under both the spheres of nature and of grace. Areas such as science, politics, law, and logic had roots in the covenant of works" (p. 7).

Here Weir touches on the area of science and in the conclusion he suggest that the federal theology had significant implication for the subsequent rise of science in the seventeenth and eighteenth centuries. Unfortunately Weir never develops this in any detail and refers mainly to the doctrine of the State for examples of the implications of the federal theology: "At times, the covenant of works was called the 'natural covenant' or the 'covenant of creation'. Theology and religious activity could be related to the covenant of grace. Ideally the categories were not to conflict (e.g. the Church-State problem is a major consideration at this juncture), but both should complement and assist each other, and both were under God and his law. There would come a time, in the new heavens and the new earth—the *eschaton*—when there would be no conflict between the two spheres, because the sphere of grace will have restored fallen nature to its original perfection" (p. 7). These examples of the implications of federal theology for the doctrine of the State are intriguing; it would, however, have been helpful also if other examples had been given, particularly in the areas of science and logic.

There may also be a problem here with the statement that "Theology and religious activity could be related to the covenant of grace" if some separation between the sacred and the secular similar to the mediaeval schema is being proposed. Science and logic are intensely religious disciplines in one sense, though not theological disciplines in the strict sense. However it is not clear that this is being suggested. The reference could be to the religious cultus and theology proper. As Weir says "Christianity spoke both to the areas of the created world and to the areas of grace and redemption," and later he points out that the Reformers broke with the Thomistic nature-grace schema (p. 24).

More importantly, Weir suggests that the federal theology provided a basis for the reconstruction of northern European society and culture: "With the loss of the traditional institutions of the Church and its sacraments, and the demise of canon law, northern European society was searching for an adequate base for its social ethic. How could men be forced to live a Christian life-style when you were not sure that they were under the covenant of grace and that their hearts were 'turned unto the Lord'?" (p. 7f.). As Weir points out, the mediaeval answer was to include all men under grace by means of the sacraments and Church membership. As long as men partook of the sacraments and were faithful Church members they were considered saved. The Reformers rejected this. As Nicholas Tyacke commented, "at this period the degree of emphasis placed by an English theologian on predestination was usually in inverse proportion to that which he put on baptism, thus bearing out Max Weber's dictum that 'every consistent doctrine of predestined grace inevitably implied a radical and ultimate devaluation of all magical, sacramental and institutional distributions of grace, in view of God's sovereign will'. Indeed the grace of predestination and the grace of the sacraments were to become rivals for the religious allegiance of English men and women during the early seventeenth century" (*Anti-Calvinists* [Oxford: Clarendon Press, 1990] p. 10).

But if not all men could be included in the Church as a result of the rejection of a sacramental and institutional view of grace in favour of a predestinarian view of grace, how was the Church to claim moral authority, and how was the Christian State to find legitimacy for its decrees and rule over non-believers?

It is here that the federal theology provided a new basis for the Christian doctrine of the State according to Weir: "Not all men had 'hearts turned unto the Lord', yet the Protestant wanted all men to live godly lives. One possible solution for the Reformed camp was to adopt the idea of the covenant of works, which bound all men to keep the law of God through Adam and yet did not place them, perhaps falsely, in the realm of grace" (p. 8).

Again, however, it is Weir's identification of the law with the covenant of works which leads him to this conclusion. As a result he claims too much for the prelapsarian covenant of works. It was the Puritan belief that the *law* remains binding on all men, regenerate and unregenerate alike, that provides the basis for the State. Though all men are under a covenant of works in Adam they are delivered from that covenant upon conversion by union with Christ, which places them under the covenant of grace. The law continues to bind them as a rule of life however. In federal theology the abiding validity of the law is a separate issue from the covenant of works. All men are required to keep the law and the State is a divinely appointed institution for enforcing God's law in the judicial sphere. The requirement to obey God's law is logically and historically distinct from the idea of a covenant of works.

Weir next looks at theological conceptions of the covenant prior to the development of the federal theology. Although in Calvin's doctrine of the covenant the two testaments are the same in substance and reality and differ only in administration, according to Weir Calvin makes no mention of the prelapsarian covenant with Adam. There is evidence, however, claims Weir, that "at least to a certain degree, Calvin considered the Edenic relationship between God and Adam to be covenantal in nature" (p. 10). This evidence Weir finds in Calvin's view of the sacraments. "For Calvin a sacrament is a sign of a covenant between God and man." Sometimes sacraments are miraculous and sometimes natural. Calvin cites the tree of life in Eden as an example of a natural sacrament (*Institutes*, IV.xiv.18). Since a sacrament is a sign of a covenant the Edenic relationship between God and Adam must therefore be covenantal in nature. This is an inference from Calvin's doctrine, however, and the covenantal nature of the Edenic state is not explicitly stated by Calvin, nor does he refer to a covenant of works with Adam. Likewise, according to Weir, Bullinger, although he gives the covenant idea a central place in his theology, makes no reference to a prelapsarian covenant with Adam.

At least two theologians did propose a prelapsarian covenant before Ursinus, however. These were Augustine and Ambrosius Catharinus (1487–1553). According to Weir only Augustine among the fathers of the Church spoke of a prelapsarian covenant: "Actually, for Augustine" he writes "it was a prelapsarian *testament*. In his *Civitas Dei*, Book XVI, Chapter 27, Augustine makes one very short reference to a 'first covenant': 'But the first covenant, made with the first man, is certainly this: "On the day you eat, you shall surely die."' This is placed in the context of a discussion of the Abrahamic covenant and its relationship to circumcision, in which the question of infant salvation is brought forward" (p. 12f.). For Augustine, the infant has original sin because in Adam he has broken the covenant that God made with Adam. The idea is not developed further by Augustine however.

This question came up again at the Council of Trent in 1546. According to Paolo Sarpi, who had access to the records of the Council and who wrote a history of the Council of Trent (1619), Ambrosius Catharinus, a Nominalist theologian troubled by the Realist view of the transmission of sin, suggested that just as God had made a covenant with Abraham he had also made a covenant with Adam. Weir cites Sarpi's history:

"And hee explained his opinion in this forme: that as God made a covenant with Abraham and all his posteritie, when he made him father of the faithfull, so when he gave originall righteousness to Adam and all mankinde, he made him seale an obligation in the name of all, to keep it for himselfe and them, observ-

ing the commandments; which because he transgressed, he lost it
as well for others as himselfe, and incurred the punishments also
for them; the which as they are derived into every one, so the very
transgression of Adam belonged to every one; to him as the cause,
to others by virtue of the covenant; so that the action of Adam is
actuall sinne in him, and imputed to others, is originall; because
when he sinned all mankind did sinne with him" (cited on p. 14).

Although Ambrosius corroborated his argument with citations
from Augustine himself as well as Scripture he was opposed by
Petrus de Soto, who maintained the Augustinian Realist doctrine
that all men are guilty because they were *in* Adam when he sinned
and not simply represented *by* Adam covenantally when he sinned
(the difference between these two views can perhaps be summed
up by saying that for the Augustinians all men are guilty because
they inherit sin, whereas in the covenantal view all men inherit sin
because they are guilty, i.e. constituted sinful on account of Adam's
sin).

It is not known whether Reformed theologians in the late sixteenth century were aware of this discussion but Weir does not
think that the context of Ambrosius' teaching, i.e. the transmission of original sin, was what led to the proposal and adoption of
a prelapsarian covenant of works by Reformed theologians. Rather,
he sees this development as a result of the predestination controversy, and particularly the supralapsarian-infralapsarian dimension of that controversy. It is Weir's contention that "the idea of
the covenant of works, or prelapsarian covenant, was introduced
by Reformed theologians to help resolve this question of God's
providence and Adam's original sin" (p. 22). Calvin and the Reformers had affirmed both the absolute sovereignty of God and
human responsibility. Thus, although all things happen according
to God's inscrutable will God is not the author of sin and man
must bear the responsibility for his own conduct. But, according
to Weir, "When Theodore Beza moved the discussion of predestination from Calvin's credal form to a situation where the doctrine
of predestination is formulated around the decrees of God, there
was much greater danger for falling into the error of ascribing to

God responsibility for sin, especially Adam's original sin" (p. 16). Weir sees the prelapsarian covenant with Adam as "a means by which orthodox Calvinists of the late sixteenth century, some of whom adopted the Bezan form of explaining predestination, could maintain the tension between prelapsarian Adamic human responsibility and divine sovereignty." (p. 16)

However, the prelapsarian covenant of works should not be seen as a device for softening the absolute sovereignty of God. "Late sixteenth-century Reformed theology taught that God, in his mercy and providence, condescended to Adam in a way that was comprehensible to him, that is, in terms of covenant. This covenant gave moral responsibility to Adam, and yet it was also the means by which the sovereign decrees of God concerning Adam were carried out. For the Calvinist of whatever variety, the prelapsarian covenant with Adam did not 'soften' the decrees of God concerning the Fall; rather, it affirmed it, expanded it, explained it, and worked it out" (p. 16).

Weir next examines secondary sources which deal with the history of the prelapsarian covenant. This brings us to the end of the Introduction, which covers 50 pages in all (almost a third of the text since the last 84 pages of the book comprise a bibliography and an index). Weir's thesis is set forth in the Introduction and in the following chapters the historical development of the federal theology is examined.

In Chapter 1 Weir considers the lexicographal and biblical treatment in the sixteenth century of the various words used in connection with the idea of covenant: *berith*, *diatheke*, *foedus*, and *testamentum*. The surprising conclusion here is that Sebastian Castellio, remembered mainly for his religious toleration and humanistic liberalism, seems to have been a catalyst in the development of the federal theology. In his Latin translation of the Bible he abandoned the word *testamentum* as a translation of the Hebrew *berith* and the Greek *diatheke* in favour of *foedus*. Thus in Mt. 26:28 he translates the Latin Vulgate "hic est enim sanguis meus novi testamenti" (this is truly my blood of the new testament) as "hic est enim sanguis meus novi foederis" (this is truly my blood of the

new covenant). The only time Castellio uses *testamentum* is in Hebrews 9. "He changes all the instances of *testamentum* in the Vulgate
Old Testament to *foedus*. What he did contradicted the translators
of the Septuagint, for he affirms that *foedus* expresses *berith* better
than *testamentum* or *diatheke* does, and that *berith* is an Old Testament concept which has been obscured by *diatheke* and which is
illuminated by *foedus*." (p. 59) As Weir comments: "The most hotly
disputed words of the sixteenth century had been altered. Such a
radical break with centuries of tradition could not fail to go unno-
ticed."

Weir sees it as significant that Zacharias Ursinus, the first Reformed theologian to propose a prelapsarian covenant, visited
Castellio at Basle "just as he (Ursinus) was making the decision to
leave the Lutheran fold and join the High Calvinists." This visit
also "coincided with the height of the burning controversy over
God's sovereignty and Adam's Fall," which, ironically from the
point of view of the subject under discussion, "pitted men like
Castellio against Calvin and Beza."

Chapter 2 deals with the predestinarian controversies of the
decade between 1550 and 1560—in which Castellio played a large
part. Here Weir contends that "the doctrine of a *foedus* with Adam
developed in response to this problem [i.e. the problem of reconciling God's providential sovereignty and Adam's Fall—SCP] as a
'milder' orthodox elaboration and explanation of the seemingly
harsh decretal doctrines of Theodore Beza" (p. 63). However, this
does not follow necessarily. Why is the federal theology a milder
orthodoxy? It does nothing to mitigate the supposed harshness in
God's decrees as formulated by Beza. Oddly, Weir has already
admitted this in the Introduction: "the prelapsarian covenant with
Adam did not 'soften' the decree of God concerning the Fall; rather,
it affirmed it, expanded it, explained it, and worked it out" (p. 16).
Weir goes on to contradict himself again on this point when he
writes: "in his technical theological treatises Ursinus is careful to
assert God's absolute sovereignty, even over the Fall, along with a
denial of God's responsibility for evil. At the same time he wants
to explain how the Fall happened. The prelapsarian covenant in

creation does not mitigate the decree of God respecting the Fall; it merely explains it more fully" (p. 108). It is difficult to see why, in the light of these statements, Weir contends also on page 63 that the prelapsarian covenant was a "milder" explanation of the seemingly harsh decretal doctrines of Beza. While the prelapsarian covenant explains more fully the relationship between God and Adam and thus throws light on how the Fall occurred, it does nothing to soften the decree of God respecting the Fall.

Chapter 3 deals with the prelapsarian covenant as proposed by Ursinus. This is the first stage in the growth of the federal theology. Chapters 4 and 5 look at the second stage in the growth and development of federal theology, namely its rise in three key Reformed schools in the German Rhineland: Heidelberg, Neustadt an der Hardt, and Herborn in Nassua. After 1590 the federal theology becomes much more widely integrated in the thinking of Reformed theologians.

Following this there is a brief conclusion. Weir sums up his argument: "The early federal theology between 1560 and 1590 developed in two stages: the first stage culminated in 1562, after a tumultuous decade of discussion about how Adam's sin worked into God's plan and could be reconciled with God's nature. The second stage is 1584–90, when the idea was developed and combined with the Ramistic system of organization by such men as Dudley Fenner. Since the Ramistic system was dominated by dichotomies, the covenant of grace started to appear as a 'foil' to the covenant of works. After 1590 the idea of the prelapsarian covenant appeared all over Reformed Protestant Europe and the whole area of covenant thinking took on especial importance in all areas of life in the seventeenth century" (p. 158).

Furthermore, "The rise of the federal theology has nothing to do with sacramental theology, the theology of Church and State and their internal and external relationships, the threat of Pelagianism, or the morphology of conversion. Its rise came primarily as a result of the questions about God, his nature, and his relationship to man and the universe. It seems to stem from systematic, dogmatic thinking, not from exegetical study of Scripture. None of

the sixteenth-century commentaries on Genesis 1–3 mention the
prelapsarian covenant until after 1590." Federal theology did have
significant implications, however, which, according to Weir, were
sometimes more important and far-reaching than its origins: "The
theology of the sacraments, the relationship between Church and
State, the morphology of conversion, the problem of Pelagianism,
the doctrine of creation and the subsequent rise of science, the
celebration of the Christian sabbath, the doctrine of justification,
and Christian ethics are all areas in which the federal theology
would leave its mark during the seventeenth and eighteenth centuries" claims Weir (p. 158). The relationship between the Church
and the State was just one area where the implications of Christian thought had very significant and far-reaching effects in England only fifty years after the cut-off date for Weir's study. These
implications affected not only how people *thought* about this relationship, but also the nature of the English constitution. The development of federal theology in the late sixteenth century should
not be underestimated as a contributing factor to the Christian
world-view that produced such changes, but it is doubtful that Weir
has identified in the prelapsarian covenant of works the crucial
factor in the development of the Puritan doctrine of the State.

I found this book a fascinating read. The Introduction is highly
stimulating, though perhaps the material could have been organised
a little better—but this is a small point over all. More problematic
is Weir's identification of the law as coterminous with the covenant of works. For the federal theology the law was of course an
important part of the prelapsarian covenant. But to identify the
law and the prelapsarian covenant as coterminous is incorrect.
This is a fundamental flaw in Weir's understanding of federal theology and thus in his argument. This flaw also throws considerable doubts on his use of the State-Church relation as a valid example for his argument, and since he does not give other examples
it is difficult to determine whether and to what extent he is correct
in his claims for the extensive implications of federal theology. For
example, Weir claims that federal theology had implications for
the doctrine of Creation and the rise of science. The biblical doc-

trine of Creation was fundamental to the world-view that led to the rise of science in the seventeenth and eighteenth centuries, but it is doubtful that federal theology was a vital factor in this doctrine or that it had the significant implications that Weir suggests.

Although this was a fascinating read, and highly informative on the historical development of federal theology, Weir has fundamentally misconstrued his subject matter at an important point and consequently a good part of his thesis does not hold up, or at least has not been proved. This part of Weir's thesis needs to be researched further and re-written therefore. This is rather disconcerting since the book had its origins in a doctoral thesis submitted to St Andrew's University in 1984, and one would have expected that this major flaw would have been discovered and ironed out before the degree was awarded. The doctoral thesis also won a prize from the American Society of Church History.

INDEX OF BIBLICAL REFERENCES

GENERAL INDEX